The Lullaby Illusion shines with passion and cou...

—*Review* D...

This is a powerful book, one that reminds us of the indomitability of the human spirit. Rich in characters, in tragedies, in cultural and political events, Susan opens her very personal diary and the result is a vastly entertaining book. Recommended.

—*Grady Harp (Los Angeles, CA)*

Five stars

The Lullaby Illusion is a tragic and uplifting story about life, loss, and facing those things beyond which we have no control -- and figuring out which ones we do. The story traces a certain period in the life of the author when her tranquil existence in Cyprus is suddenly blown up, figuratively, but also literally, by war. The experience of coping with, surviving, and then escaping for safer ground plays out in interesting parallel with other traumatic events in Joyce's Young life -- namely, the loss of her baby and multiple miscarriages, as well as the revelation that her husband is not who she believes him to be. Joyce's relationship to her vivid dream life, as well as her artistic spirit, guide her through these tragédies to stable - and fulfilled- ground. A must read for anyone who is interested in stories that trace survival and resilience in times of duress.

—*Kristin Louise Duncombe*

Five stars

The Lullaby Illusion is an exquisitely executed memoir, which leaves you spell-bound as you follow Susan's metamorphosis; as she loses herself in her husband, the enigmatic Charles, following their dream travelling the world.Through miscarriages, betrayals and escaping war torn Cyprus to her re-awakening in Germany as an accomplished artist, Susan eloquently tells her story. The characters leap off the page, you can actually hear the dialogue, feel her fear, sadness and joy - it is easy to forget that this is a memoir and not fiction. I would love to see The Lullaby Illusion made into a film, and I hope she writes more about her life, and soon."

—*Janet Hughes*

Five stars

There is so much more to this book than the aspect I am going to rave about. So often I have read books, and seen films, that either gloss over, dramatise or make war appear heroic that I think that when this is well done, as it is in the book, it is well worth highlighting. Here is a writer who describes being caught in cross fire with al the grim realities and slightly surreal disbelief that it is happening to her. A more realistic and consequently more terrifying account I have yet to read. As for the other aspects of the book - read and find out, this lady has had quite a life.

—Cuica

A Journey of discovery … beautifully expressed with the right measure of creative detail. interspersed with moments of great humour.

I came at Lullaby Illusion from a professional curiosity in all honesty with a philosophical head that was not for turning, what I found instead was a study in the laws of attraction and the power of positive thought and with it, the strength of a human spirit, not only to endure but to reinvent and remould the path to a personal destiny.

—C.Martin (France)

Definitely a five star

The Lullaby Illusion is a wonderful and kaleidoscopic personal journey. Although Susan Joyce passes through gruesome moments: a miscarriage, life in the cross fire zone of the civil war in Cyprus, a marriage breakup where her husband was close to killing her and the loss of her best friend to AIDS, she paints these facts with gentle strokes as the artist she is in "real life" and creates a lovely picture out of them. What I most liked about the book was that, like a certain James with the same surname as herself, Susan's style is a stream of consciousness where she goes there and back in time involving the reader, not only in her interesting history but also in her psyche. To do this, she takes us into the realm of her dream life which, in her case, is a very powerful and mysterious tool with dealing with the hardships she finds on her way. Her smooth cruising above hard times, her inner equilibrium and her successes make the reader feel good about their existence. The author also shows an uplifting capacity for enjoying the best things in life such as true friendship and love and has the power to make everything and everyone she touches seem special.

—Richard Klein, author of Lost Samba

Would Make a Great Movie

What intrigued me most were the illusions, and how the writing style---rich in dialogue, conversation, mystery and interesting events---would make for an incredible thematic movie. While this unique writing aspect tilted the pacing, in neither a slow nor fast pace albeit, it overall contributed to a different well-written reading experience.

Overall filmmakers, and readers who enjoy personal travel stories set in the 70's/80's, will be drawn to the events centered largely around a mysterious husband and wife's (the memoirist) travels enduring great hardships attributed to living in countries wrought of turmoil, along with experiencing personal tragedies born out of a troubled marriage.

—RYCJ VINE VOICE

The Lullaby Illusion is an ode to the human spirit - a testament to a life lived fully and well and made strong by the experience."

—Wussyboy (Surrey, UK)

The book turned out to be much more than an escape from a war zone; Susan Joyce engages in an exploration of dreams, of fulfilling one's destiny and seeking life's path to true happiness.

—Karen Guttridge "Karen" (Paphos, Cyprus)

THE LULLABY ILLUSION

A Journey of Awakening

JOURNEYS—BOOK 1

Susan Joyce

Peel Productions, Inc. • Vancouver, Washington

Published by Peel Productions, Inc.— www.peelbooks.com

Follow the author's blog and find supplemental material, incuding interactive maps, at susanjoycejourneys.com

Printed in the USA

Library of Congress Cataloging-in-Publication Data

Susan Joyce, 1945-
The lullaby illusion : a journey of awakening / by Susan Joyce.
        pages cm
ISBN 0-939217-88-5 (trade paper : alk. paper)
1. Joyce, Susan, 1945---Travel. 2. Authors, American--20th century--Biography.
3. Children's literature--Women authors--Biography. 4. Self-realization in women. I. Title.
        PS3560.O886Z46 2013
803'.54--dc23
[B]
2013006811

CONTENTS

CHAPTER 1

HE'S DEAD!

Pátzquaro, Mexico—2008

"D-e-a-d. He's dead!"

I said it slowly, listening to the sound of my own voice. I took a deep breath, and dialed Diane's phone number in Germany. Busy.

This is so unreal. "He's dead." I stroked our cat, Zeus, asleep in his basket on top of my file cabinet. I hung up.

How odd to have news of his death interrupt my life now. A man I had married and divorced years ago. A man I never felt I knew. A man I last saw—in a Chinese restaurant in Frankfurt, Germany—over 27 years ago. Twenty-seven years? Was it that long ago?

Diane and I met when Charles and I lived in Stuttgart-Vaihingen, Germany. Charles worked for a Swiss firm, sold electronic audio-video equipment to military bases in Europe and traveled frequently. With little to do, I decided to apply for a job at the new audio club on the United States European Command (EUCOM) base near us.

Diane, a slender, graceful, raven-haired beauty, had also applied as manager of the photo department.

After our interviews—we were both hired—the manager introduced us to each other. We talked for a few minutes, laughed together, and a friendship began.

Diane hailed from Virginia. Since our first meeting, I had always loved to hear her say, "Hey!" Sometimes she'd say, "Hi-dee-doo," just to tickle my ears with real "Southern speak."

Being from LA, I swore I didn't have an accent, but Diane always smiled, as though she thought otherwise.

When Charles's firm assigned him to cover the Middle East market, we moved to Cyprus. I was sad to say goodbye to Diane. A brief and lovely connection in southern Germany—but now I was on my way to a new life in the Middle East. I tried to stay in touch with Diane, but my letters sent to her Stuttgart address were returned. Like me, she had moved on.

Five years later, after Charles and I split, I moved to Frankfurt.

One sunny weekend, as I strolled through the Römerplatz in Frankfurt, I was surprised to see to see Diane sitting at a crowded Weinstube table. Divine! I waved at her.

I ran to meet her. "Incredible," I said as we hugged. It was as if no time had passed; we picked up where we left off our last conversation, five years before.

I told her about my recent move to Frankfurt and the end of my marriage to Charles.

She shared that shortly after my move to Cyprus, she had married Steve and they moved to the Frankfurt area with his job. She was involved in photography and modeling fashion wear.

We talked for hours about where life's road had taken us. An amazing friendship revived by a chance meeting.

And now, years later in the chaos of Mexico, I dialed Diane's number again and listened to it ring.

"He's dead. Charles is dead," I whispered to myself.

My mind drifted, as the phone warbled, to my first meeting with Charles. I sat behind the information window at the main switchboard in the lobby of the Tucson Medical Center hospital in Arizona, relieving the switchboard operator during her break.

Plugging and unplugging cord lines—in and out, switchboard ports flashing incessantly—I noticed a tall, handsome man patiently waiting on the other side of the receptionist window. He looked serious, resembling Dr. Ben Casey from the TV hospital drama.

As the Emergency Room secretary, it was my job to admit all patients during the 11:00 p.m. to 7:00 a.m. work shift. For now, I had relative calm, sitting in for a few minutes during the switchboard operator's break. Nice to get away from the gore and craze of the Emergency Room, where most patients were desperate people in dire need of immediate help from auto accidents or gunshot wounds. Plugging and unplugging phone connections, I thought, Nice. No blood, no trauma.

I nodded, to let him know I'd be with him as soon as possible. Perhaps he had a pregnant wife waiting to be admitted.

When the switchboard finally offered a respite, I stood and went to the window to assist the stranger.

"Sorry to keep you waiting," I said. "How can I help you?"

"I'd like to treat you to coffee, or something, when you take your break later," he smoothly offered, smiling at my shocked expression.

"Are you a doctor? A cop?"

"No. My name is Charles." He pulled an identification card out of his wallet. "I'm in charge of installing the new closed-circuit television system in the hospital. My crew has been working here for several weeks now. I live in LA. Perhaps I can get to know you before I head home next week."

I looked at the card and shook my head in disbelief. Wild! I glanced up at the smiling stranger. "Amazing," I said. "I'm moving to LA end of this month." I was. I had a job offer from Pacific Telephone. "Next week is my last week of work."

"Hey, perfect. I'll show you around. I know all the hot spots."

Tick-tick-tick-tick.... The clock sounded the passing seconds. In my reverie I had stopped rehearsing the words. I barely heard the ringing telephone. In fact, I'd forgotten I was on the telephone.

Diane and I chatted frequently by telephone over the years. Thanks to overseas package telephone plans, it cost pennies now to speak for long periods of time. Amazing to think that twenty-five years ago it cost a small fortune to call long-distance anywhere, even to a neighboring town.

"Hello," a voice answered, sounding out of breath.

Oh yeah, I was on the phone. "Diane!"

"Yes."

There was a pause. Diane asked, "Susan? Is that you?"

"Yes. He's dead."

"Dead? Who's dead?"

"Charles. Charles is dead."

"Oh my," she gasped. "When? How did you find out?"

"I received an e-mail from his cousin in LA this morning."

"You're still in contact with his family?"

"Not for years. But his cousin contacted me through our company website this morning and said he had news of Charles. I knew he had died."

"How did he die?"

"They don't know for certain—lots of unanswered questions."

"Oh my god. How do you feel?"

"You mean, knowing he's dead?"

"Yes."

I stopped; thought about the question. The reflections of the previous moments swirled away, as if down a drain.

"Relieved," I heard myself say, "I feel relieved."

There was a long pause before Diane spoke. "I understand. Didn't you have a dream about his death?"

"I had several."

"I remember the beautiful widow dream. Years ago, after he decided he didn't want a divorce."

"Yeah, that. I remember it well. A difficult time. A difficult decision to divorce him after all those years together. But the marriage was long over, and I wasn't going back."

"So you dreamed him dead."

"My love for him died years ago."

"I know."

I paused to collect my scattered thoughts. "He was always secretive. Similar to some trick puzzle you can never solve. Long after our divorce, every time his life was in trouble, he'd call me. Out of the blue. We were divorced for over twenty years, the last time he called. I was shocked that he knew I was in San Francisco, visiting Michael for the last time. He always knew how to find me."

"Spooks usually do."

"Yes, and spooky to know I probably lived with a spy all those years, without even knowing it. I finally asked him why he was calling. It was our last conversation. I asked if he was part Italian."

"Part Italian?"

"He didn't get it either. I had to explain. Italian men think they have a claim on their ex-wives—especially the first one. I told him not to contact me ever again, and hung up."

"Did he die alone?"

"Yes. His landlord found him, a few days after his death. His last ex-wife, Katherine, contacted his family in California, about his death and details of his memorial service. She said Charles had been depressed for months. She had encouraged him to seek help, but he refused. He died from some kind of coronary-related issue."

"A heart attack?"

"Not sure."

"Is Katherine the English woman who lived with him on the French Riviera?"

"Yes. He also lived there with his German wife, Inge, before they split."

"Jeez! What about his children?"

"Charles and Katherine divorced several years ago. She said that Charles had disowned all of his children—the two sons he had with her and a daughter from his marriage to Inge. Nice guy."

"How bizarre, since he wanted a divorce from you because—"

"—he wanted his own children," I added, finishing Diane's sentence. "Thought they would guarantee happiness."

"That's quite a burden for a parent to put on a child. And after having them, he disowns them?"

"Charles was never a father, just a sperm donor."

"I guess children weren't his ticket to happiness after all."

"I sent a note to Katherine, expressing my condolences," I said.

"Have you received an answer?"

"No. I just sent it this morning. I also asked some personal questions, such as who Charles worked for while they were married, and asked if she found a manuscript about Cyprus."

"Do you think it's foul play?"

"It's possible. He didn't have a history of heart problems. But knowing Charles, silly me. No one ever knew Charles."

"Sure appears that way."

"His brother called me from San Francisco a few months ago."

"How'd he get your number?"

"He phoned my brother in Portland and left a message for me to call. He said he had important information about Charles. My brother phoned me. I returned his brother's call, using a calling card. I didn't want him to know my number. He told me it was urgent that I telephone Charles in England as soon as possible. I told him I didn't want to speak to Charles, that we weren't friends. He begged me to please just call Charles and say hello. I refused. He asked me if I still loved Charles."

"After all these years?"

"Yes, strange."

"Ridiculous."

"He wanted to know what happened to us, what went wrong. I told him Charles wasn't an honest man. He asked if I could ever get back with him. He went on to tell me that Charles always loved me and felt guilty for the way he treated me. He told me that Charles was writing a book about Cyprus and needed to tell me something important—before it was too late."

"Too late? Sounds serious. Is this the brother you told me about? The one who also thought Charles was an agent?"

"Yes. As did other members of his family."

"What was he writing about Cyprus?"

"Dunno. The last time I saw Charles, in Frankfurt, he was living in Hong Kong and mentioned writing a book on doing business with China. Hopefully his wife will let me know if she finds a manuscript on Cyprus."

"Maybe that's why he died."

"Who knows? All these years I've lived in fear of him finding me. Showing up at my door, unexpected, but expected. I always wished he would go away forever, disappear into ether. And now he has." I hesitated.

The conversation was getting lopsided.

"So, how are you and Steve doing?" I asked.

Diane sighed. "We're fine. Busy as usual. Steve's out of town. I'm catching up on reading. The girlfriends are meeting for dinner tonight."

"Where?"

"Our favorite Italian restaurant."

"Romanella's. Oh my! I can taste their lasagna now! There's no lasagna in Pátzcuaro, unless you make it yourself."

"Too bad. What's new with your construction in Mexico?"

"It's a sunup to sundown operation with workers everywhere. Except Sunday. Thank God we have the casita to live in while it's happening. We hope to have it finished by Christmas. Wish us luck."

"Oh, I do."

"If only we had a good Italian restaurant in our little Mexican village. The closest one is in Morelia, about an hour's drive from here. So, what's the occasion for the girlfriend get-together?"

"We're celebrating Rosetta's birthday. Wish you were here to join in the fun."

"Me too! Say happy birthday to Rosetta! Tell her I wish I could fly in and show up in my special birthday suit."

Diane laughed, "I'll tell her. We all vividly remember that suit."

"Thanks for listening. I'll call ya again soon. Give my love to Steve and the girlfriends."

"Hugs to your guys. Take care. Love you."

"Love you too."

Placing the telephone back in its cradle, I stared out the window and stroked Zeus's head. He purred loudly and reached a gray paw out to touch me. I picked him up and carried him outside. We sat on the big wooden bench in our new courtyard garden.

I scanned the climbing splendor and explosion of color—the pink, red, and purple bougainvillea—almost covering the outside wall. The yellow-flowered Mexican honeysuckle grew wild alongside the wandering jew plant, and twisted and turned to fill in the medley, between the orange-blooming aloe vera plants. As if color were music.

"Imagination is everything," I told Zeus, recalling a quote from Albert Einstein, "it is the preview of life's coming attractions."

Plants grew quickly here. Not long ago, this courtyard had been an overgrown jungle of weeds and junk. When we arrived in Mexico, in January 2007, to start building our home, we cleared the yard of rubble and trash. Each evening I sat in the courtyard and imagined what would grow and bloom there. Months later, it was a feast of colors. A dream—imagination manifested. A delight.

I thought back to that first meeting with Charles. Later that same morning, over coffee, we shared our life adventures and expectations.

I told him about my great-aunt sending me postcards from her travels around the world, and how as a child I dreamed of seeing London, Paris, Tokyo, and other faraway places. How I would place the postcard over my heart, and pretend it was a magic carpet which could transport me to all those exotic foreign ports.

He revealed that he spoke some French, loved to travel, and yearned to explore other countries and cultures. "First stop LA," he said, smiling.

I knew instinctively that we had met for a reason of momentous significance, of great importance.

Looking back, I thanked the universe for that fateful meeting of human souls, determined by destiny to explore life and the world together. For better or for worse.

Ahh, destiny. As a child, my days passed as sometimes-here, sometimes-there, but I was always aware of an inner voice as true as anything my eyes delivered. With no television allowed in our home, I tuned into my surroundings, saw and heard things others didn't perceive. My parents called it my "wild imagination."

But my inner voice taught me to use my imagination and trust. I listened. Not that it made my life easier.

My father was the preacher of a small church in Tucson. Small, as in not many people. So when one Sunday eleven showed up—parents and nine kids!—he was ecstatic.

When the service ended, my father summoned us (eight children plus Mom) to meet the newcomers. The father of the new family reached out to shake my hand. Backing away from him, I blurted out, "He's evil."

My parents, shocked and embarrassed by my strange behavior, told me to apologize to the man.

I refused. "He is."

A year later, he drowned two of his nine children in a lake nearby. I remembered hearing the news and shuddering at the thought of a father purposely drowning his own children.

Playing cowboys and Indians with my brothers and sisters, along the slopes of the wash near our house, was great fun. Our elaborate forts were built to last forever! Of course the next flash flood washed them away in an instant.

But I also treasured my time alone. Well, almost alone.

Our dog, Brownie, a brown-and-white-spotted dalmatian with bad breath, was my constant companion. He followed me deep into the desert, exploring nooks and crannies, as we made our way to the top of a large, flat, always hot rock. We would sit for hours watching magic happen.

From our high perch, we surveyed the groves of barrel cacti and watched cars wind their way up the road, past Sabina Canyon, to Mount Lemon.

Each evening, about the time mom would call us home, the rock had cooled way down, and we would retrace our steps home—always in time for dinner.

"What do you do all day in the desert?" Mom asked one evening as we entered the house.

I explained that Brownie and I had a secret spot—a place where we could see magic happen all around us.

"Magic?" she asked.

"Yes. We watch rocks grow and cactus flowers bloom and die. One day we saw an oasis. It looked like a landing strip."

"You were just thirsty," Mom said. "Why do you go?"

"We're waiting on the spaceship to pick us up," I informed her.

"Oh!" She looked bemused. "Why ever would they do that?"

"Because they left us in the wrong place—with the wrong family."

Mom hugged me, assured me I belonged. "You're a real dreamer," she said, with a loving smile. As if dreaming were a bad thing.

My childhood was wild. I dreamed and listened. My imagination went wild—too wild! But I heard a voice within. Dream more, it said.

By the time I moved to Los Angeles, childhood was long gone. Life became hectic.

I had a new, high-pressure job with the telephone company. I began dating Charles, and after a few months, we decided to get married. We bought a new home with a large fenced back yard. Perfect for our new pedigree puppy. And children.

Sunup to sundown, my days filled with long hours working and commuting on the four-lane LA freeways—the inevitable rat race of adult life.

Or so I thought.

The peace of the desert succumbed to busy-ness in the City of Angels, to the point where reflection appeared anathema in the face of the chrome, neon, and tinsel fantasyland of LA.

For many years, the static of my busy, buzzing life drowned out my intuitive insight. And I lost sight of myself—the self that once listened and trusted a still, small voice. Until Cyprus.

CHAPTER 2

WHAT KIND OF HAT?

Kyrenia, Cyprus—1973

"Shhhh," I whispered, patting my enlarged belly to quiet the baby kicking inside. I must finish the dream.

The baby kicked again.

"Oww," I pleaded. "Shh child, please. This dream's important."

But the baby kept kicking.

"Please settle down," I begged, turning over on my side.

The kicking continued.

I opened my eyes. Still dark. Brrrr. I pulled the covers up around my chin. Warm. Please.

Bang. Slap. The howling wind banged against the shutters.

Again, the baby kicked.

"OK, I'll get up," I muttered, trying to sit up in bed. Instead, I slumped back against the pillow. Damn. I felt drunk.

The baby kicked again, urging me to move.

I opened my eyes to check on the gas heater. No light. No flame. I tried again to sit up, but couldn't. I felt faint and sick to my stomach.

The baby kept kicking. Move! a voice warned. Get out of here.

I rolled over to the edge of the bed, slumping down onto the cold floor.

Crawl, the voice insisted—loud and clear.

On hands and knees, I inched forward, toward a sliver of light under the hallway door. As I got closer, I could sense fresh air.

I reached up to open the door, but it wouldn't budge. I sat down to rest. Just for a moment.

Move, get out of here now! the voice said.

I was leaning against the door. No wonder it won't open. I slid my heavy body over, with great effort, and tried the handle again. The door opened a crack. "Help," I cried out.

No answer.

I opened the door wider, and crawled out into the long hallway. "Help! Help me!"

Still no answer. Of course, Charles is gone. Where? Europe? The Middle East? I collapsed on the cold tile floor and wept.

The baby tapped my belly, a gentle drumroll.

"Thank you," I said, talking to the soul in the body growing within me. "If you hadn't told me to move, we'd both be dead."

Shivering, I crawled to the living room and pulled myself up onto the soft suede sofa. I covered my body with the wool blanket my mom had knit for me last Christmas. I drifted into a deep sleep and let the dream continue.

> *The sun shone bright in a bustling old European city. A mountain peak towered in the background. People were walking to and from offices, shops, and restaurants. Waves of people and bobbing heads on the sidewalk below. So vivid, I thought, like a movie of a crowded city street scene.*
>
> *What's this? I spotted Charles's dark, curly 'Afro' hairstyle in the crowd. Standing tall, crossing the street in three long strides. But with a woman beside him, with a dark scarf, in a dark skirt and a white top? A uniform perhaps? Walking fast to keep up. Talking and laughing together—they know each other.*
>
> *Where are they? What city? It looks familiar.*

And where are they going? I follow the pair as they turn from the crowded sidewalk, walk up steps, enter a revolving door into the lobby of a grand old hotel.

Wham. Bang. Slam. "Oh, my god! Of course." I threw aside the blanket, pushed myself to my feet, and walked back to the bedroom. The wind blew out the flame of the gas heater. The strong gas smell permeated the room. Wow. A close call.

I turned off the gas heater and opened the doors and shutters to let the wind cleanse the room.

I cleaned my face and teeth, combed my long hair, and walked to the kitchen to turn the teakettle on. What a night!

Hearing the faint tinkling sound of sheep bells, I knew it was just past seven in the morning. I returned to the living room and opened the balcony door to watch the daily procession of shepherd and sheep. A sea of fluffy white animals and an orchestra of bells and whistles floated past. I waved to the shepherd.

He nodded and in a commanding voice steered his flock forward, down a dirt road. My eyes followed them until they faded into the distance.

My thoughts drifted to the hills overlooking Jerusalem and my visit to the holy Wailing Wall last year. Like thousands of other pilgrims, I had written a prayer wish on a small piece of paper, stuffed it into a crevice in the thick, corroded limestone wall, and prayed that my wish for a healthy child would be granted.

Brrng. Brrng. The ringing doorbell startled me. I looked down to see Ronit, an Israeli woman who worked for El Al, standing below on our front doorstep. I smiled. How wonderful! A visitor, and I can practice my Hebrew with her.

Our landlord's daughter, a sensitive young woman, brought Ronit by one afternoon for a visit. She knew Ronit's husband's family, and knew Ronit (a new arrival in Cyprus) was lonely for friendship. She knew that I had lived in Israel and decided it would be good for us to get to know each other. It was.

Pretty and slim. No big belly there. I called to her, first in English and then in Hebrew, "Good morning. *Boker tov.*"

Ronit looked up and waved. Pushing her windswept black hair aside, she called back, *"Boker tov."*

The teakettle whistled. I pushed the buzzer to open the downstairs door.

"Just in time for tea," I said, as she rounded the top flight of stairs.

"How are you feeling?" Ronit asked, giving me a hug.

"Much better now. The wind blew out the gas heater flame."

"Oh, no," Ronit exclaimed, closing the door.

"This one," I pointed to my belly, "saved my life."

"How?"

"He kept kicking me, telling me to move."

"He did?"

"Yes. I felt drunk. When I slid to the floor, he kicked me awake."

"From the gas?"

"Yes. His voice kept commanding me to move out of the bedroom."

"Amazing."

"I know. I owe my life to him. Would you like breakfast?"

"Just tea. I can't stay long. I work today."

"You look stunning in your new uniform." I motioned her into the kitchen. "Tell me about your new job."

"I work at the check-in counter."

"El Al is lucky to have you. You speak so many languages."

"English and Greek come in handy for sure. Sit down. You should be off your feet," Ronit said, carrying the breakfast tray to the table.

"Thanks." I sat down. "So you enjoy working the check-in counter?"

"It's fun. And unbelievable what passengers carry on flights with them."

"What do you mean?"

"Americans carry books or magazines. Greeks carry olives. Turks carry bottles of raki, the licorice liquor. But it gets better. The Russians carry beets and vodka."

"Are you serious?"

Ronit laughed. "Sometimes they carry potatoes. Doesn't matter; it's nice earning money again. We weren't making it on Andreas's income, even with his part-time job at the embassy."

"Gas is expensive. Driving to Nicosia all the time must cost a fortune."

"It does. Hey, everything's expensive when you don't have enough money." Ronit chuckled at her statement of the obvious. "We're looking for an apartment in Nicosia, near the airport."

"Makes sense, to save on gas. How's married life?"

"Nice." Ronit smiled.

"Your wedding was such fun."

"I loved getting all that money pinned to my dress. Just for dancing."

"A great custom. Newlyweds need money more than stuff."

"Yes, but living next to his family isn't fun. You're lucky to live in a beautiful, big villa overlooking the sea."

"It's way too big for us," I replied, "and freezing cold in the winter. We're hoping to find a place in town after the baby's born. One with fireplaces."

"Your view of the Kyrenia harbor is spectacular."

"True. Especially at sunset. That's when the old castle sparkles and shines. Watching sunsets has become my evening tonic during this difficult, stay-in-bed pregnancy. When my doctor first told me he recommended it because of my previous miscarriages, and for my health and the health of the baby, I thought I'd go crazy."

"Months in bed would drive me *mashugi*—really crazy."

"*Mashugi*. A great Hebrew word for crazed. Thank goodness I'm not *mashugi* yet. I'll do anything to have a healthy child. Besides, friends stop by and check on me."

"A good thing."

Ronit glanced down at the table, stiffened, held her nose, and pointed at the jar of Marmite on the table. "Do you eat this stuff? I thought only Brits liked Marmite."

"My doctor says it's good for me. Lots of vitamins and minerals."

"Yuck. I'd rather eat seaweed."

"It's good for you too. But not as convenient as Marmite."

I poured more tea.

"You were what, two years in Israel? Did you enjoy your time there?" Ronit asked.

"1968 was an exciting time to be there, after the Six-Day War."

"How did you ever end up in an ulpan? In the Negev Desert?"

"Charles and I both wanted to see the world, and Israel had the ulpan study program. New immigrants could learn Hebrew and study Jewish history at an ulpan institute in the Negev Desert village of Arad—with free room and board. Sounded interesting and the price was right."

"But Arad's in the middle of nowhere."

"The Dead Sea's nearby."

Ronit chuckled. "Did you try to swim there?"

"Not possible in incredibly salty water, but I had my photo taken. Not something I'd show off of course. Arms and legs flailing about wildly."

"A funny pose."

"We called the ulpan Noah's Ark, because it had two of everything. Two American families, two South African, two Russian, two Polish, two French, two Spanish. There were even two men from Uruguay there. We helped pave the first road and plant the first trees in Arad."

"*Achla!*" Ronit said.

"*Achla!*—Awesome! Great word. Is it Hebrew or Arabic?"

"Both. It comes from Arabic. Did your teacher speak English?"

"Oh no. *Rok Evret*—Only Hebrew." I wiggled my index finger, mimicking the strict teacher who insisted students speak only Hebrew in class. "Learning Hebrew came easier for me than some of the other students."

"Why?"

"I had dyslexia as a child. I used to say things backwards and I wrote letters and numbers in reverse—right to left."

"Like Hebrew. Of course. Hebrew's written from right to left. So that made sense to you."

"Yes. My dad nicknamed me Dutch."

"Well, sure—with your blonde hair and blue eyes."

"No, because he couldn't understand me when I talked. He called it 'Dutch talk.' Seeing things differently is not necessarily a bad thing. When Charles and I first arrived in Israel, we visited the Haifa Zoo. I knew, before I even saw a live elephant, that I stood in front of the elephant's house."

"How?"

"Because the sign, in Hebrew letters, looked similar to a pictograph of an elephant."

"It's true. Weird."

"I'm a visual learner, and I recognized the letter *pei* (English P) looked to be an elephant ear. The letter *yod* (English Y with a long E sound) looked like an elephant's eye, and the letter *lamed* (English L) looked similar to an elephant's trunk."

"Peel. Elephant in Hebrew." Ronit smiled.

"Standing outside the elephant house that day, I thought, if I ever write a story about an elephant, I'll name him Peel. It was a strange thought which rang true. I've always admired elephants. Who knows, maybe one day I'll write a story about an elephant."

"And name him Peel?"

"Definitely!"

"But maybe it was a vision of your future."

"Yeah. Who knows what the future holds?" I said, laughing at the thought of writing a story about an elephant.

"Greek was easy for me to learn," Ronit explained, "because many of the letters in the Greek alphabet have similar names to Hebrew letters."

"Interesting. Ancient languages and pictographs fascinate me."

"So what did you do for entertainment in Arad?" Ronit asked.

"I studied, kept a journal, read books, and wrote letters home. Charles played poker most evenings. On our day off we often went to the cinema."

"Arad had a cinema?"

"A small one. A fellow student from Poland, who spoke a mix of Hebrew, Polish, French, and English, loved going to the movies with us. In Poland he had worked as a projectionist at a local cinema. One night the film kept messing up. It appeared blurred, out of sync, and he kept yelling at the projectionist to 'Fuckus it. Fuckus it.' The audience roared laughing. From then on when any film got out of focus, people began chanting, 'Fuckus it. Fuckus it.'"

"That's wild." Ronit chuckled. "Only in Israel."

I poured more tea and finished my breakfast.

"Where's Charles this week?" Ronit asked.

"He's supposed to be in Istanbul, but I had a dream that showed me he's in a different city."

"A dream? Where do you think he is?"

"Looked like Sofia. We were there in 1970."

"Bulgaria? Why would he be in Bulgaria?"

"I don't know. But in my dream I saw a mountain behind the city. Istanbul doesn't have a mountain, but Sofia does. A large mountain. There's a medieval church in the foothills with amazing frescoes."

"Sounds like a beautiful place."

"Stunning," I replied, "but."

We sipped more tea.

"Do you believe in dreams? Visions?" Ronit asked.

"Yes. I do. I think they focus on things we're not consciously aware of— like seeing beyond our normal senses. Charles of course, thinks dreams are orderly mental activities which occur during sleep—same as clerks putting papers away in a filing cabinet. He thinks my dreams are imagination gone wild."

"Did you actually see Charles in your dream?"

"Yes. Walking with a woman in a crowd of people."

"Another woman? Did you know her?"

"No."

"Do you trust him? Will you ask him about your Sofia dream?"

"Well, so far he hasn't given me any reason not to trust him. Not yet. I'm not sure about confronting him."

"I don't trust Andreas, even though he's my husband."

"Why don't you trust him? Has he ever given you a reason?"

"No. He's so handsome and friendly with everyone. I get jealous and worry about it."

"Silly to worry about something you can't control."

"True." Ronit smiled and nodded.

"Where did you live after Israel?" Ronit asked.

"Stuttgart, Germany. Charles got hired there by a Swiss firm."

"How did he get a job with a Swiss company?"

I glanced out the window. A lark circled the hanging bird feeder.

"He answered an ad in the *International Herald Tribune*," I said. "They were looking for an electronics engineer to sell electronic products in different countries." *An American would have politely changed the subject now. But not a curious Israeli. When I lived in Israel, I was surprised by the personal questions they would ask. They wanted to know all about you.*

"Who does he work for now?" Ronit asked.

I watched another bird zoom in for food.

"Same Swiss firm," I answered. "You Israelis are a curious lot."

"Always." She smiled a strange smile. At some subliminal level, it didn't fit. More than idle curiosity.

"I lost a baby while we were in Israel," I told her, recalling the whole awful ordeal. "An ambulance took me from Arad to a hospital in Be'er Sheba. They kept me on a bed in the hallway because no rooms were available.

Wounded soldiers kept arriving on stretchers. Broken bodies and blood. Not exactly a maternity ward."

"I'm sorry. In Israel, soldiers have first priority. I had an abortion when we lived there."

"You did?"

"Yes. Andreas and I were always fighting about religion, and he didn't want to get married."

"Did he want you to have an abortion?"

"No, he got angry when he found out." Ronit studied the checkered floor tiles. "And now, people always ask us when we're going to have children," she added, lifting her head.

"I answered that question for years. Family, friends, even strangers wanted to know. It got old. One time, I was sitting in the lobby of a bank, and a woman pulled out her wallet and showed me photos of her five children. I told her they were adorable. She announced that she gets pregnant at the drop of a hat."

"What does that mean? What kind of a hat?'

"No special hat." I laughed. "It's a strange expression in English meaning something happens easily."

"Ah, English. So many strange expressions."

"The woman asked if I had children, did I want children. I replied, of course one day, and told her we were trying. When she left, she told me to keep trying and God would bless me with many children. She smiled. I waved goodbye, glad to see her go.

"Some strange man, also sitting in the lobby, nodded at me, and joked, 'Trying is the fun part.'"

Ronit gasped. "He said that?"

"Yes. People are strange. No wonder they're called strangers. Being a parent should be a personal choice. Some people make lousy parents."

"Susan, how many miscarriages have you had?"

"Five."

"Five?" Ronit gasped.

"Yes. If anything happens to this one, maybe it means I'm not meant to have babies, to sing lullabies. Maybe I'll try something different."

"Like what?"

"Be an artist, a writer—do something creative with my life."

"But what about your natural instinct? The biological clock?"

"Maybe it's a different clock ticking."

"A different clock?" Ronit looked puzzled.

"We all have something unique to bring to life. Maybe it's a creative clock that's ticking. Maybe I'm not meant to be a mother just now."

"But if you wait until you're too old, you might have regrets."

"I'll only regret if I live an empty life and don't make my dreams come true."

I poured more tea.

"Andreas thinks the abortion did permanent damage."

"Have you had tests done?" I asked.

"*Kin*—yes. The doctor says I'm fine. Andreas won't go to a doctor. He thinks God is punishing us because of the abortion."

"Charles says he wants children, but he doesn't want to adopt. When we first moved here, I didn't get pregnant for a year. Charles was convinced I needed hormones. So I went to a doctor and asked for hormones. The doctor told me to send Charles in for a sperm test. Charles refused, said he wouldn't jack off for some nurse. So guess what I did?"

"What?"

I made an *OK* sign with my thumb and forefinger, and moved my hand up and down. "I told him, if you won't jack off for a nurse, then I will. I had a clean jar ready, collected my sample, and raced off toward Nicosia."

Ronit sat speechless, mouth agape, and burst out laughing.

I continued. "The doctor told me sperm should be tested as soon as possible after ejaculation. So I only had 30 to 40 minutes to get there. I screwed the lid tight, and ran to the car. When I put the key in the ignition, the steering wheel locked. It took me five minutes to start the car. I placed the jar upright on the passenger seat and drove like a madwoman, up and over the mountain pass, all the way to Nicosia."

"That's a half-hour drive, at least. What about the checkpoints? Did you get stopped?"

"Several times. The jar kept falling over. I thought the guards were going to ask me to explain the strange milky substance in the jar. Definitely a Woody Allen movie scene. I kept placing the jar upright and checking the lid to make sure it was tight."

"So what did the test show?"

"That Charles had a low sperm count."

"And what did he say when you told him?"

"He didn't believe it; thought the doctor, or lab, had made a mistake." I let out a long sigh. "Trying to get pregnant is not fun. Takes the romance out of sex."

"I admire you for being so determined." Ronit glanced at her watch, and stood to leave. "I better be going or I won't make it to work on time. I'll stop by again soon."

"Thanks for the visit." I hugged her goodbye.

"*Laheatraoat.* See you later," we said in unison—in Hebrew and English— as Ronit disappeared down the stairs and out the front door.

CHAPTER 3

DO I DARE?

Nicosia, Cyprus—1974

"I want to see my baby," I said, propping myself up.

"He was stillborn," the doctor replied, motioning a nurse to take the bundle away.

"I know." My eyes welled with tears.

"I'm sorry. I think it best you don't."

"Please, let me hold him. Just for a few minutes. I need to touch him, to say goodbye."

"I know how much you wanted this child." The doctor patted my outstretched hand. "It was him or you. I chose to save you. I'm sure that's what your husband would want too."

"Please let me hold him. I need to know he's normal," I pleaded.

"Nadia." The doctor motioned to me. "Let her see her son."

The nurse placed the small wrapped body in my arms.

"Thank you," I said. "I need time alone."

"Are you sure?" she asked.

"Yes, I'll be fine. Give me a few minutes."

My eyes followed the doctor and nurse as they left the room. When they had gone, I opened the blanket with care, then lifted the small body and held it in my arms.

I placed the baby by my side and studied his little body—head to toes. *What a big bold head.* I smelled his hair. Touching his firm clutched fingers, I counted. Ten. I smoothed his reddish hair and ran my fingers over his little nose, eyes, and ears. "Thank you," I whispered. I studied his long legs and chubby feet. "Thanks for kicking me awake. You saved my life." I patted his soft belly and then counted his toes. Ten. "You're perfect. Because of you, I took time to dream, to think, to examine my life." I kissed his head. "I'll miss you, child," I said. Burying my head in his body, I let my tears flow.

The doctor returned and took the lifeless bundle from my arms. "I'm so sorry, Susan. Time to rest."

A voice called my name, I awoke. My British neighbor Beth, a bubbly blonde, stood next to my bed, holding my hand.

"Hiya. All right?" she asked.

My eyes brimmed with tears.

Beth squeezed my hand. "Blimey, you did all you could do."

"I did my best," I said, wiping tears from my eyes. I held her hand tighter.

"Quite. That's all any of us can do in life."

A cloud slid by and suddenly sunlight filled the room. I smiled, remembering an image which occurred right before I was wheeled into surgery.

"Something strange happened," I told Beth.

"What? When?"

"Moments before they took me to surgery, I saw myself standing alone in a cold, still, dark tunnel. I tried moving forward, but couldn't because I couldn't see anything. A flicker of light from a candle lit my way. A voice told me to 'follow the light, wherever it takes you.' The voice said that we would meet again. I followed the candlelight, into bright sunlight, and felt warm again."

"Sounds a comforting dream."

"Oh, it was." I smiled.

Beth patted my hand.

I turned and stared out the window. The sky shifted and changed, as wispy feather clouds sailed by.

I turned back to Beth. "Thanks for checking on me. I don't know what I would have done without your help."

"No worries. That's what neighbors are for." Beth placed her hand over mine.

"I know what the dream means," I told Beth.

"What?"

"I've been putting life on hold for years, trying to have a child. I've been stuck in a cold, dark place for a long time."

"You can always adopt. There are many children who need good homes."

"I know. I've suggested adoption to Charles. He refuses to even discuss it. He wants his own flesh and blood."

"I'm adopted," Beth said.

"You are? You've never talked about it."

"I don't talk about it because my adopted family is my family. My parents died in a car accident when I was quite young. I lived in an orphanage for two years until I was adopted. They've been my family through thick and thin."

"You're lucky. How wonderful they must be." I looked into my friend's warm hazel eyes, which shifted from light brown to bright green when she smiled.

"They are wonderful."

"Do you know if Charles knows about the baby?"

"I telephoned the American Embassy. They said they would try to contact him through his company."

"He'll be upset. Probably think I didn't obey doctor's orders."

"Don't be daft. He'll be happy to know you're okay. Kate and Ilene telephoned earlier to check on you. I told them you're fine and resting. Your Israeli friend is coming by later to visit."

I smiled, then gazed again out the window. "Do you think the boat ride around the harbor caused any harm?"

"The boat ride around the harbor?"

"Perhaps it jarred something."

"Surely no harm came from that. It was a short, gentle ride weeks ago. So gentle, I fell asleep."

"I remember. I couldn't tell if it was you snoring or the boat's motor."

Beth laughed.

"Getting out certainly helped boost my spirit," I said, "after those long months in bed."

"Did the doctor say what caused your water to break?"

"Severe vomiting, probably from food poisoning. Tainted tuna. Because of internal bleeding, he decided to induce labor to save my life." I choked back tears.

"I'm glad you're alive."

"Me too."

"How long will you stay in the hospital?"

"A few days. They want to do some tests and I've asked them to do an autopsy on the baby."

"Oh? Why?"

"I want to know the time and cause of death. I think the baby died just before I went into surgery."

"Oh?"

"I told you about the night the gas heater flame went out."

"Yes. I remember."

"The voice that told me to move that night, is the same voice that told me to follow the light out of the dark tunnel. When the vision ended, I looked at the clock. I need to know when he died."

"Understandable. I'd be curious too."

"This entire pregnancy has been filled with voices and visions. T.S. Eliot poems have been swimming in my brain for months now."

"I adore his poems. Bizarre lines. Do I dare?"

"Disturb the universe?" I quoted. "In my beginning is my end. *Four Quartets* has been drumming my brain for days."

My eyes closed and I drifted far away—back to my first view of Cyprus.

Charles and I were living in Israel. Since Cyprus was a short boat ride away, we decided to take a three week vacation there. We sailed on a large ship from Haifa to the old Cypriot port of Famagusta.

As the ship made its way, Charles talked about the ancient history of the island. He explained how Cyprus's geographic location caused it to be influenced and occupied by many other civilizations over the centuries. This gave it, historically, a pivotal role in many cultures. A prized piece of land fought over by Egyptians, Persians, Greeks, Huns, Romans. "The list goes on," he said.

How exciting, I thought. I can visit all the ancient archaeological sites.

Charles explained that in 1878 the United Kingdom was given the protectorate right to defend, control, and occupy Cyprus by the Ottoman Empire—in exchange for military support, should Russia interfere with Ottoman territories in Asia.

After Russia threatened to occupy Turkey, the Ottoman Empire entered into World War I in 1914. It joined the Central Powers of Germany, the Austro-Hungarian Empire, and Bulgaria. The Ottoman Empire declared war on the Entente Powers of Britain, France, and Russia. And the Ottoman Empire collapsed.

Britain annexed Cyprus in November of 1914. But, the indigenous population of Cypriots felt it their natural right to unite with Greece.

I thought about the turbulent history of this beautiful island as Charles continued his history lesson.

During World War I, Britain actually agreed to turn Cyprus over to Greece, if Greece would agree to attack Bulgaria. Greece refused. So in 1925 Britain declared Cyprus a Crown Colony. Greek Cypriots sought union with Greece. They called it *enosis*. Britain was opposed and the situation deteriorated into violence in the 1930s. And into the 40s.

In 1948, the king of Greece declared that most Cypriots wanted union with Greece and sent a petition to the United Nations. The UN accepted the petition and it became an international issue.

The British rejected it. Greece and Turkey joined NATO in 1952.

A guerrilla war against British rule by the National Organization of Cypriot Combatants (EOKA) launched in 1955. It failed.

Cyprus was declared independent in 1960, after Greek and Turkish Cypriots agreed on a constitution—which stated no partition between the Greek and Turkish populations, and no union with Greece. Makarios became the country's first elected president.

But, fighting between Greek and Turkish Cypriots flared up again in the early 1960s, and a UN peacekeeping force was sent to the island in 1964.

All's well that ends well, I thought as the ship neared the old stone dock in Famagusta. What a history!

I heard Ronit quietly talking with Beth in the background. I opened my eyes and smiled at her.

"*Shalom,* my friend. How are you feeling?" Ronit asked.

"I'm alive," I answered.

"I'm happy you are." Ronit patted my arm.

I drifted again—in and out of sleep—listening to my friends discuss the beauty of Cyprus.

I reflected on how awestruck I was when I first saw the stunning sight of white sandy beaches, olive groves, old rock walls, castles, and fields of pink, purple and yellow wild flowers.

I smiled, recalling the long winding road over the mountain pass, down the corridor into the northern port village of Kyrenia, and my first glimpse of the dazzling Kyrenia Castle crowning the northern coast harbor.

And I was thrilled when a few years later—while living in Stuttgart—Charles announced that his employer (the Swiss firm) had promoted him to be in charge of the Middle East market. We were moving to Cyprus. Yeah!

"*Ta* to the Greeks, the Romans, the Phoenicians, and all the others who decided to leave their mark and cuisine," I heard Beth say.

"It is a paradise," Ronit added.

"A cultured country where everyone speaks the Queen's English."

Ronit laughed. "Makes it easier for you Brits to understand."

"Very civilized. And the locals couldn't be nicer."

"Except when they fight over land," Ronit remarked.

Dreams and images kept floating through my head. The dreams appeared real. The images of saner, happier days in Cyprus, less so.

During my long months of bed rest, I often viewed the castle and harbor from our rooftop terrace. Using binoculars, my eyes followed ships at sea as they zigzagged their way across the blue Mediterranean and steered into the old port to dock among the small boats, gently bobbing about.

"They have some strange Middle Eastern customs," Beth said.

"I like *Kataklysmos,* the Festival of the Flood," Ronit replied, "where people celebrate by sprinkling each other with water."

"Have you seen the miniature body parts they string on lines in churches?" Beth asked.

"Oh, of course! They stick prayers to them to help heal sick people."

"I believe in all that balderdash and I'm not even religious."

"Have you had your coffee grounds read?" Ronit asked Beth.

In my drifting mental state, I smiled, imagining overhearing that amidst the hustle and bustle of Los Angeles.

"Several times. Have you?" Beth asked Ronit.

"Oh yes, my mother-in-law reads mine often. I think she does it to give me marriage advice."

I stirred, remembering the reading Andreas's mother did for me a few weeks ago. I opened my eyes and propped myself up on pillows.

"Hello," Ronit said. "Welcome back."

"Ronit's mother-in-law read my future with coffee grounds, not long ago," I said.

"What did she predict?" Beth asked.

"She studied them for a long time, kept turning the cup around and around, then told me she saw a bird in the bottom of the cup."

"A bird in the bottom of the cup? I've studied dream symbols," Beth said.

"You have?" I asked.

"Yes. Birds generally represent happiness."

Ronit busied herself, rearranging a vase of flowers on the bedside table, pointedly ignoring our conversation about the reading.

"Um," I said, looking her way for a clue.

A nurse appeared at the door to check on me. "How are you feeling?" she asked with a smile.

"Better," I answered.

"I need to check your temperature," she said, pulling out a thermometer and placing it under my tongue. "I see that you ladies are having fun, but Susan needs her rest."

"We understand," Ronit and Beth said in unison.

The nurse removed the thermometer and noted the reading.

"Time to sleep." She gave me a pill.

Ronit kissed my cheek. "Take care."

Beth patted my hand. "Good kip."

They waved and smiled as they left my hospital room.

Kip, I thought, a perfect British name for a nap.

As the sun went down, I watched the blue sky fade to silver. Clouds of white danced outside the window.

> *I thought I saw an angry face in a single dark cloud spinning by. Charles? I called out. But the face spun around and disappeared. Slower, billowing clouds followed. Surrounded by gold and pink light, they formed a train of light clouds floating across the silvery blue sky.*

> *"I see skies of blue." I listened to Louis Armstrong's voice fill the sky with music. I wanted to climb aboard the clouds and go with the train of light.*

Smelling chicken broth, I opened my eyes. I saw a light in the hall outside, and heard voices.

A nurse entered my room with a tray of steaming food.

"I hope you're hungry," she said, placing the tray on my table.

"Smells good." I sat up and looked all around the room.

"Do you need anything else?" the nurse asked on her way out.

"No thanks. But I do have a question."

"Please," the nurse said, nodding.

"Is there a music system in the hospital?"

"No, we're not that fancy." She smiled.

"I swear I heard Louis Armstrong singing before I drifted off to sleep."

She shook her head. "It's been very quiet here this evening. No emergencies. No telephone calls. What was he singing?"

"'A Wonderful World.'"

"A beautiful song. Enjoy your meal."

"I will. Thank you."

CHAPTER 4

PARADISE?

Kyrenia, Cyprus—1974

"Lovely to see you, Susan," a smiling Kate said, opening the front door to her spacious home. "Glad you could make it to our *Before Summer Madness party.*"

"Summer's crazy," I said. "But especially for you and Alex with the restaurant and tourists."

"We count on the tourist season for income, but sure do enjoy the peaceful Cyprus we locals know, before the throng descends."

Kate's husband, Alex, a strikingly handsome Greek Cypriot, waved to me from a corner of the crowded living room as he made his way through the crowd gathered.

Both Kate and Alex had dark hair, dark eyes, and olive skin. They looked so much alike, they could have been brother and sister. Kate, a native Londoner, met Alex when he studied at university there. Proud parents of two young, blond, freckled boys, they moved the family to Kyrenia when the boys were toddlers. "Why raise children in a crowded city, if you don't have to?" Kate had explained. "Life here is safer and better for us all."

Now they owned and operated a large Greek restaurant in the harbor overlooking the port of Kyrenia.

"Glad you could make it," Alex told me, as he finally made his way to the door.

"Thanks. Good to see you," I replied.

"Sorry to hear about your loss."

I nervously chewed my lower lip. Tears welled and I wiped them away with the back of my hand.

Kate reached out and put an arm around me. "A tough time for you."

"It is."

Alex patted my shoulder, and left to greet another guest who arrived behind me.

"Time helps heal," Kate said.

"It's true. I feel better with each passing day."

"You're young. Get your mind off it. Paint."

"That's exactly what I'm doing." I smiled. "I got a telephone call the other day from an acquaintance who's arranging an exhibit of foreign artists for an opening at the Hilton in September."

"How exciting."

"He's invited me to exhibit some of my art."

"Terrific. Congratulations!"

"Susan!" I heard a voice from across the room.

I turned to see my vivacious Scottish friend, Ilene, approaching. A gregarious, light-complected, ginger-haired beauty, Ilene was often my bridge partner.

"Ilene," I called, "nice to see you."

"Aye. So sorry to hear about the baby. How are you doing?" Ilene asked.

"Getting better."

"Was Charles home when it happened?"

"No. He arrived home a few days later."

"How did you get to hospital?"

"My neighbor Beth drove me. I'm fortunate to have her nearby."

"Especially with Charles gone so often. What happened?" Ilene asked.

"My water broke. Food poisoning."

"Oh, you poor dear." Ilene patted my arm. "Is Charles here?"

"No. He's in Tel Aviv for a few days."

"Whatever for?" Kate asked.

"He flies there often—to keep his private pilot's license active."

"Do you ever fly with him?" asked Kate.

"When I get invited. I love flying in small planes. Great views. One day an eagle flew alongside us."

"An eagle? Loover-ly," Ilene remarked.

"Quite the feeling flying eye-to-eye with an eagle," I said.

"I prefer big planes. More metal to protect me," Kate added.

"Susan," called another familiar voice. I turned to see Gundy, a German woman and Kate's next-door neighbor, approaching.

"Sorry to hear about the baby. Are you okay?" Gundy asked.

"Thanks. I'm getting better."

"I heard that you and 'The Lawrence' won the Kyrenia Club Bridge Tournament. Congratulations. Did you realize you were playing with a famous man?"

"No, not until it was over. Someone told me later. Lawrence Durrell apparently sees no need to introduce himself."

"He's like that," Kate said. "Rather stand-offish."

"Snobbish," Ilene added.

"I suspect he wasn't too keen on having me as his partner." I smiled.

"It's your young, blonde, California hippie look that fooled him."

"He didn't have a choice. After all, he was the last player to arrive."

"He must have been appalled by your poker bidding." Ilene chuckled.

"Bet his tune changed when you won," Kate said.

"He nodded at me."

"Well now, that's no wee bit of approval from him." Ilene teased.

"He's strange, but I admire his writings," I remarked.

"He still has a house in Bellapais, which he visits from time to time," said Kate. "He lives most of the year in the south of France now."

"I heard he sold the Bellapais property," Gundy added.

"He's a private man," Ilene said. "So, who knows."

"Maybe my bridge partner wasn't 'The Lawrence' after all?"

A waiter presented a tray filled with a colorful array of hors d'oeuvres. I helped myself to several.

"Yummy," I said, tasting a roasted eggplant tart.

"Have you tried the feta and olive one?" someone asked.

"Delicious too. Kate, great food," I told her.

She smiled. "Thanks."

"Susan, are you buying the old hacienda?" Gundy asked.

"The one you're renting?" Ilene queried.

"If the government allows. We love living there," I replied. "But they have to approve the sale."

"Why wouldn't they?" Ilene asked.

"They want to make it into a museum. They're trying to make it illegal for foreigners to buy architectural antiquities," I answered. "Can't blame them, I guess."

"It would make a wonderful museum," Gundy said.

"You even have your own private chapel out back," Ilene added.

"I pray there daily." I smiled.

"You do?" Kate questioned.

"I'm kidding. There are snakes and spiders everywhere."

"How old is the place?" Gundy asked.

"Seven hundred and fifty years," I replied. "Originally built by a wealthy Turkish merchant."

"I love the old hand-carved olivewood doors. And those shelves around the top of the walls," Ilene remarked.

"They're called *raf* in Turkish," Gundy explained. "I learned this from my Turkish mother-in-law. Perfect for displaying beautiful dishes and things."

"Dust-catchers, but they look good. And all the fireplaces work."

"That's good. I like the merchant's room, with the raised floor where animals slept in the old days," Gundy said.

"Bet that room stayed toasty warm," Kate added.

"When the horses and dogs stayed in," I explained. "Not anymore."

"Think of the history made there," Ilene remarked.

"Does it have one of those small, secret doors which links to the courtyard and the harem?" Kate asked.

"None I've discovered. Perhaps they did it in the open."

They chuckled.

"Is it true, that part of the new Peter Sellers movie will be shot there?" Ilene asked.

"The producers have asked to rent the house for a month. Maybe they'll shoot scenes in it," I answered, "but they don't consult with me." I took another bite of the eggplant tart.

"My friend Helen has a bit part in it," Gundy said.

"I heard she plays a tart." Kate smiled.

"A strumpet? Our Helen?" Ilene laughed.

"Helen says it's a dumb movie," Gundy added. "About a crazy crewman on a pirate ship who kills the captain, after learning where the hidden treasure is buried. Then the crewman loses his memory. The actors get stoned or drunk, forget their lines, and keep falling overboard."

We laughed.

"Think I'll save my bobs for better entertainment. Unless your place is featured in it. Maybe they'll find that secret door," Ilene announced.

"Drinks for you ladies?" asked a roving waiter, presenting a tray filled with glasses of champagne and wine.

"Yes, please," I answered. "A bit to wet my lips."

"Aye, just a wee." Ilene nodded, taking another.

"Cheers," we toasted, clinking our glasses.

"Here's to Susan's premiere art exhibit," Kate declared, toasting again.

"An exhibit? Where? When?" asked Gundy.

"The lobby of the Nicosia Hilton in September." I smiled.

"Fabulous. A solo show?" Ilene asked.

"No, I'll exhibit with other artists," I answered.

"Congratulations!" Ilene raised her glass. "Here's to you."

"Congratulations!" Others chimed in.

"Thanks," I said, "Feels great to be creative."

"And to Cyprus," Kate added.

We clinked raised glasses again.

"We've noticed an increase in violence since Grivas's death. Alex and I are actually quite worried," Kate said. "EOKA is pushing even harder for *enosis*."

"Wasn't Grivas a terrorist? Isn't EOKA a terrorist group?"

"EOKA is a Greek nationalist group, started in the early fifties," Gundy answered. "They're determined to control Cyprus. And yes, Grivas was definitely a terrorist, a murderer. EOKA's original objective was to drive the British out and to unite the island with Greece."

"Makarios is trying to strike back by purging EOKA's sympathizers from the Cyprus National Guard," Kate added.

"Grivas's return to Cyprus, only three short years ago in 1971, reignited the troubles," Gundy replied.

"Is Makarios nicknamed Black Mak because of his black priest garb?" I asked.

"Yes," Kate replied. "As archbishop, and leader of the Greek Orthodox church, he wears it all the time. The priest-politician. A shrewd one, too."

"But Cypriots surely don't want to be ruled by Greece, do they?"

"Not the intelligent ones," Ilene answered.

"I'm seriously thinking of taking the children to England until things calm down," Kate said. "We can live with my parents."

"Probably a good idea. Something's definitely stirring. Tension's mounting," Ilene added.

"People are on edge, a bit nervous. Do you think there'll be a coup?" I asked.

"Our Greek neighbor says it's only a matter of days," Ilene answered.

"Our Turkish friends agree," Gundy added, ominously.

"Maybe we should ask the FBIS people?" Ilene nodded in the direction of a group, clustered together across the room, who worked for the US Foreign Broadcasting Information Service.

"Mum's the word there. Even if they knew they wouldn't talk about it," Gundy whispered.

"Or couldn't," I said.

"Does Charles know anything?" Ilene asked, glancing sideways at Gundy.

I shook my head, perplexed by the question. "Charles?"

"I thought he might have heard rumors," Ilene remarked. "You know, traveling as he does."

"What would he know?" I asked, feeling a deep furrow wrinkle my forehead. My question was followed by an awkward silence.

"It was tense here in the sixties too," Gundy said, changing the subject.

"You were here?" Ilene asked.

"Yes," Gundy replied. "Cyprus joined the Commonwealth of Nations and the United Nations in 1961. We had just arrived. Fighting between Greek and Turkish Cypriots erupted many times, with fear of a possible coup led by Grivas."

"Turkey has been threatening to invade Cyprus since 1963," Kate said.

"Turkey wants Turkish troops on the island to offset the influence of the Cypriot National Guard, which everyone knows is dominated by Greek officers," Gundy explained.

"That's fair," I said.

"We had hoped for an end to the troubles when UN peacekeepers arrived in '64," Kate said.

"I remember an attempt on Makarios's life by radical Greeks in 1970," Ilene said. "We'd just moved here from Dubai. Shortly after that, Grivas returned from exile and the troubles escalated."

"Look at the recent problems in Greece. General Ioannidis toppled Papadopoulos last November. I'm sure his dictatorship is pressing for the removal of Makarios," Gundy cautioned.

"The Greeks are out to get him because he doesn't want union with Greece," Ilene concluded.

"And according to my husband Aydin, Greece wants total control of Cyprus," Gundy revealed. "Of course Aydin is Turkish, but still."

"Surely most Cypriots just want a peaceful island, without foreign troops. Don't they?" I questioned.

"I'm sure they do, but major powers will never let that happen. Last I heard, the Russians and Chinese are pressing Makarios for bases on the island," Ilene remarked.

"According to Turkish news, Makarios has asked the United States and NATO to withdraw their troops," Gundy added.

"Several governments would like to see Makarios fall," Kate observed.

"If there's a coup, Turkey will surely invade," I said.

"Well, Susan, you know they'd be in their right to do so, based on the 1960 Treaty and the Cyprus Constitution." As usual, Gundy knew the details.

"Surely NATO and the US won't let them invade now," Ilene interjected.

"The place is already crawling with tourists," Kate added.

"You think they could stop the Turks this time?" Gundy asked.

"They stopped them before in '64," Kate reasoned.

The bartender refilled our glasses with more wine and champagne.

"Let's hope for the best." I raised my glass. Why can't people just get along? I wondered.

"Here's to many more years in paradise," Gundy toasted.

"Here's to peace," Kate offered.

"I'll drink to that," said Ilene, emptying her glass.

"Here's to the sky not falling," I added.

This time, the clink of glasses sounded clunk-like to me—echoing our insecure thoughts as the tensions around us mounted. The rocky ground was shifting beneath our feet.

CHAPTER 5

FREEDOM CARDS?

Frankfurt, Germany—1977

I watched the moon ascend above the silhouette of buildings on Schweizer Strasse, Sachsenhausen's main boulevard in the old part of town. I reflected on my garden "hinter house" apartment.

Ideally located on the south bank of the Main River, within a short walking distance of downtown Frankfurt over any Main River pedestrian bridge, my building sat behind a large apartment building. Quiet, private, and cozy. *Good choice.*

I looked around the small but comfortable room. My thoughts drifted to the larger houses I had shared with Charles over the years. And the last, huge apartment we lived in during the final gasping days of our dying marriage. *Cold, opulent. Eight oversize rooms for two people. Ridiculous. Never felt like home.*

As the sun set, the sky turned to soft violet, accenting the large oak tree outside my living room window.

Almost bare of its leaves. I made a quick note.

From green, the leaves turn gold, then gone.

Stripped bare, the bones stand all alone.

Like me, I thought, getting out my sketchbook. After the Cyprus War killed my chance of an art exhibit at the Hilton in Nicosia, I wondered how long it would be before another exhibit opportunity came my way.

I smiled, remembering how the invitation happened. Diane invited me to a restaurant for dinner one evening and introduced me to the owner.

He dabbled in art, and knew many actors and artists who frequented his restaurant, located downstairs from the Frankfurt theater. A few paintings were hanging on the walls, with lots of empty wall space. When he expressed interest in getting more to brighten the place, Diane suggested using the walls as exhibit space for local artists to show their work.

"An opening night would be fun," he said.

"And, it would bring new customers into the restaurant," Diane replied.

He thought that was a brilliant idea, and asked if I'd like to show my work there.

"I'd love to," I said, excited at the thought of showing my art. I also liked the idea of possibly earning some money.

I began drawing the tree—from the ground up. Over the months—season to season—I had sketched this magnificent tree in its many states of change, hoping to use some of my rough sketches for batik paintings for my upcoming and first art exhibit.

When I finished the solid trunk, I sketched the main branches, paying close attention to light and shadows, and added to my notes.

New buds in spring, new life will bring.

The drawing was complete. I poured myself a glass of juice, arranged a small plate of cheese and crackers, and placed it on the overly large marble coffee table, which also served as my dining table.

I settled into my new Ikea love seat, which also served as a guest bed.

No music. No lamplight. No need. No one to see. Nowhere to go. Here now—with the lingering evening light, as it fades into the dark of night.

Sipping and munching, I sat for hours letting my mind roam—snapshots, sound clips of my life before Charles, with Charles, and my life now, as a single woman. Without Charles.

With Charles, money was never an issue. Certainly not a problem. But after the Cyprus War, he opened bank accounts in his name only, and I became financially dependent on him. Because he had always taken care of me, this raised no red flags. Now however, with divorce looming, I saw it as ominous.

What was that saying? I thought, trying to remember the old sailor adage about a red sky.

"Red sky at night, sailor's delight." No red sky tonight.

"Red sky morning, sailor take warning." Was it a warning or just an old wives' tale?

One day Charles had informed me, "We have no children, I owe you nothing." The bastard.

Initially Charles had filed for divorce, and hired an attorney to handle the case. A few months later, he changed his mind and asked me to try again to make the marriage work.

For me it was over. He had lied to me and cheated on me. I no longer trusted him. I didn't want to see him, or touch him, ever again. My feelings for him were stone-cold dead. So I refused.

Since I wasn't willing to give it another try, he felt I should pay the attorney and court fees.

But German law requires financial support until a divorce is final. So Charles reluctantly agreed to send a check each month for the small amount required.

Instead of mailing it, he elected to deliver it in person, each time acting as if gifting me a million deutsche marks. I suspected he did this to check on me, because he always asked to be invited inside my apartment. I always refused.

One day he asked if I still had the research papers I'd organized on Cyprus after the war. He wanted me to give them to him. Unwilling to do that, I reminded him that I was the one who spent long hours in libraries researching and taking notes on the Cyprus War, and that the Cyprus papers and mementos belonged to me.

Angry, he left in a huff.

Shortly after I moved into my apartment, I began a job search, but a bad bout of pneumonia forced me to bed for several weeks. Short of money, having no health insurance, I kept putting off a doctor visit. Instead I relied on friends who stopped by and looked after me.

One morning, trying to get to the bathroom, I collapsed. Regaining consciousness, I realized I needed help.

I telephoned Serena, my neighbor, who was a nurse. Serena had met and married her husband, a German writer, while serving in the US Army in Germany. They had two children together. Although Serena and her husband eventually went their separate ways, they never divorced. Serena had explained it was the European way to keep the family and money together.

Serena stopped by, did a brief examination, and immediately telephoned her doctor friend Gertrude.

Gertrude arrived within a few minutes. She took my temperature, listened to my lungs and heart, and determined that I could be treated at home with antibiotics. She gave me a shot, told me to drink lots of water and get plenty of rest, and promised to stop by the next day to check on me.

And she did, for several weeks, until I felt strong enough to be up and around. Each time she visited, I tried to pay her for her time and the medicines she brought. She refused to accept money from me.

"If I can't treat a friend who's ill, I shouldn't be a doctor," she said one day.

I broke down and cried. "Thank you! For being my friend. And for being my doctor."

During that month, friends showed up often with food and drinks, and words of encouragement. Slowly, I got better and stronger. And I realized my caring friends had become my family.

A few weeks passed. When Gertrude listened to my lungs and declared me healthy again, I began looking for a job.

I interviewed and got a full-time position as a financial analyst for the US Government Club Management in Rodelheim, a town close by. Nice group of colleagues. Interesting work. Good benefits. Excellent pay. *Cool!*

Six weeks later, when I received my first paycheck, I insisted on treating Serena and Gertrude to dinner at a nice restaurant. They encouraged me to save my money, but I insisted on paying the tab.

I explained my upbringing, and my belief of a hundredfold return, especially on good deeds. "I want to bless you as you've blessed me."

"Sow bountifully. Reap bountifully," Serena announced. "In Jamaica, we were raised the same way."

As a calm settled over the city, a piercing cry interrupted my serene thoughts. Through thin walls, from the apartment next door, came squeals of laughter and shrill erotic screams. My thoughts scattered while my heart skipped several uncomfortable beats. Damn. Two guys having sex. Loud. Hmm.

I got up and jammed the cassette of Billy Joel's new album, *The Stranger*, into the stereo. Cranking the volume to max, I no longer cared. Singing along with Billy and dancing wildly from room to room, I no longer heard any ruckus from my horny neighbors.

Long after the album finished, I got ready for bed. While cleaning my teeth and face, I observed my image in the mirror and watched my expressions change as I slowly recited lyrics from "The Stranger" song.

"We all have a face, which we hide away ... faces of a stranger...."

Getting to know you, I thought, turning off the bathroom light.

To sleep, perchance to dream.

> *I dreamed that Charles broke into my apartment. He rushed into my bedroom and pulled me from the bed. I tried to scream, but my voice didn't work. He reached for my heart and tried to pry it from my body, tried to pull it out of my chest. I cried out and motioned with my hands for him to stop. His image faded. He vanished.*

Sunshine splashed across my eyes. My heart pounded a wild beat. I breathed a deep sigh of relief. It's morning. I still have my heart. It's beating. I smiled and got up.

Juice first. I walked the few steps to my kitchen to pour my usual morning drink, a mix of pure cranberry and orange juice. I ground coffee beans, filled the coffeepot with water, and pushed the *on* button. Every day starts the same. *My very own routine. Comforting.*

I sat, sipping juice, and surveyed my home. Great light from the large windows, I thought. A dining table and chairs would be nice. But no room.

I thought about my good friend Michael's teeny-tiny apartment jokes. I smiled. "Susan's apartment is so teeny-tiny, you have to be careful when you put the key in the front door. If you push it too far, you could break the kitchen window."

I laughed and counted steps back to the kitchen. Only seven steps? *Oh well. At least it's* my own *teeny-tiny place.*

I poured a cup of coffee and walked the seven measured steps back to the living room and sat down.

A living room, a bedroom, a bathroom, a kitchen with a pantry. What else do I need? A studio—a place to do my art. And soon, I'll have the apartment downstairs for my studio. *Yes!*

Drinking coffee and eating breakfast, I planned my day and made a to-do list.

—Appointment with doctor, birth control.

—Check frame prices for exhibit.

—Finish two paintings.

—Design freedom cards.

The phone rang and I dashed to answer it.

"Hey, Sue-girl," Diane said, in her soft Southern accent. "How're you doing today?"

"Fine. How's the show going? What are you modeling this week?"

"Evening wear. It's going well. I'll be back this evening. How about meeting at the Greek Garden for dinner? Seven-ish?"

"Perfect. That gives me time to finish a painting and my freedom cards."

"Your what?" Diane asked.

"I'm making special cards to mail to family and friends when the divorce is finally final. Simple, silly images. One is of an empty refrigerator with an *Out to Lunch* sign on it. Another is a box of chocolates."

"A box of chocolates?"

"Yes, now I'm free to eat any chocolate I want. I don't have to save Charles's favorite for him anymore," I replied.

"But what about my favorite chocolate-covered cherry?"

"I'll still save those for you."

"Oh, good. Gotta run to catch the train. See you tonight."

"Tschau. Später."

I dialed the doctor's office number. Busy. A strange new thought crossed my mind. I wanted sex, but now, after years of pressure to procreate, didn't want anything more. Certainly didn't want to get pregnant. How would it be different?

I dialed the number again, got through, and made an appointment with a gynecologist for the following week. I marked it off my list.

I turned, pulled out color and brushes to finish a painting. With my first exhibit only a few months away, I had to keep working to finish my goal of thirty paintings to fill the space alloted.

Since each painting reminded me of a childhood adventure, I decided to name my upcoming, first exhibit *My Childhood* and to title each piece after something—or someone—from that period of my life.

This sketch was of my fifth-grade teacher, Mr. Monk. I sat at a desk, while he stood towering over me with a scowl on his face. But Mr. Monk never scowled. Mr. Monk taught everything in a fun way. An actor in his earlier years, he loved teaching through drama.

I remembered the time he insisted I play the part of Benjamin Franklin, the great, inquisitive inventor, during a history lesson class play. Whenever I thought of Mr. Monk, I could almost hear him say, "Be curious. Ask questions. All geniuses do."

I quickly changed the scowling mouth to a soft approving smile. Satisfied I had captured his essence, and his important influence in my life, I completed the painting in no time.

"Susan, darling," I asked myself, opening my tiny, apartment-sized refrigerator, "what would you like for lunch?" Seeing nothing much to nibble on, I gleefully announced, "Guess I'll have to take you out—it's on me."

Donning coat and gloves, I ventured into the outside world. First stop, the local frame shop, where I gasped in shock at the high prices of simple frames. *Expensive. Especially when purchasing thirty for the show.* I made quick notes.

Returning home, I walked an extra block to get a half of a roasted chicken, bread, and French fries from a local sidewalk rotisserie. The best in Frankfurt town.

By now, I could order in German and actually be understood. I smiled, remembering the time I went out for breakfast to a local café and ordered what I thought was a half pot of tea—*eine halbes Kännchen Tee*. Instead, in my beginner's German, I asked for half a roasted chicken—*halbes Hänchen.*

The waiter hesitated, and repeated my order.

I nodded. *Kännchen, Hänchen.* Sounded right.

He told me it would be a while. I pulled out a book and began reading.

An hour later, he returned with my order of half a roasted chicken. I stared at the plate of chicken, shook my head, and asked to get it wrapped to go. Embarrassed, I quickly paid the bill and left.

When I returned home, I got out my dictionary and learned the difference between *Kännchen* and *Hänchen,* and practiced using the words in sentences.

This day I ordered with confidence. *"Halbes Hänchen mit Brot, und Pommes Frites, mit Mayonnaise."*

"French fries the European way?" asked the young waiter, in English.

"Of course," I answered, smiling. "Fries with mayonnaise are delicious."

He smiled, approving.

The afternoon passed quickly as I removed wax from two finished batik paintings and stretched them onto wooden frames for hanging. *My own show! Exciting!*

Evening. Seven-ish. I entered the Greek Garden restaurant. Diane smiled and waved from the rear corner table.

"You're early," I said, hugging her. "Was Madame happy with the success of the show?"

"Oh yes. She sold all of her new creations. She promised to call me for next season, even gave me a bonus. So dinner's on me."

"That's great. Congratulations."

"Here's our wine," Diane announced, as the waiter set a carafe of *retsina* on the table. "Shall we order?"

"I always enjoy their *meze.*"

"Me too. *Meze* for two," Diane gave our order. "Why not? I don't have to worry about sucking into tight clothes for a while."

"Cheers." I raised my glass.

"*Prost.* You're looking great."

"Thanks. I remember when we first met. You were single, I was married. And I loved hearing about your exciting escapades with men."

"Some felt more escapes than escapades." Diane laughed.

"You were cuddly with lots of hunks. And along came Steve. He's definitely a keeper."

Diane nodded.

We clinked glasses.

"Then Charles and I moved to Cyprus and you married Steve." I told Diane about making a doctor's appointment. "And now, it's my turn to get cuddly with hunks and not get pregnant."

"Speaking of hunks, have you heard from that English musician you met?"

"Yes, he's coming to Frankfurt next month for a concert. We plan on getting together."

"Good timing."

We clinked glasses again and I gave Diane a progress report on my upcoming exhibit. "Remember Erik?"

"The gallery owner?"

"Yes. He telephoned this afternoon, wants to be my manager, and has even offered to pay for the frames. I'm thrilled. Frames are so expensive."

"That's great."

"I'm amazed. He believes in me—and my artistic potential. That reminds me." I opened my purse and handed an envelope to Diane.

"The freedom card?" Diane asked.

"The best one." I handed her the chocolate box card.

She opened the envelope and smiled. "Delightful. What a fun way to let people know you've survived the storm."

I told Diane about the guys next door whooping it up the previous night and about my turning up *The Stranger* album to drown out their wildcat sex sounds.

Diane chuckled.

"Do you feel you know Steve?" I asked on a serious note.

"I'm getting to know him. Kind of weird. Marriage seems to be about changing, while growing together."

"I realize now that Charles was a stranger. Someone I never knew intimately. He never really opened up emotionally. Parts of him were closed tight—totally off-limits."

"How can you know someone who doesn't communicate his feelings? Was he always like that?"

"Secretive? Yes. Even in the beginning. If he didn't want to talk about something, he just changed the subject. If I confronted him with a question he didn't want to answer, he would stare at me as if I just fell out of a tree."

"A moody man."

"And he became even more so after Cyprus."

"Did you ever go for marriage counseling?"

"I suggested it several times. He always changed the subject. Always thought hopping in bed would solve all problems—as long as it produced a baby."

The waiter returned with a tray filled with multiple small plates of colorful Greek dishes for us to nibble and share.

"Beautiful. *Schön,*" Diane told the waiter, admiring the presentation of Greek olives, cheeses, and the variety of dips and vegetables.

"Dolmades," I said, mouth watering.

"*Guten Appetit.*" The waiter bowed.

We sipped our *retsina* and nibbled on the various *meze* dishes. Some were hot, some were cold, some spicy, and some delicate and mild. All were savory and delicious.

Which I told the waiter when he picked up our empty dishes.

He smiled, satisfied that we had enjoyed every morsel. In Germany, waiting tables was a profession, not just a temporary job for aspiring actors. He was proud of his work.

After dinner, Diane and I talked of our lives of long ago. She told me about her school friends from Virginia and I told her about my days in LA, before moving abroad.

"My parents objected to my marrying Charles," I said.

"Who did they want you to marry?"

"Someone raised Pentecostal. Preferably a missionary. Certainly not a Jew. And the only person who I would have even considered marrying, raised in their religion, wasn't available."

"Who?"

"Elvis."

"Elvis Presley? Are you serious?"

"Yes, he was raised Pentecostal too. So I told my father to arrange it. Dad wasn't amused. He definitely had a missionary in mind."

"You're funny. You and a missionary? Never."

"Did I tell you about the time I saw Elvis, on the LA freeway?"

"No way! How did you know it was him?"

"He sang "Love Me Tender." Apologized for not having brought his guitar. I swooned."

She chuckled.

"Driving home from work one day, in stop-and-go traffic, an old green beater pulled up beside my shiny green Studebaker—which I fondly called 'Frog.' I turned my head to check out the old clunker and did a double take. The driver resembled Elvis. Don't be ridiculous, I told myself. Elvis surely drives a better car than this piece of crap. So I looked again. He smiled at me. Sure looks like Elvis, I thought.

"Our cars inched forward a few feet and the same old clunker was beside my car. I looked again. I shook my head no. He nodded, as if to say yes. I shook my head no. He shook his head yes again. No way, I thought. Why is he driving this old beat-up car?"

"Why didn't you just roll the window down and ask?"

"I tried, but the windows were manual and I almost had a wreck."

"That's one way to impress him."

"Our cars were side by side, one more time. I mouthed the question. 'Are you Elvis?' He smiled, nodded and did a thumb-up. The freeways split off in different directions. He went one way and I went the other."

"Oh no," Diane exclaimed. "You're saying we will never know?"

"Not at all. At the time, I lived with my aunt near Pasadena. She rented rooms in her home to single working women. That night at dinner I mentioned seeing Elvis on the freeway. The other boarders politely smiled and nodded, one rolled her eyes at another, thinking I wouldn't notice."

"Apparently not impressed by your story," Diane said.

"Apparently. Except for one young woman. She asked what kind of car Elvis was driving. When I told her an old green clunker, she casually replied that Elvis drives an old green Rambler when he wants to be alone and not be recognized.

"Another woman, obviously not believing her, asked exactly how she would know that? She explained that her boyfriend played in Elvis's band, and the car was often parked near the studio where they practice."

"Wow! That's an amazing story." Diane poured more wine. "So, instead of Elvis, you married Charles."

We both laughed.

"True story," I said, "And lived happily ever after until shit hit the fan. When I first met Charles, I thought he was so handsome. Now, he's not attractive at all. Remember last year when we were trying to adopt a child?"

"I do. You were excited, knowing you had a child waiting in Hong Kong."

"We had airline tickets in hand, when Charles decided he didn't want to adopt after all. Instead he wanted a divorce."

"I remember how heartbroken you felt. You cried and cried, and cried."

"I did. Now I can only feel gratitude that I never had a child with Charles. But I still have some doubts."

I asked Diane about her friend, an American psychologist named Mary Kaye. "Not the Mary Kay who sells cosmetics and drives a pink Cadillac," I explained.

Diane smiled. "I think you're doing fine. But I'm sure Mary Kaye would be happy to help you."

"I think I'm doing okay, but I'd like to get a professional opinion to know if I'm dealing with things in the healthiest way."

"She's got great credentials and is a wonderful person. Do you need her telephone 55number?"

"I have it. She gave me her card at your last party. I think I'll give her a call."

CHAPTER 6

I AM?

Frankfurt, Germany—1977

Viewing the foyer to Mary Kaye's office for the first time, I laughed at my silly notion of a pink Cadillac parked outside. A sign on the wall gave instructions for filling out a questionnaire in a box beneath the sign. I sat down and quickly filled in my personal information.

Within five minutes, a smiling Mary Kaye opened her office door and invited me into a bright, comfortable space.

We acknowledged meeting each other at Diane's party and commented on the fun evening.

"You look great with short hair," I observed. "Wasn't it longer before?"

"Yes. I got tired of fussing with it," she said, pushing her honey-blonde bangs aside.

"Short suits you. It opens up your lovely Irish face."

"Thank you." She motioned me to sit opposite her at her desk.

"So where do you park your pink Cadillac?" I couldn't resist.

"Wish I had one; I like pink and Cadillacs suit me."

She smiled, looked over the questionnaire, and explained the procedure used to obtain the best results in therapy sessions. "The initial visit is a time to get to know each other. Future visits will be more therapeutic in nature."

"That's fine." I nodded.

She asked me why I sought therapy and asked me to reflect on what worked, or didn't, in my present life.

I thought about the questions and answered the first one. "If therapy will help me heal faster emotionally, I'm open for it."

She nodded in agreement.

I told her about my marriage and my feelings about the upcoming divorce. I explained that Charles said he left me because I didn't produce children, but I always felt he just used this as an excuse for ending the marriage. I told her I had good days and bad days. Some were downright depressing, but overall I felt relieved he had asked for the divorce. "I would have had a difficult time initiating it, based on my religious upbringing. *'Til death do us part.* An especially depressing thought, knowing the marriage is dead."

Mary Kaye looked at me. "I can understand your feelings of depression. A divorce is a death—the death of a relationship."

"It certainly forces change. A great inconvenience."

She smiled and nodded for me to continue.

"Charles and I had an interesting and exciting life together for many years. We traveled the world and lived in lots of different countries—Israel, Switzerland, Belgium, Germany twice. Looking back, I'm grateful for all the adventures. Together, we were able to leave our small world views behind and explore a bigger, broader world by living in other cultures.

"My favorite place was Cyprus. Of course the war in '74 brought that paradise to an abrupt end. We lost everything we owned. Fortunately Charles has always earned good money, so we were able to move on without any major financial setbacks."

I stopped to reflect, then continued.

"Looking back, I realize the marriage worked as long as Charles was in control of all decisions.

"When Charles decided he wanted a divorce, I felt desperately alone. He left me with no money and no access to money. Bank accounts were always in his name, not mine.

"I became quite ill when a cold turned into pneumonia. I was bedfast for several weeks. My friends looked after me. One friend, a doctor, came by daily to bring me food and medicine. Diane stopped by often to check on me. Slowly, I got stronger and better.

"After I recovered, I found a good job right away as a financial analyst. My co-workers are supportive.

"Being creative feels therapeutic. And I spend most evenings painting—in preparation for my first art exhibit."

"Congratulations. When and where?" Mary Kaye asked.

"Here in Frankfurt. I'll send you an invitation."

"Please do. I'd love to see your work." She nodded for me to continue.

"Financially, life is still a challenge. But getting better. At least I'm following my dreams and not someone else's. And I feel stronger and better with each passing day, thanks to good friends, who are also good listeners. But I don't want to wear them out with my problems."

I stopped speaking and stared out the large window. Billowing clouds floated past. "I have strange dreams, but I've always had strange dreams. I keep a dream journal, and pay attention to them because I think they show me important things. I've learned to trust my inner voice for guidance.

"I'm an optimistic person. I often laugh when a situation is serious. Must be a Chinese past life influence. Am I sane or just imagining it?"

Mary Kaye smiled at the question and nodded for me to continue.

"Brussels was definitely the straw that broke the camel's back. My breaking point." I reached for a Kleenex to wipe my tearing eyes.

"We were living in Brussels. Charles traveled frequently with his work. When he left for his usual business trip one week, he mentioned he would be going to his office in Basel, Switzerland, and suggested I get away and visit friends in England. So I went to see friends in the English countryside.

"While there, one night I had a vivid dream. Actually a vision—so real I thought I was watching a movie on a big screen in a theater. I opened my eyes, sat up in bed, but the film kept rolling.

"I saw Charles in Paris, not Basel, with another woman. I know Paris, because I've been to Paris many times. I watched them board the Paris Metro. I could see the names of the metro stops as the train sped along underground.

"When Charles and the young woman exited the train, I noted the name of the station and watched them climb the stairs to a main street in the Latin Quarter. My eyes followed them down a winding side street. As they turned the corner, a light shone on the street sign. I watched them climb stairs and enter a two-story apartment building. I even noticed the number on the building.

"They went inside to a noisy party. They had drinks and hors d'oeuvres, visited with others at the party for a time. They climbed stairs to a second level and entered a small bedroom.

"They undressed and got into bed together. At first, she sat on top and I couldn't see her face. I kept hoping they would change places so I could figure the mystery woman out. From the sound of her voice and her French accent, I thought I knew her.

"When they turned over, I saw it was Anna, the wife of Jake—a friend from Naples. I felt shocked because she and Jake had just had their first child together.

"As Charles and Anna murmured affectionately and drifted off to sleep in each other's arms, I moaned a loud *no!* and the film ended, showing *The End* on the big screen.

"I tossed and turned the rest of the night, and tried to convince myself that it was just a dream. Maybe, not 'The End.' But I knew better. It was a vision, revealing the truth in my life.

"The next morning, over coffee, I told my English friend about the vision. She immediately quipped, 'But of course he's cheating on you. All men cheat.' She told me that her husband has been having affairs for years and whenever she questions him, he always denies it. 'Unless you want a divorce,' she advised, 'just accept it. It's norm.'

"I tried calling Charles at his office in Basel. He wasn't in.

"Seeing how upset I was, my English friend—a strong believer in astrology—began composing my natal chart based on my date, place, and time of birth. She talked about my ruling planet, my fifth house, aspects, affinity, earth, water, even mentioned an avatar point—which of course meant nothing to me.

"At some point, she seemed confused by her method of horoscope interpretation. She suggested I have my natal chart done by a pro—someone she knew in London. So I made an appointment for the following day, and met an astrologer named Liz Greene who specialized in psychological astrology.

"Liz told me Virgo was my ascendant, which gave me a brilliant mind. And Jupiter in my first house accounted for living in different countries. She spoke of powerful energy, premonitory dreams, and great potential. And was a bit annoyed that I kept asking if my marriage would work out. I didn't want to hear that my marriage was over. Brilliant mind. Greater things be damned, whether I liked it or not.

"The next afternoon, I went with my friend and her children to a county fair. People waited in a long line to have their fortune told by a well-known fortune-teller. I stood with my friend in the line. When it came my friend's turn, the fortune-teller told her about a large sum of money coming her way.

"When it came my turn, the fortune-teller shuffled the cards, and informed me she couldn't tell me anything I didn't already know. She motioned me to leave.

"What? I thought. I've paid for a reading. Seeing my confusion, she told the person who had collected my money to refund it. Bizarre, but true. My friend was confused by her refusal as well.

"Incidentally, my friend's mother died a few months later and left her a small fortune.

"A few days later I returned to Brussels—before Charles did—and telephoned Jake in Naples. I asked to speak with Anna.

"He said she was in Paris, visiting a friend.

"I asked if she was visiting her friend who lives in the Latin Quarter near the Shakespeare English bookstore on rue de la Bucherie.

"He said yes, and asked if I had met Anna's friend.

"I ignored his question and asked about the new baby.

"He said he enjoyed looking after him while Anna was away.

"I told him that Charles was also in Paris and maybe they'd get together.

"I quickly ended the conversation and hung up.

"My heart ached. Sick to my stomach and faint, I sat gasping for air for a few minutes, taking deep breaths until I felt oxygen flow to my brain again.

"After regaining my composure, I made a decision. I would give Charles one week, from the day of his return, to confess. If he didn't, I would confront him."

I stopped talking and took more Kleenex from the box.

"When Charles arrived home, a few days later, he acted as if nothing unusual had happened. I asked him about the weather in Basel. He replied with a casual, 'How would I know? I'm always in meetings.'

"The charade continued for six days. Feeling physically ill, I wasn't sleeping well. The night before the confrontation day—the day of reckoning—I had a nightmare where I pushed a screaming child, in a baby carriage, down a bumpy dirt road.

"The child kept screaming for me to push him faster. The bumpy road made it difficult to push the carriage forward, much less any faster. The child continued screaming at me to go faster.

"I stopped the carriage, thinking perhaps I could explain the bumpy road problem to the ornery child, but he screamed louder and jumped up and down, hitting the sides of the carriage with his arms and hands.

"I looked around, trying to figure out where we were and how we could find a smooth road out. There were piles of things everywhere—leaves, wood, old junk. A place for waste—a landfill.

"I leaned down to try and calm the child. He glared at me.

"Doing a double take. I looked at him again. Shocked, I took a step back and realized a miniature Charles sat in the baby carriage staring at me. An angry man in a shrunken child's body.

"He screamed again.

"'Fine, I'll push you faster,' I yelled and began running, pushing the carriage as fast as I could go over the loose, rocky bumps and potholes. He whooped and hollered with glee. I pushed it wildly, purposely trying to throw him from the buggy.

"We passed a huge pile of something moving. Interwoven colorful objects slithering in and out, in slow motion. I stopped the carriage abruptly and walked back to look. Snakes. Piles of snakes.

"Moving the carriage closer to the huge pile of long, leathery creatures, I stared in fascination. As a child I had always been afraid of snakes, but now they looked beautiful and harmless. Not frightening at all. I tried to get the miniature Charles to look at them, but he kept screaming for me to move on, to go faster.

"Ignoring his screams, I got closer to the entwined sea of serpents. They were exotic-looking creatures of different sizes and colors, weaving in and out of the pile. Resembling an exquisite tapestry or a perfectly woven braid. I knelt down next to them, reached out, and touched them.

"In an instant, I awoke to a dark sky, the sound of rain, and loud snores from Charles."

I paused again and stared out the window. Mary Kaye waited.

"I got up from bed and tiptoed to the bathroom. Examining my face in the mirror, I noticed deep, dark circles under my eyes and a very sad face. I stared at my face for a long, long time. I stared until I found a light in the reflection of my eyes."

I stopped talking and dabbed my wet eyes.

"What did the dream mean to you?" Mary Kaye asked.

I thought about the question. "An awakening on many levels," I answered. "Tired of pushing. Tired of Charles's demands. I stopped and faced my fears." I took a deep, long breath.

"You also let go of the old and stopped to see something new," Mary Kaye noted.

"I did." I nodded.

Mary Kaye encouraged me to continue.

"That morning was Day Seven of waiting for Charles to come clean about Paris and Anna. He didn't." I sighed.

"I had packed a small bag of personal belongings the night before, knowing my questioning him could be explosive. He had never hit me before, but I knew he would be livid with me for calling Jake.

"We sat in chairs, in the living room, across from each other. He sat reading the newspaper. The silence was deafening.

"I told him that I knew he had been in Paris with Anna. He lowered his paper and stared at me.

"Then he laughed. A strange laugh. A nervous laugh. 'Don't be ridiculous,' he sneered. 'Is this based on another crazy dream of yours?'

"'Yes, and I confirmed it with Jake.'

"'Jake,' he screamed, lunging at me. He threw me on the floor, put his foot on my chest, and asked how I had confirmed it with Jake.

"When I told him I'd telephoned Jake in Naples and Jake confirmed that Anna was in Paris, Charles went berserk. He tried to kill me." I placed my hands over my pounding heart and took deep breaths.

Mary Kaye waited.

"He put his thumb on my windpipe and pushed down with pressure. I kicked and turned my head and body to get loose, and get air. I couldn't. I knew I was a goner, unless he came to his senses. I could actually feel my eyes bulging out of my head. My body went limp. I must have fainted.

"'Oh my God,' I heard him say, as he picked me up from the floor and placed me on the couch.

"A few minutes later, when I came to, I opened my eyes and looked around. He was gone.

"I rested until I felt stable enough to walk, then got up, grabbed my packed bag and left the apartment. I had exactly three dollars in my wallet and some small Belgian francs. No bank account. No credit card. But I knew I had to get out.

"Fortunately, friends of ours lived in a suburb near Brussels. The husband was a friend from Poland who we met while studying Hebrew at an ulpan in Arad, Israel. He had a mouthful of gold and a heart full of soul. His wife was also very caring. I telephoned them and explained my drastic situation. Without hesitation, they invited me to stay with them until I felt stronger. They drove into Brussels and picked me up. I stayed with them for a few days until I felt ready to move on. They even gave me a loan to help me start over."

"Good friends are great assets." Mary Kaye smiled.

"I'm grateful for all of mine."

I stared out the window again, gathering my thoughts, and continued.

"When this happened to me, I could no longer ignore the fact that I didn't know Charles. He was a stranger. A great pretender. And I had been the perfect spouse, all those years, who threw great dinner parties. A 'see no evil, hear no evil' sort of Mrs. I also realized—to my horror—that Charles had been trained to kill."

"Who did he work for?"

"A Swiss firm, an international electronics firm, probably a front. My guess is that Charles worked as an agent. Undercover, or nonofficial cover, for the Americans and maybe the Israelis as well. Of course he adamantly denies it, and of course no government will ever acknowledge it.

"Anyway, after Brussels, I telephoned friends here in Frankfurt and they encouraged me to move here. So I did. My friends lived near a park and I used to run through the park every morning, waiting for ideas or solutions to fall from the sky. And some good ones did. I would come back from the run feeling refreshed—filled with creative ideas. I sketched out paintings, jotted down ideas for poems and stories. Another awakening! My creative juices were flowing.

"Just as I got back on my feet again, Charles contacted me. He decided he wanted the marriage to work. He got a job in Frankfurt, as an executive for an international publishing company, and suggested we adopt a child.

"Happily ever after? Obviously not. I no longer trusted him, but since he had never laid a hand on me before Brussels and since he begged for another chance, I tried my best to make it work. He probably did as well.

"After receiving confirmation of our approval to adopt a child in Hong Kong, we set a date and purchased airline tickets.

"Over dinner one night, he informed me that he didn't want to raise someone else's child. He wanted his own. He moved out that night. The divorce will be final soon."

We sat in silence for a few minutes. I let out a long sigh. "Thanks for listening. When would you like to see me again?"

"You don't need another appointment," Mary Kaye said. "You're doing just fine."

"I am?" I asked.

"Yes. You're dealing with your situation in a healthy way. But I'd enjoy getting together sometime as friends and seeing your exhibit. Let me put your name and number on my 'friends' list. You're a very interesting woman."

"Are you sure I don't need more therapy sessions?"

"Yes, I'm sure. You have my card. I have your number. Let's get together. Maybe lunch one day."

I cried again and took another Kleenex from the box on the desk. "Thank you." I stood to leave.

Hesitating, I asked, "What if I were to tell you I think I'm being followed?"

Mary Kaye walked around the desk, reached out and patted my arm. "You probably are. So, take care. We'll talk soon."

CHAPTER 7

THE BOX

Frankfurt, Germany—1977

"Let's sit over there." Michael nodded in the direction of empty spaces, at the end of a long table in the far corner of the room.

"Good people-watching," I said.

We settled on wooden benches, opposite each other.

"Love Wagner's. Great action and food." Michael smiled and nodded at a man sitting at a table across the room. "I'm glad you live in Sachsenhausen. Everyone here thinks I'm a movie star."

"You're the spitting image of a young Tony Randall."

"And as fastidious and fussy, I trust."

"You're not fussy. Just choosy. See any celebrities this evening?"

"Muhammad Ali just walked out."

"Muhammad Ali? Are you serious?"

"Five minutes ago."

"With his entourage of bodyguards and beautiful women?"

"Of course. A parade of beauties and brawny boys," Michael answered.

"Did he say hello?" I asked.

"Of course. He recognizes me from my Broadway performances."

"Did he remember you from the other night at the Balalaika? Rosetta introduced him to us."

"He smiled and nodded as if he knew me. I did the same."

"Wow! That's something to write home about," I said.

"That would only confuse my mother. She hasn't a clue about celebrities. She thinks their youth minister is a rock star."

I laughed. "Guess what? My landlord has agreed to let me rent the apartment downstairs for my studio."

"That's wonderful. Now you can throw dinner parties."

"Do my art and throw dinner parties."

"*Wunderbar.*"

"Truly wonderful," I agreed.

A big-bosomed waitress arrived to take our order. She pulled a pad and pencil from a pocket of the leather pouch fastened around her ample waist. The other pouch pockets were stuffed with coins and bills.

"Steak tartare?" Michael asked me.

"And *Handkäse mit Musik,*" I added.

Michael smiled. "Love that musical 'toot' one gets with raw onions?"

"Of course. Tradition."

"*Steak tartare, zwei Apfelwein und Handkäse mit Musik,*" Michael proudly ordered in German. "*Danke.*" He smiled at the waitress.

"*Ya gerne.* You're welcome," she added in English.

"Do you remember the first time we met?" I asked, touching Michael's outstretched hand.

"I do," Michael said. He smiled, placing his other hand over mine.

"When I entered the room, you were beaming at me. Glowing."

"Red wine does that."

"When Charles introduced us, we chatted like long-lost friends."

"Soul mates. And Charles wandered off in a pout." Michael glanced at me, mockingly aloof.

"He complained all the way home, accused me of chatting you up."

"Well, you did look sexy in that little red dress. And you were chatty."

"Thanks. Charles was jealous of you."

Michael chuckled. "You should have told him women weren't my type."

"I did. He didn't believe me."

"How did you ever end up marrying Charles? You're such opposites."

"Love's blind. I wanted to escape my small-world upbringing. And we both wanted to see the big world."

"You certainly have. How do you feel now, with the divorce looming?"

"About Charles?"

"About Susan?"

"The fog's lifting."

"Because you're focusing on what's important to you."

"Definitely. Being married felt comfortable for a long time. I thought I was happy. He appeared happy. Since I didn't have a plan of my own, I went along with his."

"Don't rock the boat."

"Exactly. And it worked. Until Cyprus. After those long months in bed— dreaming and thinking—I became aware of *me* again."

The bouncy waitress returned with our order of drinks and food. We clinked glasses.

"Yummy," I said, sampling the handmade cheese and chopped onions on a slice of dark bread.

"An illusion of happiness creates a foggy reality," Michael remarked.

"I guess I thought a child would satisfy all longings. Make everyone happy. Silly me."

"Did Charles tell you that?"

"Yes. And everyone else—family, friends, even strangers. Amazing how many people think having a child will save a marriage. It's fantasy to think that a baby will make everything okay again. A rocky relationship is rocky because it's broken and needs fixing. Or not. Takes two to make it work. I think the lullaby illusion is a universal myth."

"Unless you're gay and single," Michael announced. "Actually, the weak side of human nature makes us wish someone else would be in charge, be responsible. The easy life."

"The empty life."

"You're in a good place. Your art reflects it."

"Life has purpose, now that I'm being creative. I feel curious and full of wonder. My life's taking shape. I look forward to the divorce being final, so I can get on with fulfilling my dreams. I have a long list."

"What's your short list?"

"Create art that touches people. Be financially successful with my first exhibit. I want to make it with my art. It's something I feel passionate about."

"Lucky you. That's the way I felt about acting and writing. Being a businessman isn't as fulfilling, but it pays for the lifestyle to which I've become accustomed. By the way, have you received any more spacey letters from your mom?"

"With news of people I don't know and hope I never meet? None this week. How about you?"

"I brought the latest one," Michael said, removing a letter from his coat pocket. "There's only one good line. The other five pages are about people unbeknownst to me."

With dramatic flair, he read the first two lines out loud. "'Dear Michael, I've lost thirty pounds, mainly in my face and neck.'"

I stared at him, my mouth agape, and burst out laughing.

"The original pinhead," he observed, putting the letter back in his jacket pocket. "She's proud of losing weight. She's been trying for years."

"She's a good mom to stay in touch."

I turned my head and watched a familiar-looking man sit down at the end of the next long table. Alarmed, I leaned forward and whispered, "Don't look now. You can look later. Just listen. I see this man often. He gets on and off the U-Bahn every time I do. I've also seen him standing on the corner, near my apartment, several times. I think he's following me."

"When did you first notice?"

"A few weeks ago. At first I thought it had something to do with the divorce, but now I'm not so sure."

"Maybe he likes you. Europeans can be kinky that way." Michael patted my hand. "Seriously, describe him to me and I'll check him out on my way to the loo."

"Mediterranean-looking. Could be Italian, Greek, maybe Israeli, with dark, wavy hair. Dark eyes. Olive complexion. He's sitting at the end of the next table down, on the same side as you. He's wearing a dark blue turtleneck sweater."

"Does he ever acknowledge you? With a smile or a hello?"

"No, he always ignores me. Never makes eye contact."

"Excuse me. Tinkle time." Michael stood and headed to the bathroom.

Michael returned to his seat a few minutes later.

"He's gone," I said.

"I saw him before he left. Why do you think you're being followed?"

"My gut says it has to do with Charles and Cyprus."

"When did you first suspect Charles's involvement in the Cyprus conflict?" Michael asked.

"In London, right after the war. At a party for Cyprus refugees. The owner of a large hotel chain, who had hotels in Cyprus, invited Cypriot refugees to his country estate for a grill party. When we arrived, with British friends from Cyprus, I noticed people were avoiding us. Some turned and walked away when they saw us approaching. Some greeted me, but ignored Charles. These were people we had shared dinner and chitchat at parties with while living in Cyprus. People we considered friends."

"Did you ask them what was wrong?"

"No. I was dumbfounded—speechless. We were obviously being snubbed. Charles acted as if he didn't even notice and strolled outside for a smoke.

"I stood alone, when a man walked up to me and asked if I knew who Charles was. I answered, 'He's my husband.' The man yelled, 'Charles

Rubinstein is persona non grata on the Greek side of Cyprus and will be killed if he ever tries to return there!'

"Stunned by his verbal attack and the cold stares from around the room, my eyes welled with tears.

"My good Scottish friend Ilene pulled me aside and asked if I understood what was happening. I said no. I scanned the room, looking for Charles.

"She told me the Greek Cypriots believe that Charles is an agent who sold them out. I asked her why they were blaming Charles. She said it wasn't just Charles. They also blamed the British and the American governments. But Charles was one of three Americans on the last flight out of Cyprus the morning of the coup. The other two Americans on the flight were US military personnel. She asked if I knew the other men.

"'No,' I told her.

"She informed me that Charles and the other two men were seen leaving NATO headquarters in Athens together, later that same day."

"Whoa!" Michael said. "You're definitely being followed."

"Everyone in the room stared at me. I was stunned, I didn't know how to answer the questions or what to make of the accusations. I looked around the room again. No Charles in sight. I told Ilene that to my knowledge Charles worked for a Swiss firm, and not the US government. She gave me a hug and assured me she believed me. She went on to say the Greek Cypriots also thought Charles worked for the Israelis, because of his frequent flights to Israel. She believed that Greek Cypriots were naturally upset at the losses of lives, homes, and their businesses.

"I could feel the cold stares and glares. Loud, angry voices—mentions of Charles, and his frequent trips to Turkey, Greece, Israel, and Bulgaria.

"When I heard someone say Bulgaria, I nearly fainted."

Michael tilted his head quizzically.

"I knew Charles visited accounts in Turkey, Italy, Greece, and Spain," I said. "But I didn't know about Bulgaria.

"Once, during my long pregnancy in Cyprus, I had a vivid dream where I saw Charles walking with a woman into a hotel lobby in Sofia, Bulgaria. I mentioned it to my Israeli friend, Ronit, when she visited me later that day and expressed my surprise at Charles being in Sofia, because he had told me he would be in Istanbul that week."

"How could you tell it was Sofia from a dream?"

"A mountain peak—towering in the background."

"Wow. The mind is an amazing recorder of details," Michael said. "Sights, sounds, smells. So when Bulgaria came out at the party—"

"I knew the dream I had in Cyprus was true. And I knew there was truth to the accusations about Charles. A man, a facade. Who knows?"

Michael mimed the tightening of a screw.

I stopped, took a long sip of *Apfelwein*, and continued, "I found Charles outside, walking in the garden, talking with our English friends—the ones we were staying with.

"'We're leaving,' Charles informed me. We got in the car and left the party without even thanking the host.

"On the ride home, our friends discussed the anger of Greek Cypriots over the war, their losses, and how they wanted to pin the blame on anyone but themselves. The friends joked with Charles about the talk of Charles being an agent. The husband commented that he had always suspected Charles since all Americans living on the island worked for the US government in some way.

"Charles smiled.

"I waited until we were alone and asked Charles if he was in any way involved in the Cyprus war. I told him I needed to know the truth.

"He adamantly denied being an agent for anyone and assured me the Swiss firm was legit. I accepted his answer, because I wanted desperately to believe him."

"Don't tip it over," Michael said. "So you think the Swiss firm was a front?"

"Yes. Probably still is. My gut tells me that Charles and the Swiss firm were involved."

"Why did you choose to live in Cyprus?"

"His firm sent us there."

"Did Charles have accounts there?"

"A small one. The navy had a base there with a small exchange. US military personnel wore civilian clothes to appear low-profile in Cyprus."

"Perhaps Charles peddled information between governments. Mind you, it could have also been a Turkish double cross."

"Who knows if I'll ever know the truth. Charles showed me a strange article he wrote a few months ago—about not being a spy, even though everyone assumes he is. He said he'd submitted it to a magazine."

"Why would he do that?"

"Trying to convince someone."

"Probably you."

I sat and thought about Michael's comment for a long time.

"Michael," I said, "I just remembered something important. Charles often flew a small Cessna plane to Israel, with another friend. An English guy named Syd. They both loved to fly and looked for places to fly into close by, to keep up their private pilot's license requirements. They had flown to Tel Aviv on numerous occasions, but one time when they flew into the airport Charles was detained—for reasons unknown—and Syd ended up having to fly the plane back to Cyprus solo. I was of course expecting Charles to be home in time for dinner. I waited and waited, and finally got a telephone call from Syd saying Charles had been arrested when they landed in Israel. I was shocked by the news."

"What did you do?"

"I telephoned the US Embassy in Nicosia and they told me to come in the next morning. I went to the embassy and told them what Syd said had happened. They asked a zillion questions, grilled me, suggested I travel to Tel Aviv and sort it out there in person at the US Embassy."

"Did you?"

"I did. But when I arrived in Tel Aviv, a day later, and telephoned the embassy for an appointment, I was told that Charles was in the airport waiting for a flight out."

"How bizarre!" Michael said.

"Sure enough, I found Charles sitting in a lounge waiting on the next flight to Cyprus. He was angry and kept yelling about the 'damn Israelis.' Over-the-top angry. I'd never seen him be so demonstrative. I kept telling him to calm down or he might get arrested again. He told me they arrested him because they claimed he took wood from a construction site when we lived in Arad. I remembered one time when our neighbor, the construction site manager, offered some scrap wood to Charles to build a coffee table. I knew Charles had never stolen any wood. It was offered to him by the site manager. And that was several years ago. We had visited Israel many times since and never once had any problems or questions."

"Was Charles was performing for you? Telling you what he wants you to believe?"

"I asked him how he was able to clear things up in such a short time. 'Money,' he answered. He suggested I try to get a seat on the flight back with him. Which I did."

"Did he ever talk about this incident again?"

"No, not that I remember."

"Did he ever return to Israel?"

"Yes, several times."

"Did you read about Makarios's sudden death last week? Died of a heart attack just shy of his 64th birthday."

"I'm sure he died of a broken heart. It's so sad that Cyprus is still divided."

"By a green line," Michael added. "Did you keep a journal while you lived in Cyprus?"

"Yes, and I researched news material on Cyprus after the war."

"Where is it?"

"In a box under my bed. Along with some correspondence from friends and photos of Cyprus and the UN camp. Disturbing photos of charred bodies and the blackened landscape, taken by a UN soldier during the war. Charles has tried numerous times to get these items from me."

"I think you need to give the box to someone for safekeeping."

"That's probably a good idea. Would you keep it?"

"Be happy to. Where did you go after you were rescued?"

"That's another long story," I said, taking a deep breath. "There were several weird twists which happened after the Cyprus War."

"Like what?"

"When we were rescued off the coast of Cyprus by the Brits, we were transferred to the HMS *Hermes*. A few hours later, the Sixth Fleet came along and transferred all Americans on board to the USS *Trenton*. We were told to line up and show our passports, as the ship was sailing to Beirut. An officer looked at Charles's passport first, then mine. When he saw that my passport had an Israeli stamp in it, he said I needed to go back to the British ship because the Lebanese wouldn't allow me to enter the country. Charles's passport didn't have an Israeli stamp in it, even though he traveled there frequently.

"At the time, I thought nothing of it. The US Embassy gave us two passports, one for Israel and another one for visiting Arab countries. I had the wrong one. But later, when I thought it through, it was weird that Charles traveled to European countries on his second passport. Like he didn't want other countries to see his frequent trips to Israel."

"Interesting!"

"So we went back to the HMS *Hermes* and were taken to the RAF Akrotiri British base and waited on a military plane to fly us to England."

"And where did you go after England?" Michael asked.

"We rented a house in Virginia Beach, awaiting word from the firm on Charles's next assignment. Charles spent his days on the road, visiting accounts on military bases near his company's Virginia office in Langley."

"Isn't the CIA headquarters in Langley?"

"Yes."

"The plot thickens."

"I spent my days visiting the Edgar Cayce Institute, and researching the Cyprus War at the public library. I spent lots of time alone trying to figure things out. By that time, I felt certain that Charles had a secret and that the company was a front."

"Were you afraid?"

"Afraid to look at the big picture, to look at my marriage, my life. Yes. Afraid to tip the boat over in the middle of a deep, dark ocean. One night while home alone in Virginia Beach, I had a vision."

"A dream?"

"A clairvoyant vision."

"A clear vision of something actually happening?"

"Yes. My mind floated around the sky. I heard the loud sound of jets landing and taking off at the military base nearby."

"Langley! Of course."

"As I zeroed in, I could see planes being loaded with weapons and taking off for different destinations around the world. I saw Charles and his firm arranging and organizing the deliveries."

"Weapons for wars. That's a vivid vision," Michael surmised.

"When Charles returned, a few days later, I told him about the vision. He dismissed it as part of my overactive imagination and suggested earplugs so I could get a better sleep."

"I'm surprised he didn't also recommend blinders."

"I realized the truth of Charles, his firm, and what they did."

"Whoa!" Michael said. "I was living in London in 1974, dating a Greek guy. We watched the Cyprus disaster unfold every evening on the news. Since Greece and Turkey were both part of NATO and the US supplied arms to both, the Cyprus situation was an explosive one. The US couldn't stand Makarios for lots of reasons. He was the number one enemy of their junta friends in Athens. He had Communist support and they thought he was in cahoots with the Arabs."

"A clever man, Makarios knew that the junta was planning to overthrow him," I said.

"He warned everyone in interviews. By 1974, the nuclear arms race was full speed ahead between the US and the Soviets. So Cyprus, in its strategic location in the Middle East, was key in the monitoring of nuclear tests. The US did not want to lose its spy bases in northern Cyprus. Watching the coup and the war unfold, I remember thinking Kissinger had masterminded a plan to divide the island and save the spy facilities from a possible Communist takeover. The Turkish invasion left the British bases intact and US spy stations free to continue spying on Russia and the Middle East. A no-brainer."

"You pieced all of that together?" I asked. I marvelled at Michael's intellect.

"Yes, and Aphrodite would turn over in her grave if she knew what has happened to her beloved island."

"She would. When I looked out the window of the plane, as we were leaving Cyprus, and saw the charred remains of a place I knew as paradise, I broke down and wept."

"There's no paradise on earth. Not anymore." Michael signaled for the check. "One day I want to hear the details of the war and rescue."

"I remember every detail and actually feel blessed to have experienced and survived the Cyprus War."

"A tragic event can be a positive experience."

"It definitely shapes one—for better or worse."

"I'll walk you home and collect the box. Promise me you won't walk the streets alone after dark."

"I won't. Unless it's a necessity."

CHAPTER 8

HURRAH?

Nicosia, Cyprus—15 July 1974

"Oh my God," I gasped, steering the Pininfarina convertible through the roundabout, nearing the Nicosia airport. "Soldiers are everywhere."

"Probably military exercises," Charles said.

"They're on both sides of the road, all the way to the airport."

"Black Mak—Makarios is probably coming or going."

"Considering the seriousness of this past week's events, I think it's a coup."

"Nothing to worry about." Charles tried to assure me, patting my knee.

"As soon as I drop you off at the airport, I'm getting the hell out of here," I told him.

"Don't forget to stop by the mechanic on the way home. Have him adjust the brakes."

"I will."

"Good luck." Charles kissed me goodbye, grabbed his bag from the backseat. "See you next week."

"Have a good trip."

He waved before disappearing through the sliding glass doors of the Nicosia International Airport terminal.

I started the engine and pulled into the exit lane from the airport. Steering onto the exit road, I noticed even more armed soldiers gathered. Scores stood alongside the road and in empty fields nearby.

I turned the car radio on to BBC. Just static. I tried other stations. Static. More static. I switched it off.

Nearing the roundabout, I noticed an army tank approaching from the direction of the Greek army camp. I pushed down on the gas pedal and sped around the traffic circle onto the frontage road, in the direction of George's garage.

Behind, a sudden burst of rapid gunfire shocked me to the core. My legs trembled. "Oh, my God," I gasped. "This is it." I raced away from the airport.

Screeching brakes brought the car to a halt in George's parking lot. I jumped out and ran inside.

"*Kaliméra*—good morning," George greeted me calmly. "How are you? Is the mister off flying again?"

"He's off to Athens. What's happening?" I asked, pointing in the direction of the roundabout.

"Where?" George asked.

I pointed toward the main traffic circle again. "Gunfire. Soldiers are everywhere. Tanks too."

"Perhaps a car backfiring, or a military maneuver. Would you like coffee?"

"No thanks, I'm in a hurry. Something's happening."

"You Americans, always in a hurry." George laughed.

"Sorry, I'm just trying to get home as soon as possible."

"What's wrong with the car?"

"The brakes need adjusting."

"Let's take a look." George motioned me to follow him outside.

As we neared my car, gunfire exploded. Bra-ta-ta-tat! Bra-ta-ta-tat! I grabbed George's arm and clung to it.

"Machine guns. Oh my God." He pushed me toward his office. "Quick, get inside."

Bra-ta-ta-tat! Bra-ta-ta-tat! The sound continued. Louder. Getting closer.

I watched him run onto the service road, parallel to the main highway, and look in all directions.

Gunfire continued. He came running back inside, grabbed the telephone, and dialed zero.

He muttered something in Greek, hung up and dialed another number. He shouted at me. "Leave now. Drive to Kyrenia. They've attacked the main police station. It's a coup. Go." He pushed me out the door. "It's not safe here."

I dashed to my car, got in, and sped away, in the direction of the road to Kyrenia. A military bus, turned sideways, blocked the roundabout. Cars stopped and backed up, trying to escape the chaos unfolding. Gunfire continued.

My mind raced, trying to figure out what to do next. I can't go that way, I must go back.

Constant, loud gunfire bombarded my thoughts. Bra-ta-ta-tat! Bra-ta-ta-tat! Dakka dakka!

Ka-boom! Ba-Ba-Ba-BOOM! A line of tanks appeared, rumbling over the rise of the hill.

Shaking and sweating, I put the car into reverse and backed all the way to George's garage.

"Do you want to get killed?" he screamed, running toward my car. "Leave here. Drive to Kyrenia."

"The road's blocked."

"Go that way, past the police station," he said pointing to the right. "No, no. Too dangerous. Police stations will be a prime target for the insurgency."

"Where can I go?" I asked desperately.

"To your friends. Ronit and Andreas. Their apartment is just across the highway. Go. Don't stop for anything," he shouted. "Don't stop for anything."

I jumped into the car and sped away, taking side roads to the main road.

At the main road, I stopped and looked left in the direction of the Presidential Palace. No cars coming. A lone woman ran past a kiosk.

Just as she passed, the stand exploded in flames behind her. She kept running. I gasped in horror.

I looked right, in the direction of the roundabout, and to my terror saw a long line of tanks rumbling toward me, firing big-barrel guns in all directions. Oh, my God. I gasped.

Ka-boom! BA-BA-BOOM. BA-BA-BOOM. Columns of smoke rose as shells hit their targets.

A sickening wave of fear flooded my mind. *Do I wait for them to pass? Do I cross the road in front of them?* This is it. I'll be killed. My heart pounded. My hands trembled. My knees knocked together.

Don't stop for anything. I could hear George yelling.

Ka-boom! BA-BA-BOOM. BA-BA-BOOM. The deafening sound surrounded me.

I knew I had to cross the road and get to the safety of Ronit's apartment. Legs shaking, heart pounding, I pushed in the clutch, put the car in first gear, and pressed down on the gas pedal.

The car lunged and jerked forward as I shifted to second, third and fourth, and raced across the road in front of the firing tanks.

Clear of the tank fire, I took a deep breath and sighed. I made it. Only then did I look back in the mirror to make certain tanks weren't following me.

I watched as they rumbled on by, on the main road, in the direction of the city and the Presidential Palace.

Ba-Ba-Boom. Ba-Ba-Boom. The gunfire now sounded much farther away.

I slowed the car and turned right, onto the street where Ronit and Andreas lived, and parked in an empty space under their building.

Removing the key from the ignition, I slumped over the steering wheel and cried tears of joy for having made it to safety.

Getting out of the driver's seat, I realized that my summer dress, wet from sweat and urine, clung to my body.

I pushed the bell for apartment 3B and waited. No answer. I tried it again. Still no answer. *What's the name of their neighbor? The Cyprus Air pilot. Perhaps he's home.*

"*Me za?* Who is it?" a sleepy voice asked in Hebrew.

"It's me, Susan."

"Susan? *Shalom.*" The buzzer released the door lock. I climbed the stairs to the third floor.

Ronit stood in the doorway, in her nightgown. She smiled at me and kissed the brass *mezuzah* on the door post.

Ba-Ba Boom! Ba-Ba Boom!

"*Ma ka rah?*—What's going on?" Ronit asked.

"Tanks."

"Sounds like thunder." Ronit motioned me inside the dark apartment and closed the door. The *rolladen* shades—rolling shutters—on the windows were always closed during the hot summer days, to keep the inside air as cool as possible.

"Military tanks. They're everywhere. Look outside." I pointed to the kitchen window.

Ronit opened the kitchen shade enough to peer out through the slits and view the main road below. "Oh, my God. Tanks are everywhere. They're ripping the pavement. Why are they firing?"

"To clear the streets. Where's Andreas? He'll know what's happening and why."

"He's on guard duty at the Israeli Embassy. Look. A bus is blocking the roundabout."

"I know. I tried to get through earlier. They're blocking all roads, in and out of the city."

We watched cars heading for the roundabout stop, turn in circles, then speed away along side streets, trying to steer clear of the danger. Tanks continued firing.

"Oh God," Ronit said, and began crying. "Andreas. My *mana mou*. Andreas."

I put my arm around her. "We're safe here, for now. Andreas is safe there. I hope Charles is okay. I left him at the airport. I don't know if his flight to Athens even took off."

Ronit left and returned with a portable radio. She turned the dial back and forth, first to Kol Israel, BBC, then Cyprus Broadcasting. Only static and music.

Moments later, we heard a tremendous explosion. Glasses and plates rattled. The apartment building shook.

We scurried to the kitchen window and watched in shock as a huge ball of fire about a mile away erupted, filling the sky with billows of black smoke.

"The Presidential Palace," Ronit gasped.

Explosion after explosion rocked the area around us. We ran into the living room, stood in the center of the room, and waited for calm.

An uneasy quiet followed. We returned to the kitchen window and looked out again. Fires and smoke filled the air. People were running along the main road and scurrying through empty fields nearby.

"I hope they make it," Ronit said. "Wish we had a phone. Our British neighbor Garth has one, but I can't go there."

"The Cyprus Airways pilot? Why not? I'd like to call the airport."

"Andreas is jealous. He thinks we're too friendly."

"But you're neighbors."

"You go."

"Do you want me to phone the embassy?"

"*Kin.* Yes." Ronit wrote the number down and handed it to me.

"Oh, Ronit." I hugged her. "I'm sorry. I'll be right back."

I crossed the hall and rang Garth's doorbell. No answer. I waited, then knocked on the door.

Moments later, a sleepy, pajama-clad Garth opened the door.

"I'm sorry. Did I wake you?" I asked.

"Hell, no. The construction workers did. Listen to that pounding."

"It's a coup. I'm Susan, Ronit's friend from Kyrenia. Can I use your phone?"

"Of course," he mumbled, motioning me inside. "I remember you from a beach party. Your husband's the big guy who looks like the *Fugitive* actor. I was just talking with my ex-wife in London when the phone went dead. Electricity's off too."

"Have you looked outside? Tanks are all over the place. We're in the middle of a revolution."

"A revolution? Bloody hell. Priscilla won't believe this." He picked up the telephone. "Still dead. Damn. I'll get my radio. There must be some news on about this."

He returned with a small radio and spun the dial. "Good God. Nothing."

"I've got to get back. If you hear any news, please let us know. I dropped Charles at the airport for the Cyprus Air flight to Athens."

"No planes will fly into or out of Cyprus today. I'll let you know if I hear something."

"Thanks," I said, leaving.

"I'm in the kitchen," Ronit yelled as I closed the front door.

"Garth's phone is dead."

Ronit motioned for me to join her at the kitchen table. "Thank God for gas stoves. I made coffee."

"Thanks. Can I shower first? I'm soaking wet."

"Of course. I'll get you some fresh clothes."

I showered and changed into a loose-fitting shift of Ronit's, and returned to the kitchen.

Ronit poured hot coffee into two large mugs and turned the radio on. Static on Kol Israel. British Forces Broadcast asked listeners to call in and request a song. A Cyprus station was playing Greek military music.

To our surprise, BBC broadcast a crackling live announcement, accompanied by marching music and a patriotic song.

> AT 0830 HOURS THIS MORNING, AS ARCHBISHOP MAKARIOS WELCOMED A GROUP OF SCHOOLCHILDREN FROM CAIRO TO THE PALACE, TANKS SURROUNDED THE GROUNDS AND OPENED FIRE. A GROUP OF COMMANDOS ENTERED THE PALACE, SHOUTING, "DOWN WITH POPE CAESAR.' THE FATE OF THE ARCHBISHOP AND THE CHILDREN IS UNKNOWN.

> INSIDE KYKKO WERE ABOUT 60 PRIESTS AND NOVICES, GUARDED BY UNITS OF MAKARIOS'S SPECIAL TACTICAL RESERVE, A PARAMILITARY POLICE FORCE SET UP BY THE ARCHBISHOP WHEN HE UNCOVERED EOKA-B CELLS AMONG THE REGULAR POLICE. A DOZEN SHELLS BLASTED THE FACADE OF THE TWO-STORY BUILDING, AND MACHINE GUN BULLETS RAKED THE WALLS. ONE EYEWITNESS SAYS PASSERS-BY WERE CAUGHT IN THE FIRE. THEIR FATE AND THAT OF THE PRIESTS IS UNKNOWN.

"Oh, my God," we exclaimed in unison.

Heavy gunfire began again. We ran to the kitchen window. Clouds of smoke filled the sky surrounding the presidential palace.

Looking left, I saw lines of cars at the roundabout, still blocked by the bus and tanks.

A man opened his car door to get out. Soldiers rushed toward the car with rifles pointed. The man backed into his car seat.

A tank opened fire, in our direction, over the top of the man's car. Seeing the ball of fire blasting through the air, we fell to the floor screaming and crawled into the living room. We huddled together on the couch until the gunfire subsided.

The silence was broken by a familiar summer sound, the shrill chorus of male cicadas screaming their song. The loud, high-pitched calls, from sunup to sundown, had been a daily occurrence this hot summer—

drowning out most other sounds. *Funny. I didn't remember hearing them earlier this morning.*

When we next peered out the kitchen window, I saw bushes and brush ablaze in the empty field between the roundabout and Ronit's building.

Ronit turned the dial to Kol Israel. "No new news." She turned the radio off. "I don't know what to do."

"Not much we can do right now."

"No. About Andreas. He wants a divorce."

"Do you?"

"No, but I don't want to live like this. We're always fighting."

"I'm sure things will work out. You've been together a while."

"We've been together for seven years total. Five years in Israel. My family thought we were married and thought he was Jewish. Maybe he's got the itch?"

"The seven-year itch?" I asked. "I think people use that as an excuse to play around."

"I don't think he has a girlfriend. We fight over money. And religion. And Israel versus Cyprus." Ronit's voice trailed off.

"Coming from different cultures can create problems, unless you accept the differences."

"We're both too stubborn for that."

A knock on the door. Ronit ran to open it. "Hello," she greeted Garth.

"My phone's still dead. But I heard that the Cyprus Air 8:05 flight took off. The only flight out today," Garth announced. "They allowed it because Greek officers' families were on board and they wanted them out of this bloody mess. I'd be surprised if they let civilians fly out with them."

"Charles had a meeting in Athens this morning."

"Let's hope he got on it," Garth said. "The report only mentioned Greek military families leaving. I'll let you know if I hear more."

"Thanks," I replied, as Garth headed back to his apartment.

We heard distant cracking sounds of rifles and short bursts of automatic weapons as we closed the front door.

Kol Israel interrupted its programming with a news bulletin at 1100 hours.

THERE APPEARS TO BE A REVOLUTION IN CYPRUS. THE SITUATION IS CONFUSING. THE PRESIDENTIAL PALACE IS UNDER ATTACK. STAY TUNED.

Hoping to conserve battery power, we agreed to listen to news only every half hour. At 11:30 Ronit turned the radio on again. We listened intently to a new Cyprus Broadcasting report in English.

THE CYPRUS NATIONAL GUARD INTERVENED TODAY TO STOP INTERNECINE WAR. THE MAIN PURPOSE OF THE NATIONAL GUARD IS TO MAINTAIN ORDER. THE MATTER IS AN INTERNAL ONE AMONG GREEKS ALONE. THE NATIONAL GUARD AT THIS MOMENT IS IN CONTROL OF THE SITUATION, AND MAKARIOS IS DEAD. ANYONE WHO PUTS UP RESISTANCE WILL BE EXECUTED AT ONCE. A 24-HOUR CURFEW IS IN EFFECT IMMEDIATELY.

"Makarios is dead," Ronit whispered, tears streaming down her cheeks.

"I met him at a christening once. A stunning-looking man with dancing blue eyes," I said.

"Not anymore."

Heavy gunfire continued in the distance. The coup was meeting resistance.

"Andreas, my *mana mou,*" Ronit cried out. "Where are you?"

I reached over and hugged her. "He'll be all right," I tried to assure her.

Later in the day, we listened to another BBC report.

A COMMUNIQUÉ ISSUED BY THE GREEK NATIONAL GUARD (WHICH CARRIED OUT THE COUP) BROADCAST OVER THE CYPRUS BROADCASTING RADIO THAT ARCHBISHOP MAKARIOS WAS DEAD. OTHER SOURCES SAID HE WAS ALIVE AND HAD ASKED THE UNITED NATIONS FOR

HELP. HE ALSO ASKED THE GREEK CYPRIOT COMMUNITY TO CONTINUE TO RESIST. THE GREEK NATIONAL GUARD SAID THAT THE MATTER WAS AN INTERNAL ONE. THAT IT WAS IN FULL CONTROL, AND WARNED THAT ANYONE OFFERING RESISTANCE WOULD BE SHOT.

SHOOTING AND EXPLOSIONS CONTINUED. REPORTS SAID THAT THE COMMANDER OF THE TACTICAL RESERVE FORCE, MAJOR PANTAZIS, HAD SURRENDERED. GREEK MILITARY AUTHORITIES DECLARED A TWENTY-FOUR-HOUR CURFEW THROUGHOUT THE GREEK SECTORS TO ENFORCE LAW AND ORDER AND SAID THE ARMY HAD TO INTERVENE TO PREVENT A CIVIL WAR.

"It's weird that Charles left and now a coup has occurred," Ronit remarked.

"If he got on the plane."

"Maybe Charles is involved."

"Charles? I would surely know. You can't live with a man for so many years and not know."

"People at the Israeli Embassy have asked me. You have lots of official American friends."

"We have lots of friends of different nationalities. Most foreigners here work for some government. Look at you and Andreas. You work for El Al. He works for the embassy."

"As a guard," Ronit answered.

"Charles works for a Swiss firm. He sells electronic equipment," I insisted.

"Why does he travel to Greece, Turkey, Bulgaria, and Israel so often?"

"He sells equipment to NATO all over the Middle East."

"What kind of electronic equipment?"

"I'm not sure. He doesn't talk much about his work."

A knock at the door startled us. Garth stood, car keys in hand, asking if we needed anything from the store.

"No, thanks," Ronit told him.

"There's a curfew. Be careful," I called after him. "Gotta love the Brits and that stiff upper lip," I remarked to Ronit as she closed the front door.

During the next several hours all radio stations continued to carry the CBC report of the coup and the death of Makarios.

Ka-boom! BA-BA-BOOM. BA-BA-BOOM. Tanks were firing again. We hurried back into the living room and sat on the couch. The distant sounds of sporadic gunfire continued for hours.

Finally we heard a new report from BBC.

THE ACTING TURKISH MINISTER AND MINISTER OF NATIONAL DEFENSE, MR. ISIK, MADE A STATEMENT ON THE DEVELOPMENTS IN CYPRUS.

"IT HAS BEEN LEARNED THAT A COUP HAS TAKEN PLACE IN CYPRUS. ALTHOUGH, REPORTS SAID THAT THIS HAS BEEN DIRECTED ONLY AGAINST THE GREEK CYPRIOT ADMINISTRATION, THE CYPRUS ISSUE IS AN INTERNATIONAL QUESTION. AND IT IS AN ISSUE BASED ON FUNDAMENTAL RESPONSIBILITIES, OF TURKEY, GREECE, BRITAIN AND THE TWO COMMUNITIES IN ACCORDANCE WITH THE AGREEMENTS. IT IS NATURAL THAT TURKEY WILL NOT ALLOW THE VIOLATION OF THE FUNDAMENTAL STATUS BY THIS MOVE. CYPRUS WILL REMAIN AN INDEPENDENT STATE WITH BOTH COMMUNITIES NOT DOMINATING EACH OTHER. THE TURKISH GOVERNMENT IS CLOSELY FOLLOWING UP THE DEVELOPMENTS WITH UTMOST IMPORTANCE AND WILL NOT FAIL TO TAKE NECESSARY MEASURES."

"It's strange, that you live here, but Charles doesn't work here," Ronit observed, when the report ended.

"We live here because it's paradise," I answered.

"Not anymore." Ronit wept again.

"No. Not anymore," I agreed, staring into space.

A screech of brakes below startled us. We ran to the balcony as Andreas's car pulled into the garage below.

"Where have you been?" Ronit called to him.

"Guarding the embassy," he answered, running up the stairs. "I had a front-row seat of the action at the palace. I could see everything. The tanks open fire, the explosions, the black smoke. A helicopter made several futile attempts to land, but was driven off by gunfire."

"Did they kill Makarios?" Ronit asked.

"I hope so. Under Black Mak, the Communists were taking over. We couldn't just sit back and let it happen. He put people through hell. Don't cry for him. There was no other way."

Confused by his comments, Ronit and I looked at each other.

"Have you heard any news about the airport?" I asked. "Charles might be trapped there."

"It closed at 8:30, right after the 8:05 Cyprus Air flight took off. All main roads are barricaded. I can try to reach it on back roads."

"No. It's too dangerous," I cautioned. "Hopefully he made it."

Andreas headed down the hall to shower and change clothes.

When we heard the bathroom door close, Ronit whispered, "I'm shocked. I didn't know he was for unity with Greece."

"Pro-*enosis*? I'm surprised too."

Andreas whistled a patriotic song as he entered the living room, after his shower. "It's a great day for Cyprus. As foreigners, you have nothing to fear. Absolutely nothing. Have you prepared dinner?" he asked Ronit.

"I can. There's a chicken in the fridge. We don't have bread."

"I'll go get bread and wine," he announced, leaving.

I followed Ronit into the kitchen to help with dinner. "I'm glad you're here," Ronit said. "This is our first meal together in over a week. We haven't been speaking to each other!"

"He's happy to see you. I'm glad we're all alive."

Andreas returned home with bread and wine. "I tried to get to the airport, but all roads were blocked," he reported.

He turned the radio on to the Greek Cypriot radio station, and in a loud voice announced, "Nikos Sampson has taken the oath as president."

"I can't believe it," I remarked. "Isn't he the terrorist who once dressed as a Turk and gunned down Turkish soldiers?"

"Yes," Andreas answered. "But it's only temporary, until Cyprus can have free elections."

"How long?" asked Ronit.

"A few months," Andreas assured her. "It's an internal thing between Greek factions."

After dinner, Andreas turned the radio on again. Martial music played. Andreas sang along.

"What do the words mean?" I asked. "The tune is familiar."

"When Johnny comes marching home again Hurrah! Hurrah!" he sang.

"Hurrah?" I asked, puzzled.

We heard sporadic shooting in the distance, but all was quiet in the neighborhood.

As the sun set, a few cars made their way along the deserted streets below. We watched people arrive at their homes, and heard cries of joy as families hugged and kissed each other.

Ronit lit candles. Andreas suggested we play a game called Risk. Since I hadn't played it before, I asked Andreas to explain it to me.

"It's a strategic board game about world domination," he explained. "Players control armies and try to capture territories from other players."

"Like real life," I remarked. "Can we play gin?"

"Sure," Andreas said, bringing out the cards.

Ronit brought three glasses filled with an Israeli liqueur.

Later that evening, we listened to a news bulletin from the British Forces Broadcasting Service.

BFBS REPORTS THAT TEL AVIV HAS PICKED UP A CLANDESTINE RADIO STATION TRANSMITTING FROM PAPHOS. THEY MONITORED WHAT IS PURPORTED TO BE THE VOICE OF PRESIDENT MAKARIOS. "I AM NOT DEAD. I AM ALIVE. AND AS LONG AS I LIVE, THE CLIQUE THAT HAS REBELLED WILL NOT RULE CYPRUS. SO. I LIVE. SUPPORT ME. RISE UP AND FIGHT."

"It's propaganda," shouted Andreas. "Makarios is dead. They just want his supporters to fight on. I saw the attack on the palace. No one could have escaped from that." He quickly turned the dial to Cyprus Broadcasting in Greek.

"What are they saying?" I asked.

"Makarios is dead," Ronit answered.

CHAPTER 9

DEAD OR ALIVE?

Nicosia, Cyprus—16-17 July 1974

I rubbed sleep from my eyes and listened to the rumblings of jeeps and tanks moving about in the streets below. Is he dead or alive? I wondered.

The July sun was blazing hot; already the air was stagnant. *Oh for a breeze. A puff of air.* Within an hour or so the heat would be unbearable. I drew the bedroom window shade open a few inches. A gray haze of smoke hovered over the city of Nicosia. I closed the shade.

Ronit sat at the kitchen table, sipping coffee and turning the radio dial to different stations.

"*Boker tov!* Good morning," I greeted her. "Is Andreas up yet?"

"*Boker tov.* He's still asleep."

"The tanks are still at the roundabout," I announced, peering through a small slit in the kitchen window shade. "Only army trucks and jeeps are moving."

"At least it's quiet. Would you like coffee?'

"Yes, please. Is Makarios alive?"

"Reports say he is and hiding somewhere near the coast."

"It's a miracle, if it's true."

"Andreas wants him dead. He says the resistance will die if Makarios is dead."

"Unfortunately, I don't think the Turks will sit back and do nothing."

"Andreas says the Americans will stop them. They stopped the Turkish navy from landing during the trouble in the sixties."

"With Nixon's impeachment, and Kissinger—who thinks he's Henry the King—in charge, I don't think they'll stop the Turks this time. There's too much bad blood between the US and Greece. And after Vietnam, Americans are tired of war. I'd love to be wrong. I love this island."

"Oh, me too," Ronit agreed.

We listened to the latest report from the BBC.

> FIGHTING BETWEEN THE SUPPORTERS OF MAKARIOS AND THE GREEK OFFICERS NATIONAL GUARD, WHO THEY SAY MAY HAVE SEIZED POWER, IS CONTINUING IN NICOSIA AND THREE OTHER MAJOR TOWNS: LIMASSOL, LARNACA, AND FAMAGUSTA.
>
> REPORTS FROM PAPHOS SAY THAT THE BISHOP OF PAPHOS HAS SENT A MESSAGE TO THE GREEK CYPRIOT REPRESENTATIVE OF THE UNITED NATIONS, MR. ROSSIDIS, REQUESTING TO PLACE A COMPLAINT WITH THE WORLD BODY ABOUT WHAT HE CALLED AN ATTEMPT AT A COUP BY GREECE AGAINST THE LAWFUL GOVERNMENT OF CYPRUS. HE IS REPORTED TO BE ACTING ON BEHALF OF ARCHBISHOP MAKARIOS, WHO IS AGITATING RESISTANCE AGAINST THE MILITARY.
>
> DESPITE STRONG WARNINGS BY THE NATIONAL GUARD AGAINST ANY ATTEMPTS TO ORGANIZE MEETINGS OR DEMONSTRATIONS SUPPORTING MAKARIOS, A LARGE CROWD HAS DEMONSTRATED IN NICOSIA SHOUTING PRO-MAKARIOS SLOGANS.

Static interrupted and Ronit turned the dial to get better reception. The CBC reported:

> THE NATIONAL GUARD HAS ORDERED ALL RESERVE GREEK OFFICERS TO REPORT FOR DUTY IMMEDIATELY, IN UNIFORM. RESISTANCE HAS DIED DOWN THROUGHOUT THE ISLAND. THE NATIONAL GUARD SAID THEY HAVE BEEN ORDERED TO SHOOT ON SIGHT.

DIPLOMATIC CIRCLES IN NICOSIA ARE FOLLOWING THE EVENTS CLOSELY. ONE FOREIGN DIPLOMAT DESCRIBED THE EVENTS AS A "WISELY PLANNED ATTEMPT BY GREECE TO OUST MAKARIOS."

Looking tired, Andreas entered the room. "Good morning," he greeted me.

"Good morning," I answered.

"Would you like some coffee?" Ronit asked him.

"You bet," he answered, taking control of the radio. Greek music played on. "The news will be on shortly. What did Kol Israel report?" he asked Ronit.

"Makarios is alive and believed to be somewhere in the Paphos area," Ronit answered.

"I'll have to hear it to believe it," he muttered, turning the dial. Only static.

He turned it back to CBC and listened to the news in Greek. "No mention of Makarios being alive. It's baffling."

After breakfast Andreas took the radio out to the balcony, hoping for better reception. After several attempts, he left to listen to news on his car radio.

I switched the radio to the BFBS, hoping to hear news in English. There were only announcements to the British Forces, advising them to observe the curfew and stay off the streets for safety.

Ronit tapped me on the shoulder and pointed to a house down the street. Two military jeeps had stopped in front of the house. Several soldiers got out and went to the door. Others stood with machine guns in hand, facing the house.

A woman appeared at the door. A man joined her. He gently pushed the woman back inside, and left with the soldiers.

Andreas came back up the stairs. Ronit asked him if he had heard any of the conversation at the house where the military stopped. He motioned us inside before answering.

"Whatever you do, don't ever discuss politics in public. It can get you killed," he said in a hushed tone. "The man has been taken in for questioning. Probably a man of importance during the Makarios reign. Nothing will happen to him. Or you. You're foreigners. Only pro-Makarios people will be questioned and released, unharmed. Unlike Makarios.

His police force rounded up dissidents and tortured them, sometimes ripping out their fingernails."

"Oh, my God!" Ronit gasped in horror

I felt sick to my stomach, and shuddered at the thought.

Seeing our anxiety, Andreas reassured us that no harm would come to foreigners. He turned the radio on once more. We listened to a BBC World Service report.

> THE TURKISH PRIME MINISTER, MR. ECEVIT, CUTTING SHORT HIS VISIT TO OPIUM-PRODUCING AREAS, HAS RETURNED TO ANKARA FROM AFYON TO ATTEND A MEETING ON CYPRUS. HE WARNED THAT TURKEY WILL NOT ALLOW ANY NATION TO INFRINGE ON THE TURKISH CYPRIOT COMMUNITY. IN A MESSAGE TO THE TURKISH COMMUNITY, MR. DENKTASH (VICE PRESIDENT OF THE CYPRUS REPUBLIC AND PRESIDENT OF THE TURKISH CYPRIOT ADMINISTRATION) SAID THAT HE WAS FOLLOWING THE SITUATION CLOSELY. HE CALLED ON TURKISH CYPRIOTS TO AVOID TRAVEL. "I AM SURE WE WILL OVERCOME THESE DIFFICULT DAYS WITH THIS COMMON SENSE OF OUR COMMUNITY AND OUR ATTACHMENT TO OUR NATIONAL STRUGGLE AND MOTHERLAND TURKEY."

"Motherland Turkey?" Andreas anguished, with a look of disgust. He changed the station back to the CBC.

Ronit whispered to me, "He doesn't want to hear bad news."

> MR. NIKOS SAMPSON, WHO WAS SWORN IN BEFORE THE EX-BISHOP OF PAPHOS, WAS INSTALLED AS PRESIDENT BY THE MILITARY. HE SPOKE IN AN EXCITED VOICE TO THE GREEK CYPRIOT COMMUNITY WHEN HE ANNOUNCED THAT THE PROGRAMS OF HIS NEW GOVERNMENT WOULD BE ANNOUNCED SHORTLY. HE SAID THE NEW GOVERNMENT WOULD MAINTAIN THE NON-ALIGNED POLICY AND FRIENDLY RELATIONS WITH ALL COUNTRIES. HE PROMISED THAT FREE ELECTIONS WILL BE HELD WITHIN A YEAR TO ALLOW THE PEOPLE TO DECIDE THE KIND OF GOVERNMENT THEY WISH TO BE GOVERNED BY.

"If only Grivas hadn't died," Andreas said, turning the dial again. "He would have been president."

"Wasn't Grivas a terrorist?" Ronit asked.

"No," Andreas gruffed. "He formed the EOKA movement to liberate Cyprus from British rule, and unite Cyprus with Greece."

"Oh," Ronit said.

"But why Nikos Sampson?" I questioned.

"He's a thug," Ronit said, "and reason enough for Turkey to invade. Turks don't want to live under the Greek junta."

Ignoring her comment, Andreas turned the radio dial again.

A PRO-MAKARIOS RADIO, FREE VOICE OF PAPHOS, ANNOUNCED THAT AN EMISSARY OF ARCHBISHOP MAKARIOS ARRIVED THERE WITH A MESSAGE FROM THE ARCHBISHOP ASSURING HIS SUPPORTERS THAT THEY WOULD WIN. THE RADIO SAID ALL GREEK ARMY OFFICERS IN THE PAPHOS REGION HAD SURRENDERED TO THE PRO-MAKARIOS ELEMENTS.

"Who can you believe?" I asked.

"The Greeks," Andreas answered.

"Which ones?" Ronit questioned.

"This is a domestic affair. It's about Greek Cypriots, nothing to do with the Turks!" Andreas insisted.

"Let's hope the Turks agree," Ronit offered.

The rest of the day, and into the evening, we listened to conflicting reports on who was in charge, and whether Archbishop Makarios was in fact dead or alive.

By Tuesday night, all news outlets in English—and Kol Israel—were reporting that Makarios had indeed survived the attack on the palace.

WE HAVE CONFIRMED THAT ARCHBISHOP MAKARIOS IS ALIVE AND WELL ON THE ISLAND OF CYPRUS.

"No more resistance," Ronit said.

"I don't believe it," Andreas protested. "It's propaganda. They want to confuse Cypriot people. Makarios won't get off this island alive. Even if he survived, they will get him. In London, America, wherever he goes. He'll never return to this island alive."

"Andreas," Ronit interrupted his tirade. "I'm shocked at your feelings about Makarios. You've never mentioned any of this before."

"No. Not even to my brothers. Cypriots don't talk freely about how we feel. We've learned from our past. In the last troubles, if family members were on different sides someone always ended up dead."

"Isn't Cyprus a democracy?" Ronit asked. "Wasn't Makarios elected? So, only a minority of people don't like him."

"You're wrong. People are frightened to show how they feel. Once the world knows he's dead, you'll see how many people feel as I do." Andreas's face twisted in a pained grimace. He got up and walked out the front door.

"You think the Turks will invade?" Ronit asked me.

"Yes. They won't stand by and watch this happen to Turkish Cypriots. The Greeks have gone too far this time."

"How soon?"

"Soon. I need to get home, feed the cat, and pack a bag. I think it's best to leave Cyprus as soon as possible. I'm not sure where I'll go. But—"

"I can get you on a flight to Tel Aviv when the airport opens."

"Thanks. I can always stay with friends there until I hear from Charles. What will you do?"

"I'll stay with Andreas. He's in great pain."

"I understand."

Andreas returned an hour later.

"Electricity's back on," Ronit told him. "I'll make dinner."

"By tomorrow, life will return to normal," Andreas assured us. "You'll see."

At 2200 hours that evening, the British Forces station confirmed that Makarios was alive and had been taken off the island.

ARCHBISHOP MAKARIOS, WHO WAS OVERTHROWN AS
PRESIDENT OF CYPRUS IN MONDAY'S MILITARY COUP,
STAGED BY THE GREEK-OFFICERED NATIONAL GUARD,
HAS NOW ARRIVED IN LONDON. HE WAS FLOWN THERE
ON A ROYAL AIR FORCE PLANE FROM A BRITISH BASE
AT AKROTIRI.

"That traitor," Andreas mumbled. "After urging his people to fight, he flees."

The BFBS broadcast continued.

THE US FLEET, WHICH WAS SCHEDULED TO ARRIVE IN
ATHENS TODAY, IS HEADING FOR THE MEDITERRANEAN
ISLAND OF CYPRUS. THE RUSSIAN FLEET IS ALSO
HEADING IN THE SAME DIRECTION.

Knowing I was sitting in the middle of a hotbed of conflict, outside and in, I said good night and went to bed. I could hear Andreas's and Ronit's voices rise and fall, between news updates, and the rumble of jeeps and tanks in the streets below.

At around 0400 hours, a loud explosion shook me awake. I heard voices screaming and people running on the streets below. It appeared close, but in sleep one never knows.

Or does one?

Another explosion followed. Farther away.

By sunrise, all was quiet again.

Ronit greeted me as I entered the kitchen. "Tanks and soldiers are still at the roundabout, but civilian cars are moving about in the streets below. The curfew will be lifted this afternoon for two hours, so people can get food and necessities."

"What time?" I asked.

"14:30."

"Great. I'll drive home. Sam will be happy to see me."

"Who'll look after Sam when you leave?"

"Sabrina, our cleaning woman. She always cares for him when we're away."

"I wish you would stay here. According to the news, all resistance has been quashed. Government offices will return to normal hours and the airport will open tomorrow."

"Maybe Andreas is right. Maybe life will return to normal."

"Would you like some coffee? Andreas has gone for bread."

"Thanks."

Andreas arrived home with fresh bread and cheese. Just as we sat down to eat, we were startled by the ring of the doorbell.

Andreas answered it and called to me. "It's your friend Juan, the UN attorney. He's offering to drive with you to Kyrenia."

I hurried to the door. A smiling Juan gave me a big hug. "Glad you're safe. We're making our rounds, checking on the safety of UN employees, and I spotted your car. I'm driving to Kyrenia to check on others and thought you might like an escort home."

"I can leave my car here, if it's a problem."

"You'll need it to get to the airport when you leave."

"True, but I'm frightened to drive alone."

"Another UN attorney is with me. He'll ride with you. We'll be two vehicles traveling together. Just be calm and follow me. By the way, Charles was listed as a passenger on the Athens flight."

"Really? Thanks for checking."

I hugged Ronit and Andreas, and dashed down the stairs.

Bart, the other UN attorney, said hello and got into the front passenger seat. Juan handed him a UN flag to wave at checkpoints.

We entered the main road and turned left, in the direction of the round-about. I began shaking, remembering the harrowing ride of just two days ago. Tanks were positioned all around it, while soldiers with guns stood nearby.

Bart smiled at me. "Just take a deep breath and relax. I'll show the flag and they'll wave us through."

When we entered the roundabout, a soldier raised his hand to halt our two-vehicle procession. Juan stopped and talked with the soldier. I saw him point back in our direction. The soldier waved Juan's vehicle through.

I edged my car forward. The soldier stopped us and asked in broken English where we were going.

Bart held up the UN flag. "We're UN employees heading home to Kyrenia."

The soldier muttered something in Greek to other soldiers standing nearby. He cocked his gun.

I didn't say anything, but trembled knowing they recognized my unique turquoise convertible, and me. I had crossed this checkpoint frequently during my time in Cyprus.

Another soldier walked to my side of the car. "You're not a UN employee. Where are you going?"

Bart repeated that we were UN employees and demanded respect for the UN status. "We're going home," he firmly stated.

I looked at Bart.

"Put your foot on the gas and slowly drive forward," he instructed calmly.

Legs shaking, I put the car into first gear, put my foot on the gas pedal, and steered the car forward.

Soldiers began shouting and waving for us to stop.

"Keep the car rolling," Bart said, nodding forward. "Don't stop at the next checkpoint."

I shifted into second gear, pressed down on the gas, and drove on. My body quivered.

The soldier stationed at the next checkpoint appeared busy, talking on the telephone.

Bart waved the UN flag. "Keep moving," he said, as we cleared the last Greek checkpoint. "Good job."

I could see the guard frantically waving in the rearview mirror.

"Stop!" he yelled in English, and chased after us.

I kept the car rolling forward and faster.

Our two vehicles were the only ones on the empty road from Nicosia to Kyrenia, and we quickly passed into a "no-man's-land" and entered the Turkish zone.

Seeing the UN flag waving, Turkish soldiers smiled and waved us on through their checkpoint.

"Strange that the Turks didn't stop us," I commented.

"It's life as usual in the Turkish areas," Bart said. "Very quiet. A quick takeover. No resistance. On the surface."

"I feel safer already," I said. "The air is certainly fresher."

We rounded the last curve and headed down the mountain to the village of Kyrenia.

"Always a magnificent view on a clear day, with the old castle jutting out to the azure sea," I remarked. "And look how clearly you can see Turkey today."

"Only 36 miles away." Bart replied.

"Cyprus sits so close to Turkey, wonder why Greece claims it's part of Greece. Weird."

A stunning view indeed, I thought. And so ironic with freedom at stake.

I saw roadblocks, soldiers, and army trucks everywhere as we neared the first crossroad.

Juan pulled his car off the road ahead of us and stopped.

"Take side streets home," Juan advised. "It's safer."

"Thanks! Thanks too for escorting me home."

"Good to meet you," Bart said, getting out. "Best to leave the island until things quiet down."

"I plan on it. Thanks for riding with me," I said as we parted.

A Greek soldier, guarding the next corner, asked me where I was going.

"Home," I answered.

With a confused look, he nodded, then motioned me forward with his outstretched hand.

At the next corner, I turned left onto our cobblestone road. No armed guards in sight. Whew!

As I steered the car into our carport, I saw our American friend Pete standing near our front door, writing a note.

"Good to know you're safe. Paula was worried about you."

"I've been in Nicosia with friends. I got stuck there after taking Charles to the airport. Is it safe to go shopping?"

"The curfew lifts at 1600 hours. If you need anything, give us a call."

"A working telephone?"

"Yes. Telephones are working locally, but not to the outside world." He wadded the note into a ball, smiled, and waved goodbye

CHAPTER 10

WORST OVER?

Kyrenia, Cyprus—17-18 July 1974

Feeling relieved to have made it home safely, I took a deep breath and sighed, "Ahhh!"

I walked up to the immense carved wooden door, unlocked the heavy iron bolt and pushed it aside. I lifted the long wooden bar and opened the door.

Peering into the courtyard, everything appeared peaceful. But I sensed I had walked into a world which was fading fast. "The calm before the storm," I muttered to myself.

I crossed the cobblestone foyer, looked past the archways into the large garden.

"Sam, I'm home. Food time," I called to our cat.

All was silent. I walked toward the fish pond and turned on the electric pump for the fountain which refreshed the water. *Oh good, electricity's on.* I tossed food to the eager fish and searched for Sam near the fish pond.

"Sam," I called again.

Moments later, I smiled, hearing the pitter-patter of Sam running down the stairs. "Meow-meow." Always vocal, he had to announce his arrival.

"Oh Sam." I picked him up and cuddled. "How've you been?"

He purred.

"Sorry to be gone so long. I got stuck in Nicosia."

107

He continued purring.

"How can you be so calm when the world is falling apart?" I asked, putting him down on the floor.

Opening the kitchen door, I reached for cat food, filled his bowl to more than usual, and watched him devour all of it.

I picked up the telephone. A dial tone. *Great. Perhaps Charles will call.*

No sooner had I hung up the phone than it rang again.

"Hello."

An anxious Ilene wanted to know where I'd been for the last few days. I recounted the drive to the airport with Charles, and my harrowing days in Nicosia during the coup. "So scary!"

"My God," she said. "You poor dear. It's been so quiet here. If it wasn't for the curfew in effect, I wouldn't even know a revolution was happening."

We discussed what to do next: stay put or go elsewhere until things settled down.

"I definitely plan on getting out of here, as soon as I can get on a flight," I told her.

Ilene suggested I pack a bag and stay with them in the meantime.

"I'm fine. Sam needs my company and I need his," I answered. "If I change my mind, I'll let you know."

I telephoned my neighbor Beth to let her know I had made it home. I mentioned my plans to leave the island and await news of Charles in Tel Aviv. She told me they were packing to leave on the next available flight.

I dialed my friend Kate's number to see how her family was doing. Kate expressed her alarm at the recent arrests of prominent Greeks who were pro-Makarios. Many had been arrested and interrogated by the new military regime. Although she and Alex were not politically involved, Alex's brother being a Makarios cabinet member did concern them. Still, they had sent their sons to a friend's house, just in case. They didn't want their children to witness an arrest. Kate and the boys planned to leave on the next flight to London. They would stay with her family until things settled down in Cyprus.

My, how quickly things had changed since their recent party, when I mourned the loss of my stillborn son.

The phone rang. American friends assuring me if the situation became serious the US government would evacuate its citizens.

I made a checklist of things to be done before departure and a list of items and important documents to take. I opened my suitcase and began packing.

Sam sat purring on the bed.

I took a break and sat down beside him. Stroking his head, I thought about the peaceful life in Cyprus. On the surface—still and calm. Feels eerie, knowing a catastrophic storm sits offshore. A storm of such immensity it will blow this paradise into a million pieces. Cyprus will be changed in the blink of any eye. Changed forever.

A knock at the front door interrupted my packing. I ran downstairs.

To my surprise, our British neighbor David stood smiling at me. "I saw your car pass on the main road; I'm glad to know you're safe. Did Charles catch his flight?"

"Yes. And I ended up smack dab in the middle of the coup. I plan on leaving as soon as I can get a flight out. Are you going to England?"

"I'll join the family for holiday in a few weeks. In the meantime, I'm on my way to the harbor to have afternoon tea with friends."

"The harbor? What about the curfew?"

"Afternoon tea can't be canceled because of a coup. I predict that by tomorrow, life will be normal again."

"You Brits and your tea." I waved him goodbye.

When the curfew lifted at 1600 hours, I grabbed a shopping bag, got on my bike, and headed down the hill to the local Turkish supermarket. The place was packed with people, many of whom I knew. After greeting and exchanging stories, most were convinced that come tomorrow, life would return to normal. But, just in case, they frantically grabbed as many items as they could carry.

The grocery shelves were almost empty. I managed to get tins of soup, crackers, and lemon squash—my favorite concentrated summer drink.

I saw Ilene's husband, Syd, in the checkout line. He insisted I take my bike and groceries home, and ride with him to their house for a short visit.

Approaching home, I spotted my cleaning gal, Sabrina, a Greek Cypriot, and her husband, a Turkish Cypriot. I stopped and talked with them about the coup and how bad it had been in Nicosia. They were torn over what to do, but had decided to stay in Kyrenia.

"It's our home," they uttered in unison.

I asked Sabrina if she would look after Sam and the fish for me for a while.

"Of course, I fed Sam yesterday."

"That Sam." I smiled. "He pretended he hadn't eaten for days. Cats? You never know them."

After securing groceries at home, I spent an hour visiting with Syd and Ilene. Their plan was to leave on Saturday's flight to London. They urged me to get off the island as soon as possible.

"The Turks will invade," Syd said.

We talked more. They tried to get me to stay the night.

"I need to finish packing. Hopefully I can get a flight out to Tel Aviv soon."

We said our goodbyes. Syd drove me home.

Beth telephoned, insisting I stay the night with them. She said that Patrick, her husband, could meet me halfway.

"I'm fine alone," I insisted. "I'll call if I change my mind."

Dusk descended, and I quickly changed my mind about staying home. I packed an overnight bag and raced down the cobblestone streets on my bicycle. No cars in sight. The streets were empty. What critters were out and about scampered away as I pedaled fast to Beth and Patrick's home.

Beth welcomed me with a big hug. "Nice you changed your mind. It's not a night to be alone. Patrick will grill steaks for dinner."

We had dinner on the terrace, by the glow of the fire. Civilized conversation until we talked reality—the coup, Sampson installed as the new president, and the probability of a Turkish invasion.

"It's not a matter of if, but when," Patrick declared. "We'll leave on tomorrow's flight. Fortunately, as an employee of the airlines, we have guaranteed seats. I'd recommend you get on the first flight out to anywhere."

"Do you know a pilot who needs a pretend wife for a day?"

"Bet we can find one for you," Beth said, laughing.

"Ronit thinks she can get me on an El Al flight to Tel Aviv tomorrow or the next day. I have friends there I can stay with until I hear from Charles."

"It makes more sense than going to England," Patrick said. "Have you heard about Alex's arrest?"

"No. I spoke with Kate earlier today. He was home."

"They picked him up for questioning."

"Alex is such a gentle soul. How is Kate holding up? Is she alone?"

"No, their nanny's with her," Beth answered. "She plans on flying to England with the boys. Our next-door neighbor also got arrested. They released him the next day. When Patrick asked him about it, he said he couldn't discuss it with anyone."

After dinner Patrick and Beth's landlord, Sabri, a prominent Turkish businessman and a friend to all foreigners, came wandering in to chat and share a drink.

"Have any Turks been arrested by the new government?" I asked him.

"They wouldn't dare. If they lay a hand on a Turk, all hell will break loose," Sabri replied.

"Do you think Turkey will invade?"

"They certainly won't sit back and let a thug like Sampson be president. It's a matter of time. I heard on the news this evening that Turkey is preparing to protect the Turkish Cypriots. Of course they'll invade."

We saw a car pull into the driveway, lights glaring. I cringed.

Patrick called out, "Who's there?"

"Just me," a man answered in English as he got out of the car.

"Just you?" Patrick asked, recognizing a pilot friend.

"I've been checking on friends and thought I'd stop by for a gin and tonic," he announced as he sauntered toward us.

I laughed. "You Brits are accustomed to revolutions."

"We've started a few," he said.

We listened to the BBC news report at 2200 hours, and also listened to local news on the Cyprus Broadcasting station.

All government offices and banks would be open for business, as usual, the next day. The Nicosia International Airport was also scheduled to reopen. All scheduled flights would resume.

After hearing the news, I went to bed. Feeling soothed by the fresh air and quiet, and a few gin and tonics, I slept soundly, making up for my sleepless nights in Nicosia.

We were up at the crack of dawn the next morning. A radio report assured us the curfew had been lifted and we were free to move about until 1700 hours.

Beth packed suitcases while Patrick made coffee. I set the table for breakfast. *Linen place mats and napkins.* So civilized. Still?

After breakfast, we said our goodbyes and I rode my bike home. The streets were filled with people. I sensed they were glad to be out and about—shopping, sharing their stories of the siege, and worrying together about what the future held.

Home! First things first, I opened the front door and called to Sam. He ran to me for a cuddle and food—of course. I put a load of laundry in the washing machine and went upstairs to finish packing my suitcase.

Clothes, toiletries, underwear, socks, shoes.

Who knows how long I'll be gone?

I opened desk drawers, sorted through important papers that we might need if gone for a while. Passport, address book, birth certificates, insurance papers, Barclays checkbook, Swiss bankbook. *What else?*

I went for the key to the padlock on Charles's office door. No key in its usual place. *Strange. Perhaps there's something important in there I should take for safekeeping?*

Charles kept the door locked when he was gone because of the valuable electronics stored there. When home, he holed up in the small room, spending hours every day listening to broadcasts from around the world and practicing languages. His latest interest was Chinese.

Where was the key? Puzzling! It always hung on the hook by the bedroom door. Chinese? Why is he learning Chinese?

A knock on the front door. Unexpected. I dashed downstairs to open it.

Sabrina stood smiling. "Ready to clean," she said.

"Oh, good." I instructed her to hang the laundry out to dry. "I need to run errands."

I drove my car to the bank and waited in a long line to get money out. Next stop was the local travel agency. They couldn't book a flight because telephone lines to Nicosia still weren't working. They recommended I drive to the airport in Nicosia. "I'll check back tomorrow," I said as I left. On my way home, I filled the car's gas tank.

I had just finished packing clothes and toiletries when I heard the front door open.

"Honey, I'm home," Charles called out.

"Unbelievable," I muttered, dashing down the stairs. "What are you doing here? People are trying to get off this island, not back on it."

"No need to worry. The worst is over." Charles smiled and gave me a hug.

"The worst is not over," I responded. "If you believe that, you're a fool."

"Trust me. I know."

"The Turks are going to invade. They're not going to sit back and do nothing."

"The US won't let them."

"How will they stop them?"

"You'll see. Were you able to get the brakes done on the car?"

"The brakes? No. I've been dodging tanks and bullets since you left. The coup started as I left the airport. Surely you know about the coup?"

"Actually, I didn't know until I landed in Athens. The airport was abuzz with the news."

"Soldiers and tanks were everywhere." I began crying. "The road to Kyrenia was blocked by a bus."

"Where did you go?"

"I drove from George's garage to Ronit and Andreas's apartment."

"Thank God you made it."

"Tanks were firing in all directions along the main road. It was a miracle that I made it across the road and to their place alive."

"When did you get home?"

"Yesterday. The UN escorted me. That was scary as hell too."

"I came back early because I knew this would be frightening for you."

"For everyone. It's been a nightmare."

"I'm sorry you had such a difficult time," Charles consoled, putting his arm around my shoulder.

"How did you get back here today?" I asked.

"I conned my way onto a special press flight, the first back to Cyprus."

"How?" I wanted to know.

"People in high places. Aren't you glad I'm home?"

"No, I'm not. I plan on leaving Cyprus on tomorrow's flight to Tel Aviv, if I can get a seat."

"There's no need. Things will settle down. You'll see."

"Charles, the Turks are going to invade," I said, climbing the stairs to finish packing.

Charles followed me up to the bedroom. Seeing my open, half-filled suitcase, he tried to reassure me. "Listen, I came home to show you that everything will be fine."

"You don't have to show me anything. How do you know everything will be fine?"

He answered. "These things happen here time and again. History repeats itself."

"Because of its strategic location?"

"Yes."

"Because all the big powers want to control it?"

"Yes."

I hesitated. "Charles, are you in any way involved in this?" I asked.

Charles ignored my question.

"Makarios was the first elected president because he agreed to give up plans for union with Greece," I continued.

"True. But the Greeks never gave up the plans," Charles said.

"Why isn't the US demanding the removal of Sampson? He's a criminal. A terrorist, and he's just been sworn in as the new president. It's obvious Athens is behind the coup and obvious that Turks are threatened. And obvious the US condones what's happening."

"The US doesn't trust Makarios because of his ties to Communist countries and his demands that the US leave. That's why US military personnel and families left a month ago."

"The Turks won't sit back and let this happen. No way." I felt sick, sad for the people of Cyprus. "It's hopeless. They're innocent pawns in an international game of power-grab. Aren't they?"

"Yes," Charles replied.

"Where is the padlock key?"

"Padlock key?"

"The key to your office?"

"Oh," he said, "I guess I took it with me."

The phone rang downstairs. I ran to answer it.

"It's Ronit," I yelled up to Charles.

Ronit chatted away, obviously happy. She said she and Andreas had resolved some issues and that their relationship was greatly improved. She said she tried to talk him into going to Israel with her, but because he's a male Greek Cypriot the government won't allow him to leave. "They want him here to fight."

"I'm sure they do," I said.

She tried to assure me everything would be okay now that Makarios was out of the way.

"I'm happy to hear you and Andreas have worked things out," I said.

Ronit surprised me by saying they were driving to Kyrenia tomorrow and wanted to see us.

"They're coming to Kyrenia tomorrow evening to check on family," I told Charles, as he came down the stairs.

"Invite them to dinner and to stay the night," Charles suggested.

I relayed Charles's invitation to Ronit.

She eagerly accepted. They would arrive the next evening for dinner, and stay overnight.

"Andreas thinks everything will be okay now," I said to Charles, after hanging up.

"I'm sure it will," he said. "Let's walk down to the harbor and grab a bite to eat."

"Good idea."

I grabbed my sunhat and we walked down the cobblestone street to the harbor. We saw several of our friends out strolling and enjoying the beautiful day. With the curfew lifted and shops open, life appeared to be returning to normal.

Dawn of the next morning brought another beautiful Mediterranean day. Charles suggested we join English friends for lunch and a swim at our favorite new beach hotel. Designed by an Englishman of Greek descent, the Zephyros's glass facade sparkled as an architectural showpiece in the shining sun, set against the blue Mediterranean Sea.

Before lunch, I went for a swim in the almost empty Olympic size pool. The only other swimmer was a young German woman.

When I commented on having the pool to ourselves, the young woman described her situation. "Most tourists left yesterday after the German Consul ordered us to leave. They even provided a plane to evacuate us. I stayed on to finish my tan. Guess I'll have to pay my own way home."

"Let's hope you make it out in time." I shook my head in disbelief. Daftness at its finest.

"I plan on finishing my tan and my vacation."

"Good luck," I said, getting out of the pool.

Over lunch at a poolside table, conversation with our British friends kept circling back to what Turkey would do.

One friend puzzled, "Appointing a thug like Sampson as president is reason enough for the Turks to invade. Turkish Cypriots remember in great detail the 1955 troubles when he personally dug graves for Turks out of a personal vendetta."

"He's an asshole," one said.

"He also murdered British citizens," another added.

"Sampson's efforts to assure Turkish Cypriots it's an internal problem is laughable," someone commented.

"Certainly naive," added another.

"The Turks will never buy that line. Turkey will invade," I said.

"Turkey won't accept the status quo," someone else added.

"I witnessed firsthand the destruction in Nicosia," I said. "The coup was a bloodbath. Cyprus is a volcano. The eruption will be dangerous and deadly. An invasion is imminent. I keep trying to convince Charles to leave."

"If the situation is of real danger to Americans," Charles said, "the US government will know and evacuate citizens before an invasion."

"Unless," someone commented, "the US wants their citizens to stay put—like sitting ducks—to convince the world they'll stop the Turks."

Charles smiled. "I met with the top military brass in Athens this week. The American intelligence community in Cyprus has no shortage of sources for information, as far as Cyprus is concerned. There's the FBIS, the State Department's Radio Relay Organization, and a naval security station. All of these organizations are operating in Cyprus and all have multi-language experts gathering information. When the top brass assure me that the Sixth Fleet is on its way to stop an invasion, I believe it."

"Here's to the Sixth Fleet protecting paradise," one friend toasted, raising his glass.

"Paradise is past," I remarked, cringing.

After lunch, we said our goodbyes, and agreed to be in touch if anyone learned anything new.

We stopped at the local butcher shop to buy steaks for dinner.

Selection was limited. We bought the best we could find. As we were leaving, we witnessed an accident between an army truck and a private vehicle. The young woman driver of the car sat sobbing.

"Everyone's so nervous," I commented.

"No need to be." Charles shrugged.

When we arrived home, I put groceries away. Charles switched on the radio for the latest news from BBC. Not good.

A TURKISH FLEET OF THIRTY-FIVE SHIPS WAS REPORTED TO HAVE SAILED FROM A PORT IN SOUTHERN TURKEY, ABOUT 45 MILES FROM CYPRUS FOR AN UNDISCLOSED DESTINATION. MOST OF THE FLOTILLA WAS REPORTED TO BE TROOP-CARRYING LANDING CRAFT.

IN AN INTERVIEW RAUF DENKTASH—THE FORMER VICE PRESIDENT OF THE REPUBLIC OF CYPRUS—WAS ASKED, "WHAT IS YOUR ANTICIPATION OF A TURKISH INTERVENTION? A MILITARY INTERVENTION?"

HE ANSWERED, "I THINK IT IS NOT TOO DISTANT A POSSIBILITY."

"DO YOU EXPECT ANY RESISTANCE?"

"I THINK HALF THE GREEK POPULATION WILL WELCOME THEM AS SAVIORS."

The report gave me the jitters. Once again I tried to convince Charles that we needed to leave as soon as possible.

"Most journalists on the flight agree with you," Charles said. "I overheard many similar conversations at the press conference I attended."

"A press conference? Where? When?"

"In Nicosia."

"Why were you at a press conference?"

"After our plane landed, an announcement was made requiring all press to attend a conference at the public information office in Nicosia."

"But you're not press."

He ignored my comment and continued. "On the way to the information office, we passed the Presidential Palace. I was amazed at the destruction."

"How did you get to the information office?"

"I rode there with another journalist. The office was crawling with soldiers, policemen, and bodyguards. All carrying guns. We were rushed into a hall where we were shown torture weapons—whips, pipes, rubber hoses— and they showed us people who had been tortured by the Makarios regime. One guy pulled his pants down and bent over to show his black and blue butt."

"Oh, my God."

"Sampson spoke in Greek. It was translated into English. He said the new government wanted to right the wrongs of the Makarios government. No need to fear anything because he would give all the people of Cyprus the opportunity to live in freedom. He promised to bring peace. Long live the Greeks. When he entered and left the room, he was accompanied by six massive men with machine guns in tow. He is definitely a puppet for the Greek junta. I'm sure he'll be replaced as soon as an election is held."

"But I still don't understand why you were there."

Once again Charles ignored my comments, and tried to convince me that he knew best. "I predict," he said, "with all the tourists gone, that the days ahead will be great. Empty beaches."

"You're not seeing the seriousness of the situation," I said, disheartened.

I left the room and climbed the stairs to prepare the guest room for Ronit and Andreas's arrival.

I phoned Kate later, and learned that Alex had been released. "He's home." I wept as I told Charles the good news.

Syd and Ilene stopped by to show us their plane tickets to London. They were excited to have seats booked on tomorrow's flight. After tea, we said goodbye and agreed to stay in touch.

A glass of wine in hand, Charles and I climbed steps to the rooftop terrace to watch the sun set.

Charles looked through his binoculars and pointed out to sea. "They're a ways away, but I see another fleet arriving. Not Turkish."

"What fleet? The news report said the Sixth Fleet was in Crete. How can they be here, if they're still there?"

"The exact location of military ships is never disclosed, but looks like US ships to me."

"Maybe they're here to rescue us." My heart skipped a beat at the thought.

The door knocker banged loudly. We hurried downstairs to answer it.

Ronit and Andreas arrived all smiles, happy to be back in Kyrenia—visiting family and friends.

Andreas helped Charles get the grill going, while Ronit helped me prepare the rest of the dinner.

After dinner Charles showed Andreas a new electronic device he had picked up in Athens and suggested they test it out in the neighborhood. Charles loved his electronic toys. This was a handheld, battery-operated FM microphone transmitter which allowed him to broadcast to any FM radio receiver.

Charles set the mike for the same frequency as Cyprus Broadcasting and they made their way through the neighborhood making phony examples of announcements.

"Boys, toys, noise," I told Ronit after they left.

Later, we sat in the garden in the cool of the evening, playing backgammon while discussing our different world views. As the Cyprus wine flowed, the conversation got louder.

"The Turks are heading this way as a show of power," Andreas announced. "They've done it many times before."

"Under the treaty, they do have the right to intervene," I reminded him.

"The junta started it all when they overthrew Makarios," said Ronit. "If only they hadn't replaced him with that gorilla Sampson."

"Turkish Cypriots have nothing to fear. No reason to attack," Andreas noted. "The US is happy to have Makarios out of the way. They'd rather deal with a puppet like Sampson than risk offending the junta in Greece."

"They don't want the Sixth Fleet tossed out of Greek ports. Russia would be eager for that to happen," Charles commented.

"The Russian fleet has also set sail," I said.

"I'm just surprised the junta removed your religious leader," Ronit said.

"He's a murderer. A Communist bastard. A religious leader doesn't torture his own people," Andreas shouted, his mouth a grimace of pain and fear. He shook his curled fists. "If he ever returns to this country, he'll be killed."

We sat in silence, shocked by Andreas's rage.

"Would you shoot him?" Charles asked Andreas, point-blank.

Andreas pulled his hand into a gun shape and pointed it at Charles. "Bang," he snarled.

After Turkish coffee and dessert, and several more backgammon games—with Andreas clearly the winner—we said good night and headed to bed.

I waited until I heard the upstairs guest bedroom close, and made my nightly rounds turning off lights and securing windows and doors, upstairs and down.

When I returned to our downstairs bedroom, Charles was already asleep, snoring loudly.

Feeling nervous, I paced back and forth around the garden before joining him in our king-size water bed. I tossed and turned, and wondered how long before Turkey invaded.

"Stop the tossing," Charles said. "Relax."

Exhausted, I slipped into a troubled sleep and an alarming dream.

> *I drove my convertible down a steep hill. Without warning, the two right tires came flying off the car. Panicked at the thought of heading headfirst over a cliff, I let go of the steering wheel to jump from the careening car.*
>
> *"Steer it to safety. Trust yourself," a voice calmly commanded.*
>
> *So I placed my hands back on the wheel and turned the car away from the cliff. With great difficulty, I steered it toward a green spot at the bottom of the hill and braced myself for a turbulent landing.*
>
> *I took deep breaths as the car slowed to a stop on a grassy knoll, just a few feet short of the cliff's edge.*
>
> *Drained of energy, I slumped over the steering wheel and cried tears of joy.*

I jolted awake in a cold sweat. My teeth clattered uncontrollably.

There's no escape. No place to run. No place to hide. Turkey will invade. How frustrated prophets must feel when they finally predict something that comes to pass, and it falls on deaf ears. I prayed to be wrong, but knew I was right this time.

CHAPTER 11
DÉJÀ VU?

Frankfurt, Germany—1977

I sat at the bar of my friend Rosetta's jazz club, the Balalaika, enjoying a glass of chardonnay and nibbling roasted peanuts.

"Rosetta will be down shortly," the bartender told me.

In Sachsenhausen, a few blocks from my apartment, the club was a popular jazz spot in Frankfurt. Many famous musicians and singers frequented it when visiting Frankfurt.

Rosetta, a jazz singer originally from New Jersey, moved to Germany after a successful concert tour in Europe in the late 1960s. Diane introduced me to Rosetta when I first moved to Sachsenhausen and we became fast friends.

"Good evening," a tall, muscular man said, standing next to an empty barstool by the entrance. "Is this seat free?"

"It's reasonable," I said, smiling.

He pushed his shoulder-length blond hair back and ordered a beer. Turning to me, he said, "Crisp evening. Fall's in the air."

"Yes. I love the change of seasons, watching leaves change colors."

"Me too." His gray eyes danced. "Do you live here?"

"I do. And you?"

"Chicago. I'm here for a few weeks, every few months with my work."

"What's your work?"

"Photographer."

"Fun. What kind of things do you shoot?"

"Whatever I'm paid to shoot. New cars this time."

"Nice to get paid for creative work."

"It's a good life. What's your line of work?"

"I'm an artist. At the moment, I'm working on my first exhibit."

"No wonder you like to watch leaves. Congratulations. My name's Dan." He smiled.

"Nice to meet you. I'm Susan."

"Hey girlfriend," Rosetta greeted me. "And look who's in town," she said, smiling at Dan. "Long time, no see. I see you two have met?"

"Yes," Dan said, nodding.

"Getting to know you, getting to know all about you," Rosetta sang.

I smiled.

"So, when is your exhibit?" Dan asked.

"November the 5th," Rosetta announced, before I could answer. "Will you be in town?"

"I think so," Dan replied. "We're scheduled to be shooting for two months."

"Well," I smiled. "You're invited. Rosetta will be entertaining."

"That's great. I'll be there."

Rosetta picked up her guitar and strummed as she made her way to a small stage in the far corner of the club. All conversation stopped when the stage light went on and she began singing an old standby, "Country Roads."

When she got to the chorus, she encouraged club patrons to join in.

As a child I often sang harmony with my sisters and loved to sing harmony with Rosetta. Everyone sang or hummed along with Rosetta, song after familiar song, until the set ended.

The audience applauded enthusiastically. Conversations resumed.

Rosetta joined me and Dan at the bar.

"Dan has photographed some very famous people," Rosetta offered.

"Cool," I said, turning to Dan. "Anyone I know?"

"Yes. Rosetta and a few other stars."

"And a few dozen Playboy centerfolds," Rosetta added.

"I shoot whatever I'm paid to shoot," he said, laughing.

Rosetta made her rounds through the club, stopping to greet guests sitting at the scattered tables.

"She's a natural," Dan said, "with her million-dollar smile."

"She sure is. And a wonderful friend."

Dan excused himself and headed to the men's room.

Rosetta returned to the bar. "Now he's someone you want to get to know," Rosetta whispered. "Good-looking. Intelligent. Fun."

"He's nice. But, I'm not quite ready."

"Probably has a girl in every port. So, no strings. By the way, Diane telephoned a few minutes ago to tell you she's on her way. Serena stopped by earlier. Maybe she'll pop in later too."

"Great. Thanks."

Dan returned to the bar and asked if he could buy me a drink.

Rosetta smiled and before I could protest announced, "A beer and a chardonnay. Coming right up."

Dan smiled. I smiled back and thought, Why not?

"Have you had dinner?" he asked.

"I haven't, but a friend is stopping by. We're going to dinner. How about a rain check?"

"It's a deal. Can I call you?"

"I'd like that."

Rosetta smiled and hummed.

Diane arrived and I introduced her to Dan. We chatted for a few minutes. I gave Dan my telephone number before leaving. He said he'd call in a few days.

"He's nice," Diane said as we walked out into the cool night.

"Nice eyes."

"What do you feel like eating?"

"Chinese. It's walking distance."

"Sure is," Diane chuckled as she opened the entrance to the Chinese restaurant directly next door to the club.

The owner smiled and invited us to sit in our favorite booth by the window. "Reserved for you. Spatial." He smiled.

"Thank you," we answered in unison.

After he had taken our order, we chuckled at his pronunciation of "special."

"We're special and spatial," I told Diane.

He returned with a pot of tea, and menus.

"Look," Diane said, pointing at the menu. 'Dan Dan Spicy Noodles' are the special tonight. Do you think it's an omen?"

"Lust is a-stirring. I can actually imagine having fun sex again. I spent too many years doing it in hopes of getting pregnant. Strange to want it and not want to get pregnant."

"Lust is a good thing to explore. You'll know when the time's right."

The owner returned for our order.

"Sweet and sour shrimp," I said.

"No Dan Dan Spicy Noodles?" Diane asked.

"Not tonight."

Diane ordered Beggar's Chicken.

"So how's the exhibit coming?" Diane asked.

"Canvases are stretched. Frames ordered. Almost finished. Just in time. Did I tell you about the Indian woman who stopped by to look at my work?"

"No. How did she know about it?"

"She collects art and said she found herself drawn to the poster on a column in the U-Bahn advertising my exhibit."

"It's an appealing poster and it's plastered all over town. Erik's done a fine job getting those out there. How did she find you?"

"She found my name and number in the telephone book. She's exotic-looking. Arrived in a beautiful pink Indian sari with a red dot on her forehead. She viewed all the paintings, then decided to buy My Guardian Angel."

"That's wonderful."

"She insisted on paying me before the show, because she said it's always good PR to have a Sold or On Loan From a Private Collector sign on display for opening night. I agreed."

"That's amazing."

"Down to my last pfennigs, I wondered where the next ones were coming from when she showed up. She didn't have the money on her, but agreed to send a check."

"It's a beautiful piece."

"The whole time she visited me, she looked familiar. As if I knew her from another place or time."

"Déjà vu?" Diane asked.

"Yes. Exactly. That night, after she left, I dreamed of my guardian angel. The one I had as a child. She always wore a long flowing robe, sort of sari-like. When I was little, she was much bigger and better at everything than me and always got me out of tight spots and helped steer me to safety.

"But this time in my dream, as I moved along an old, rickety wooden bridge, the child and the guardian angel of my youth faded away behind me. I realized I stood alone on a rickety bridge. It shook violently as a storm stirred overhead. Dark shapes lurked in the raging river below. They're only shadows, I assured myself. You're almost there. Follow the moonlight. I kept telling myself what the guardian angel used to tell me.

"Just as I reached the other side and landed on firm ground, the bridge collapsed and crashed into the river below. By following the moonlight, I saved myself."

"What a positive dream."

"Three days later, an envelope with a check appeared in my mailbox. So dinner's on me."

"Do you think she's real?"

"The check cashed. She's real. I think she found me to help her find herself. She recently went through a divorce and is finding it difficult to be alone. Her name is Aditi. I had her write it down, so I can send her a thank-you card and get together sometime."

"I hope she comes to your exhibit."

"Me too. Are you a Johnny Carson fan?"

"Oh yes. I love The Tonight Show."

"I haven't seen it in years, but I used to watch it every night, except on my honeymoon. There wasn't a TV in the honeymoon suite. When I mentioned it to the hotel desk clerk, she informed me that most honeymooners didn't need one."

Diane giggled.

"And now, I'm dreaming of Johnny Carson. It's weird. In all the dreams I'm reliving scenes from my past. In one dream, I'm attending a Pentecostal revival. Johnny Carson and Ringo Starr are there with me."

"Crazy!" Diane said.

"Honest to Johnny," I said, smiling. "In the latest Johnny dream, he invited me on the show as his guest. Feeling nervous. I tripped over electrical wires and stumbled while getting on stage. The audience thought it was part of the act and cheered me on.

"When I sat down next to him, he asked if I was nervous and I nodded yes. He said he liked my dress. I told him that since he was such a sharp dresser, I felt mentally handicapped trying to spar with him while he was dressed.

"The audience cheered and yelled, 'Take it off. Take it all off.' So I untied his tie and the audience went wild, and the lights went out. End of dream. I woke myself up laughing."

Diane burst out laughing, and laughed so hard I thought she would choke on the chicken bone she had been carefully nibbling.

"I seldom dream," Diane said, "and if I do it's always something silly about losing my purse or shoes."

"That's not silly. If you lose a shoe in a dream, it could mean you're headed in the wrong direction, or that it's a waste of time to go. Losing a purse could mean you need to be more careful with finances."

"So?" Diane asked, looking serious. "What do you think your 'undress Johnny' dream means?"

"It means I'm ready to undress an intelligent, witty, well-dressed man."

"Time for spicy noodles!"

We both laughed.

"Rosetta said you got married in Las Vegas. I thought only movie stars and people in a hurry did that."

"Actually, if you're in a real hurry, you can do a drive-through wedding. Charles and I were married in a 24-hour wedding chapel with piped in, prerecorded wedding bells. A photographer and sound man were on hand to capture the magical 'I do' moments, for a nominal fee of course. All that mattered to me was getting the legal document, so we could sleep together. I refused to have 'real' sex with him until after we were married."

"You were a virgin?"

"Blow jobs aside."

"That's not a virgin."

I laughed. "Our families didn't approve of our relationship. So we eloped. My parents objected to his being Jewish and his parents objected to my parents' objections."

Diane grinned.

"We figured with time they'd forgive and forget."

"Did they?"

"Not my parents. His family was much more supportive."

"Steve and I are lucky to have the support of our families."

"You really are. It helps."

I motioned for the bill, and suggested a night cap at the Balalaika.

"A good idea. Perhaps Spicy Noodles is still there," Diane said.

We chuckled.

✳

CHAPTER 12

CHOICES?

Frankfurt, Germany—1977

"Benvenuto," Rafael welcomed, leading me to a quiet, corner table by a large window. "Reserved just for you. Which view today?"

"The big sky."

He nodded and pulled out a chair. "Congratulations on your upcoming exhibit! I read about it in the paper. Sorry we can't make your opening night; the restaurant's hopping on Fridays."

"I understand. Let me know when you can go and I'll give you a personal tour."

"Great! *Grazie,*" Rafael said. "Your waiter will be with you shortly."

I fetched my sketchpad from my carry bag and began drawing the view of a large, old oak tree outside the restaurant entrance, paying close attention to shadows—cast and form.

Rafael returned with two glasses of champagne. "Congratulations!" he handed me a glass. "Great success."

We clinked glasses. Rafael admired the sketch. "Excellent! Are you one for lunch?"

"Two. Julie will join me."

"Ahhh, she likes me. I can tell. She eats here often."

"Well, you and your pasta. It's the best in Frankfurt."

"*Grazie!*" he bowed.

"Oh, it's our friend," he said, moving toward the entrance.

I put the sketchbook away.

With a big smile, he greeted my friend Julie, a lovely, young, dark-haired woman looking strikingly sad today.

Wonder what's wrong with Julie?

"Sorry I'm late," Julie apologized. "I had to stop at the bank for money."

"This one's on me," I said. "You know my philosophy of receiving one-hundred-times blessing in return, for every generous deed."

"Okay. Next time I get the blessing."

Rafael returned with two more glasses of champagne. "Cheers," he said, setting one glass in front of each. "Enjoy! *Gustare!*"

"*Prost!* To good friends," I said clinking my glass with Julie's.

"*Prost!* You look great! Single life must agree with you."

"Thanks! I feel great. Hey, guess who called from the States this morning?"

"Who?"

"Our friend Jennifer."

"Jennifer? Anthony's wife? How's she doing? Does she like being back in the States?"

"She loves Denver and being close to family. Their daughter Molly likes going to a school where everyone speaks English."

"Did Jennifer ask you about Marlies?"

"No!" I answered. "Everything was all about Anthony. How he visits often and telephones every week. He purchased a house for them, helped them move in, and he's paying Jennifer's way through university. She said life's working out according to God's master plan."

"God's plan? Sounds much the same as Anthony's plan. I thought he went back to get a divorce from Jennifer so he could marry Marlies."

"He asked her for a divorce, but she refused. They were married in the Catholic Church, so for her divorce is out of the question. She believes he'll come to his senses, stop screwing around, and return to his family."

"Unbelievable!"

"She says she's willing to wait for him, no matter how long it takes. And is content to be true for as long as it takes."

"She said that?"

"Yes, she said that."

"I saw Anthony with Marlies here last week. Sitting at that table." Julie pointed to a corner table. "She's ready to drop the baby any day now. Does Jennifer know Marlies is pregnant with Anthony's child?"

"She didn't mention it. I didn't tell her. It's not my place. I'm sure she'll find out soon enough."

"Let's hope he tells her before she hears it from someone else."

Rafael returned to our table with menus. "Your waiter's busy; I can take your order."

"Veal marsala, for me." I handed him the menu.

"The house cannelloni," Julie said.

"*Subito*—coming right up," Rafael announced.

"While talking with Jennifer," I said, "the thought flashed on what my life could have been, had I chosen a different path."

"A different path?"

"Yes. We have choices in love, in life. I was also raised to believe that marriage is sacred and to divorce is to fail."

"Me too."

"'Til death do us part' means something totally different now."

"What does it mean, now?"

"'Til the death of the relationship.'"

"The relationship?" Julie asked. "I'd be so lonely living alone."

"Half of my married life I've lived alone, with Charles always traveling. And now working full time and getting ready for the exhibit, I don't have time to even think about being lonely. If the show's a success, I'll find a part-time job, so I can have some time for fun."

Julie raised her glass and proposed a toast. "Here's to success, and fun!"

We clinked glasses and sipped more champagne.

"Julie, thanks for being my friend through all of this. I remember calling Charles at the office and you answering the phone. It must have been difficult for you—having him as your boss and me as your friend."

"Painful. Especially when he refused to speak with you and told me to tell you that his attorney would answer your questions. His girlfriend Inge pushed him for a speedy divorce. She told everyone in the office that they were getting married as soon as the divorce became final."

"It could've happened sooner. If I had accepted the blame."

"Blame? Why would you accept the blame? He's the one who cheated on you. He's the one who asked for a divorce."

"He wanted to blame me because I didn't produce a child."

"That's ridiculous!

"It was actually a reason for divorce under an old Roman Catholic law. I said, 'NO WAY!'"

"Hard to believe that's ground for divorce in today's world."

"Fortunately the law will change this year to acknowledge a no-fault divorce. When my attorney told me that, I agreed to proceed. And yeah, the divorce will finally be final."

The waiter arrived with our steaming lunch. *"Gustare!"* he said, smiling.

"Grazie," we said in unison.

"Inge's so young and naive. I can't imagine what Charles sees in her," Julie remarked.

"Probably just that," I retorted.

"Have you met her?"

"Oh yes! She visited me one night. Uninvited, of course."

"What nerve."

"She had a fight with Charles, and he wasn't speaking to her. He often did that to me. Sometimes he would stare at me, silent. As if I just fell out of a tree. A weird look."

Julie sighed. "I know that look from Charles. It's scary."

"Inge wanted me to explain his strange behavior. I wasn't feeling well that evening, in fact I was in pajamas and ready for bed when the doorbell rang. So I ignored it.

"About a half hour later the bell rang again. I continued to ignore it, knowing my friends would call me before stopping by. I heard footsteps and a sudden knocking on my upstairs door. I thought perhaps my next-door neighbor needed something. I opened the door. A tall, slim, long-haired, 20-something woman pushed her way in and introduced herself as Inge, Charles's fiancée."

Julie shook her head in disbelief.

"I said I wasn't feeling well and asked her to leave. She refused to go until I answered questions about Charles. She sat down in the chair opposite me and told me everything bad Charles had ever said about me. How he left me because I didn't want children with him. How I liked animals more than children. How insensitive I was to his needs.

"I don't know how I looked to her, but I certainly felt as if she had just fallen out of a tree or something. Bewildering."

Julie chuckled.

"She continued her barrage of information about her relationship with Charles. How special it was. How tuned in she was to him. How much she loved him. How hard she worked at the relationship, and how confused she felt now because he stopped speaking to her for no apparent reason.

"I told her Charles was a difficult man to know because he wasn't open and honest. I don't think she even heard me, but as she rattled on with her 'poor me' story, I began to feel better.

"I actually felt sorry for her because she was so clueless, and I felt lucky to be rid of moody Charles. I suggested she use my telephone to call Charles, let him know she had come to her senses and would be home soon. I told her to be happy for finding her perfect mate. She seemed confused by my attitude.

"I smiled, watching her go down the stairs and out the front door. Good God, I thought, she's a real Stepford wife. Those two deserve each other."

"She's attractive, but—" Julie said.

"Not very bright," I said, finishing Julie's thought.

"How did she get in the downstairs door?" Julie asked.

"She waited until my neighbor came in and claimed she was a friend of mine. What a pushy, loony broad. The next day I phoned Charles at the office. You must have been busy because he answered the phone. I told him to tell her to never come to my apartment again. Or else."

"She's definitely pushy. When she visits the office, she asks me to bring her a cup of coffee."

"Oh Lord!" I chuckled. "That night after her visit, I had the weirdest, funniest dream."

"About what?" Julie asked.

"A baby. I was sitting in a train compartment. As the train pulled out of the station, I looked out the window and listened to the rhythmic sound of the train gathering speed. All of a sudden the compartment door slid open and a young woman entered, carrying a baby in her arms.

"She sat down in the seat opposite me. The woman ignored me, but the baby cooed and smiled. An adorable child with fat cheeks and blonde hair. We were having fun playing, entertaining each other.

"When I heard the conductor coming to check tickets, I stood up to get my ticket out of my jacket pocket and noticed the baby staring at me, in the mirror. I looked down at the baby's face and gasped. The baby looked just like me.

"I sat back down and stared at the young woman holding the child. It was Inge sitting opposite me.

"She turned beet-red in the face and glared at me. She yelled and told me that Charles is furious with her, and the hospital staff. He thinks some-one has switched babies, because the baby looked like me."

"And in your dream, the baby did."

"Yes. The baby giggled and laughed out loud.

"I woke myself up giggling. End of dream," I said.

"Amazing! And funny!" Julie smiled.

"I actually wish them luck. If not, he'll be back looking for me or someone else to do his laundry." I paused a moment. "So are you still enjoying your job with the magazine?"

"It gets old dealing with the politics of editorial versus sales. Every department head thinks he knows best."

"Father always thinks he knows best. How are you and John doing? Any luck getting pregnant?"

"No," Julie answered, biting her lower lip.

"Are you okay?" I asked, seeing her wipe a tear away.

"John's moved out. He wants a divorce."

"When did this happen?"

"A week ago."

"What's the problem?"

"I'm not sure. I caught him in bed with our upstairs neighbor."

"Your so-called friend, the airline hostess?"

"Yes."

"That's a problem." I patted Julie's hand. "I'm sorry."

"I can't imagine life without John. We've been sweethearts since high school and married now for almost thirteen years."

"What a jerk, doing this to you."

"Not him. I blame her. I caught them in our bed."

"Takes two to tango. By time our divorce is final, it will be almost thirteen years since our wedding."

"Lucky thirteen?"

"When it's over, it's over. Years from now you might thank her for taking your lousy husband away."

"No," Julie sighed, mournfully.

"Well, I feel grateful someone took Charles away. I've even thought of designing a line of cards to thank exes for leaving. A 'Glad you're not here' sort of message. I've designed a few to send out when my divorce is final."

Julie pointed in the direction of a wall speaker. "Oh listen, I love this song. It reminds me of John."

We sat in silence and listened as Lenny Welch's smooth voice drifted out of the sound system singing his hit tune, "Since I Fell for You."

The slow, sad song finished playing. Julie dabbed her eyes with a Kleenex.

"Songs have a way of jogging memories," I said. "They tell you a lot about yourself and your relationship. 'Too bad. Too sad.' Best to let John go."

"But I don't want a divorce. I don't want to live alone."

"You have your wonderful dog."

"Yes. She's great," Julie said, wiping tears from her eyes.

"And she's loyal. Start imagining yourself with someone who is loyal and honest."

Julie nodded. "I know you're right."

A livelier song came on. Ray Charles belted out "Hit the Road Jack."

I sang along, "Woman, oh woman, don't treat me so mean."

When the song finished, I got serious. "Charles wasn't honest either. But our life together got me where I needed to go. And now, I'm grateful to have found my own path in life."

"You always see things in a positive light."

"What's a girl to do? Lie down and die? The first few weeks, after Charles told me he wanted out, I felt angry, betrayed, absolutely shocked. I walked around in a daze and asked the gods, why me? But, as I got stronger, I thought, why not me? I deserve to be in a healthy relationship—one of mutual love and respect."

"Men are all the same. They don't know how to be honest."

"There must be good ones out there."

"If you meet one, give him my number."

"That's the spirit." I patted her hand. "But it will be the second one."

She smiled.

"Listen, my place is small. But you're welcome to stay with me until you find an apartment."

"Thanks! Someone at the office has offered me their spare room. Dog and all."

"Nice! Here's to your next chapter," I said raising my glass.

"And to your first exhibit," Julie added, as we clinked glasses.

"Dessert?" Raphael asked, nearing the table. *"Panna cotta? Tiramisu?"*

"Choices?" Julie said. "Which one?"

"One of each. We'll share," I answered.

CHAPTER 13

EMPOWERED

Frankfurt, Germany—1977

"It's crowded tonight," Michael said, glancing from side to side, as we entered the bar restaurant near the opera house.

"There's a place." I pointed to a far corner table.

"Super," Michael said, leading the way.

Almost immediately, a waiter arrived to take our drink order.

"*Ein Pilsner und ein Chardonnay,*" Michael confidently ordered in German. His eyebrows raised as he watched the waiter swish away. I chuckled.

"I know that real conversation in a foreign language presents more of a challenge, than just ordering drinks," Michael said. "But bars and restaurants offer an easy start to a foreign language, and I've found many waiters who are willing to teach me more."

"How do you say, 'Lay down I think I love you' in German?" I asked.

"No clue, some things don't need saying." Michael scanned the packed room. "I've got my gay radar turned on."

"Always on the prowl?" I asked.

"Always," he answered. He leaned forward. "Don't look now, but that gorgeous man at the next table is quite the hunk."

I smiled, waited a few polite seconds, then glanced over to check the gorgeous one out.

"Definitely hot."

"Oh, yeah. I wonder who his female friend is."

"Probably just that. Like us. Friends."

Michael smiled.

"Hey, thanks for inviting me to the opera tonight," I said. "I've always wanted to see *Aida* on stage, ever since I visited the La Scala Opera House in Milan and saw a poster announcing it as a coming attraction. Opera is a whole new musical adventure for me. I was never exposed to operas before moving to Europe. The challenge for me is to understand what they're saying, to follow the story."

"Italian operas are the easiest to follow."

"I can usually figure the story out by following the body language."

"A program is also helpful." Michael smiled.

"The program's written in German. The opera is performed in Italian. And I'm trying to figure it out in English. Have you seen *Aida* before?"

"Many times, but not with such grand sets and costumes."

"A spectacular production!"

"The finale was the best ever. Trilling, thrilling singing."

"Why did Aida hide in the vault? She knew she would die there."

"She wanted to die with her lover. In his arms forever."

"A tragic ending."

"What would drama be without a tragic ending?"

The waiter returned with drinks, a bowl of pretzels, and nuts.

A haunting tune from the restaurant's background music caught my attention. I sipped my wine and listened intently.

"'Dust in the Wind,' Kansas." Michael clinked his glass with mine.

"It reminds me of a dream—about a ghost town."

"A faded dream?"

"No, quite vivid."

"You talk often about dreams. Are you obsessing with old memories?"

"I don't think so. I didn't die in his arms in a vault, like Aida."

"A ghost town? Sounds spooky."

"It was spooky at first, but ended up being empowering—once I took control of the situation."

"So tell me."

"I stood alone, in the middle of a vast desert. On a deserted dirt road. A ghost town loomed ahead." I stopped and took a sip of wine.

"A dark and stormy night?" Michael asked.

"No, a hot and windy afternoon. Howling wind. Shutters and doors were banging. Tumbleweeds were bouncing about."

"The tumbleweed trot," Michael chortled. "Sorry. Go on."

"The old road looked to be the only way in and out of town. The sun shone bright, blazing hot. As I walked along the road, I noticed a faded, wooden sign standing near the side of the road. It read *LAST GAS 99 MILES*. I turned and looked around, trying to figure out where I was. Jagged mountains, in the distance, surrounded the town. I read the sign again. I knew I was dreaming, but the details were so vivid. So real and intense."

"A lucid dream."

"Yes. I heard him call my name."

"Who?"

"Charles." I paused.

"Ahh. Charles. You can run, but you can't hide from Charles."

"As the wind moaned and whistled through the dilapidated wooden buildings, Charles walked toward me, grinning. A disgusting grin." I took another sip of wine.

"And then?" Michael asked.

"He grabbed my hand and pulled me toward him. I stiffened, not wanting to be close. He pointed to a boarded-up gas station—leaning, barely standing. Most other buildings had collapsed. He told me that with a can of white paint, some TLC, and the rest of our lives, we could make this place almost like new. The word 'almost' bounced and echoed all around the valley.

"'The rest of our lives?' I asked Charles, pulling my hand free.

"He walked around the outside of the building, inspecting a water pump and examining an old jalopy and auto parts, parked alongside an over-turned outhouse. The hood of the car was propped open with a two-by-four.

"Why I wondered, would he be inspecting old parts of a parked car? One that has died and will never run again. A waste of energy, I thought.

"I walked closer to look at the car. The old engine, stained by oil drippings, sat covered with cobwebs. Charles removed the piece of wood and closed the hood of the car. He patted the round fender affectionately and rubbed his dirty hands on his faded jeans. I backed away, not wanting to touch anything."

Michael broke our eye contact, glanced over my shoulder, and for a brief moment held up a thumb and forefinger. European waiters were professionals. Always watching and waiting for the diner's signal. Two fingers, two more drinks were on the way.

I continued. "Charles walked around to the front of the building and inspected gas pumps. He pointed to the price of gas. The pump showed 79 cents a gallon."

"Wow! Wait," Michael said. "The 1973-74 oil embargo put gas at that price. Prior to that it had been 35 cents a gallon for years."

"Thirty-five cents a gallon? How do you retain all this information?"

"Photographic brain. Sorry!"

"No, it's truly amazing you know so much."

"I'm spatial. Continue, please."

"Charles walked towards the front door of the gas station and motioned me to follow him."

"This is getting creepy," Michael said.

I hesitated. "You know, I just thought of something important. 1973 was when I was pregnant and bedfast. I lost the baby in Cyprus in early 1974. When Charles returned from his business trip, he accused me of not wanting children with him and said I purposely killed the baby, by taking a boat ride around the harbor. Devastated by the accusation, I knew our marriage was over. I had tried so hard, for so many years, to have a baby. For me the marriage was dirty, broken, and dead. Nothing could fix it. I also knew that he was having an affair."

"How did you know that?"

"The Sofia dream. I told you about it. Remember?"

"Yes. Profound. But back to the desert dream."

"Charles kept talking about fixing things up—getting the gas station running again and making the living quarters comfortable. I knew I didn't want to live anywhere with Charles.

"He stopped talking and smiled at me, beckoning me inside as he pushed the creaky front door open. 'Welcome back!' he said. I sensed that he wanted to carry me across the threshold.

"I shuddered at the thought and waited outside, until he had gone in. I stepped inside. but purposely left the front door ajar. The room smelled musty. When my eyes adjusted to the light, I noticed cobwebs covering everything—counters, chairs, tables, the corners."

"Creepier," Michael chimed in, pushing a bowl of pretzels toward me.

"Charles announced, 'There's a bedroom and bath upstairs.' He suggested I go up and make myself comfortable, while he fetched water for bathing. He told me, 'Cool water, in this heat, will feel good on bare skin. I stood stiff as a statue, while he fumbled with the back door knob. He finally got it to turn and opened the door. Light streamed in. He smiled and waved as he headed outdoors, in the direction of the water pump.

"I watched him pick up a bucket and walk toward the pump. My heart pounded as I waited to hear the sound of water pumping. When I heard the steady, rhythmic sound, I tiptoed out the front door and closed it quietly behind me." I paused and took sips of wine.

Michael waited for me to continue. "And then?"

"I took off running, as fast as I could, down the road. I ran so fast, I felt like a small plane getting ready for takeoff. I flew past the *LAST GAS* sign and far beyond. Exhausted, I finally slowed and stopped running. When I turned and looked back, the ghost town was far away—in the distance."

"Did he follow you?"

"No."

"The End?"

"No! I knew I had to level the ghost town."

"Wipe the slate clean?"

"Wipe it off the face of the earth."

"How did you do that?"

"I cupped my hands together and starting blowing."

"Like the wind? Whoosh-whoosh, away?" Michael asked.

"It took some time. With every inhale and exhale the ghost town swayed a little more. All of a sudden, I felt I had the power to do anything."

"Move mountains," Michael declared. "Blow a fucking town away. Whoa! And then?"

"I clapped my hands and created thunder. I shook my fists and bolts of lightening filled the sky. Dark clouds moved in and rain began pouring down, drenching me and the parched earth."

"My God, woman," Michael mused, motioning to the waiter for another beer. "Great material. I could never come up with this stuff. I can see the credits rolling now."

"Be my guest. Put it in a screenplay!"

"What happened next?"

"The storm subsided, the sky cleared. The ghost town was gone."

"To be in the middle of a storm, in a dream, means you are going through devastating personal catastrophe and loss. But you weathered the storm."

"I also created it. Directed it."

"Yes," Michael replied, taking it all in. "You did. Swept it clean."

"The next morning, when the warmth of the sun woke me up from the dream, I felt throughly cleansed. Glad to be alive. At peace with myself."

"Empowered," Michael said. He appeared awestruck, gazing into space. The hunk at the next table might as well have disappeared. Michael's "gaydar" had shut down as we talked.

Snapping out of his revery, Michael signaled for the bill.

I offered to pay, but Michael wouldn't hear of it.

"You're my confidante," he said. "It's good to keep you wined and dined. So would you like to go to Greece with me after your exhibit opening?"

"Wow! I haven't been to Greece since before the Cyprus War."

"I'll visit accounts in the area by day, and by night we can hit the hot spots."

"During the Cyprus years, I visited there often. Always stayed in Vouliag-meni, a seaside town, south of Athens."

"That's a mouthful. I know the town. I've stayed there and visited the ancient ruins. The most famous is the temple of the god Apollo."

"Yes. I've seen them. Sandy beaches. Nice tennis courts too. I played a pretend tennis game there one evening with a friend. Totally stoned."

"Pretend tennis? How exactly does that work?"

"No ball or racket. A slow-motion game where players pretend the actions."

"A singles game?"

"Yes."

"Who won?"

"A tie."

"A tie, in singles? What?"

"We reached deuce and quit. We laughed so hard, we were exhausted. People were actually standing around watching us play."

"They were probably waiting for the court."

"Of course they were." I chuckled.

"You're insane—but in a nice way," Michael said. "Promise me you'll never grow up."

"If I do, I promise not to get stale."

Michael laughed. "How about Greece?"

"I'd love to go to Greece with you."

"Great! I'll make reservations."

CHAPTER 14

NAPALM?

Kyrenia, Cyprus—20 July 1974

In the early hours of Saturday morning, I awoke to the distant drone of aircraft. Stunned, I sat up in bed and listened. Planes. Getting louder. The realization sent shivers down my spine. I placed my hands over my heart. "Oh, my God!" I gasped. "It's the Turks!"

I looked at the clock—5:20. The crack of dawn. I shook Charles, trying to wake him, but he continued to snore. I shook him again to no avail.

I jumped from bed and yelled, "The Turks are attacking."

Moments later, a series of explosions awakened the entire village of Kyrenia.

"Holy shit!" Charles said, leaping out of bed. "Quick, run for cover."

We scrambled into clothes and ran from our downstairs bedroom, across the cobblestone hall, toward the dining room.

Explosion after explosion rocked the area around us. We dove for cover under the stairs.

Ronit and Andreas came running down the stairs from the upstairs guest bedroom. We huddled together under the staircase as more explosions erupted nearby. Dust and smoke filled the air from falling debris.

I heard the deafening roar of another jet passing low overhead.

"Run!" Charles shouted, pointing to the dining room. "Get under the table."

We scurried across the cobblestone foyer into the dining room and crawled under the massive wooden table. We knelt, crouched on the floor, and waited.

Moments later, we heard a small explosion followed by a loud whistle. A great explosion shook the solid stone house—shattering windows, knocking paintings off walls, and rattling furniture. An explosion so forceful, it shifted the marble slab floor beneath us.

Another tremor and a thud overhead brought something crashing down on the table top. "Ma kara? What's happening?" Ronit screamed in Hebrew and English.

Heads bowed, we waited until the explosions stopped. We opened our eyes and looked at one another. I sighed. We had survived the onslaught.

Charles got up to see what had crashed on the tabletop. "The iron chandelier fell from the ceiling," he said.

"Thank God it's a solid table," I said. "That chandelier is heavy." Dazed, I looked around at the damage. Broken glass and shattered objects everywhere.

"Shit," Charles yelled, running from the room.

"Me too," Andreas and Ronit said in unison, running up the stairs to the bathrooms. Fortunately there were four in this big house.

I ran to another bathroom downstairs and barely made it in time. As soon as I sat on the toilet, my bowels erupted. I sobbed.

Hearing a faint whirring sound in the distance, I quickly pulled up my pants. Airplane engines. Oh, my God! They're returning. I raced back to the dining room.

We huddled together, under the table, and listened.

The onslaught had three parts. First, the screaming sound of aircraft overhead. Next, the sound of rockets being fired with a pop, a whistle, followed by an all-encompassing explosion. Heads bowed, eyes closed, hands clasped tightly together, we waited for the final sound.

I prayed that the rockets would fall in empty fields far away.

When I heard the final explosion, I gasped in relief and opened my eyes. "We're still alive." I wept, tears streaming down my face.

The planes left to reload bombs in Turkey. "Ten-minute flight time from the base in Turkey to Kyrenia," Charles said. "They'll return in thirty minutes."

"The opposition is starting," Andreas said, as we listened to the sounds of machine guns and antiaircraft firing outside.

Dear God, help! We're in the middle of a war.

During the lull between raids, Charles gave orders. "Andreas, bolt the outside doors and shutters. Susan, fill water containers. Grab pillows and blankets. Ronit, check the telephone. Get drinking water from the kitchen."

Charles left to disconnect gas tanks and check for structural damage.

Thirty minutes later, hearing the familiar sound of planes returning, we cowered again under the dining room table. Charles came back with a radio and an AC adapter in hand. With pillows and blankets in place, we waited for another round of bombs to fall.

"The phone's working," Ronit whispered. "But I couldn't get through to the embassy. The line's busy."

"A good sign," Andreas said.

Another wave of bombs filled the sky with the familiar sounds of chaos and swirls of smoke. "They're farther away," I whispered, as we listened to the rockets being fired, the pops, whistles, and final explosions some-where in the distance.

Charles turned the radio dial to BBC news.

THOUSANDS OF TURKISH TROOPS HAVE INVADED NORTHERN CYPRUS AFTER LAST-MINUTE TALKS IN THE GREEK CAPITAL, ATHENS, FAILED TO REACH A SOLUTION. A TURKISH ARMADA OF 33 SHIPS, INCLUDING TROOP TRANSPORTERS AND AT LEAST 30 TANKS AND SMALL LANDING CRAFT, HAS LANDED ON THE NORTHERN COAST.

TENSION HAS BEEN RUNNING HIGH IN THE MEDITERRANEAN ISLAND SINCE A MILITARY COUP FIVE DAYS AGO IN WHICH PRESIDENT ARCHBISHOP MAKARIOS, A GREEK CYPRIOT, WAS DEPOSED.

THE COUP LED TO FEARS AMONG THE TURKISH CYPRIOT COMMUNITY THAT THE GREEK-BACKED MILITARY

RULERS WOULD IGNORE THEIR RIGHTS AND PRESS FOR UNIFICATION FOR CYPRUS WITH GREECE—ENOSIS.

"Why are the Americans allowing this to happen?" Andreas asked.

"Shh," Ronit said, when shouting voices were heard in the street outside.

The sound of running boots passed by and the voices grew fainter.

After several minutes of an eerie quiet, I heard people moving along the street. I tiptoed to the window to see if I could see anything through the wooden slats in the shutter. "No pattern. Just people running back and forth," I whispered.

"Probably checking on friends and neighbors," Andreas said.

"Stay away from the windows," Charles warned.

A deafening explosion close by forced me to scurry back under the table.

"Whoa! Close! Just behind our back garden wall," Charles observed. I looked at him. He was being analytical. As though he was used to being around explosions.

After a few minutes of peace, Charles and Andreas climbed the stairs to the balcony to survey the damage and pinpoint where the loud explosion had taken place.

When they returned, Charles reported, "That was too damn close. There's a huge crater behind our back wall. No bodies. They must have missed their target."

"There are several areas up in smoke near the Greek army camp," Andreas said. "It's as if the sky is raining balls of fire."

"Napalm B," Charles explained.

"Napalm?" I shuddered at the thought. "Like they used in Vietnam?"

"Yes. It's a combo of polystyrene and benzene. A jellied gasoline used as an incendiary device. Impossible to extinguish. Designed to burn flesh."

Burn flesh? Did he just say that? I shuddered again.

Sporadic attacks continued as rockets and mortars launched nearby. The summer sky rained fire. The air grew thick with smoke and ash.

We hunkered down, under the dining table, and listened to another BBC news report.

IN CYPRUS THE VICE PRESIDENT ISSUED A STATEMENT:"WE ARE LIVING AN HISTORICAL DAY. THE TURKISH ARMED FORCES LANDED IN CYPRUS IN ORDER TO SAFEGUARD THE INDEPENDENCE OF CYPRUS, TO RESTORE HUMAN RIGHTS AND FREEDOM IN ACCORDANCE WITH THE 1960 AGREEMENTS. NO NEED FOR RESISTANCE. A DEMOCRATIC SYSTEM WILL BE RAPIDLY RESTORED AND LIFE IN THE ISLAND WILL RETURN TO NORMAL."

IN BRUSSELS THE NATO COUNCIL HAS BEEN MEETING IN AN EMERGENCY SESSION. GREECE HAS ACCUSED TURKEY OF AN ACT OF AGGRESSION BY INVADING CYPRUS.

TURKEY REPLIED THAT ITS TROOPS MOVED IN TO RESTORE CONSTITUTIONAL ORDER.

Andreas asked for the radio and tuned it to CBC—the Cyprus Broadcasting station. In Greek, they were telling all Greek Cypriots to join their national guard units and telling families to stay put.

Ronit took the radio next to listen to Kol Israel. Reporting in Hebrew, they announced that Nicosia and other cities were being heavily bombed and urged people to stay inside.

Charles took the radio and tuned it to BFBS—the British Forces station.

ALL FOREIGN NATIONALS ARE ADVISED TO PACK ONE SMALL BAG EACH IN THE EVENT OF EVACUATION. PETS WILL NOT BE ALLOWED TO EVACUATE WITH FAMILIES.

"Oh, Sam!" I winced.

"Sabrina will take good care of him," Charles assured me, patting my hand.

After several minutes of silence, Andreas took Ronit's hand in his, and spoke to her softly in Hebrew.

She cried.

He told her he must go and fight for his country.

Ronit swayed side to side, and begged him not to go.

"Someone has to fight the Turks," he explained.

She clung to him, tears streaming down her cheeks. "What about us?" she asked.

Andreas lifted her chin and said, "Ronit, if it was Israel, you would fight."

"Wars are senseless," she pleaded with him. "People die. Not governments. What's more important? Your government, or your life? Your government, or your wife?"

Still crying, Ronit looked at Charles and me, and begged, "Please, don't let him go."

Charles tried to reason with Andreas about the senselessness of it all, considering the Turks' overwhelming air power. The Greek Cypriots had nothing to match that.

Andreas got up and went to the foyer to telephone his parents, a few streets away. He spoke in a worried, hurried tone. When he hung up, he said the Turks were going door-to-door looking for Greeks. He said he must leave to protect them.

Ronit begged him to stay. He insisted he must leave. "You'll be safer without me."

"If they come, I'll say we're all foreigners," Charles said.

"I must go," Andreas announced. "Promise me you'll look after Ronit."

"We will. We promise."

Andreas kissed Ronit goodbye and left.

After Andreas left, Ronit became hysterical. She pounded her chest in anguish and cried out. I hugged her until her crying subsided.

Ronit jumped up to telephone the Israeli Embassy. To her surprise someone answered. She told them her location and asked if they had evacuation plans for Israeli citizens. They advised her to wait and go with other foreign nationals when she heard the radio announcement. She asked about the safety of other Israelis on the island. "I'm happy to hear all Israelis are safe," she reported.

All remained quiet for a couple of hours. We heard jets flying high overhead. "Nicosia's their destination now," Charles explained.

Feeling safer, we ventured outside to sit in the garden.

The telephone rang. "It's Andreas," Charles called to Ronit.

Ronit ran and grabbed the telephone, thrilled to hear from him. He had made it safely to his parents' house. He told her they were fine and that he would drive his family across the mountain, on back roads, to his brother's house in Nicosia. They agreed to stay in touch through the Israeli Embassy until the crisis ended. He told her he wanted her to return to Israel for now because life in Cyprus would be tough for some time. After exchanging many endearments, Ronit put the telephone back in its cradle and cried softly.

"Andreas has decided not to fight," she said, smiling.

Charles telephoned the American Embassy to ask if they had contingency plans for US citizens. They advised him to go with other foreigners when he heard the evacuation announcement. "Unbelievable," Charles complained. "They know we're stuck here." He hung up the phone, suggested I prepare sandwiches.

No one had an appetite, but I made sandwiches and coffee, and put them on the table in the garden.

"Maybe later," Ronit said.

Sam appeared at the kitchen door meowing for food. Happy to see him, I gave him a big hug and opened a tin of tuna for him. I petted him and assured him that Sabrina would take good care of him.

Charles returned from the garden with leaves and buds from his prize marijuana plants. "I'd say this is as good a time as any to enjoy the harvest," he remarked, rolling giant joints. "This will help calm you," he assured Ronit.

I turned the radio on, in hopes BFBS would make an announcement regarding evacuation. No news. I switched to BBC and listened to the same old news. "Not even a mention of foreigners in Kyrenia," I remarked, reaching for a sandwich and coffee.

After lunch, I telephoned Ilene and Syd. No answer. Hopefully they hadn't been on the road, to catch their flight, when the bombing started. God forbid.

The phone rang again. American friends called to ask if we had heard of any evacuation plans. Charles informed them that we were awaiting further instructions from BFBS and agreed to be in touch if we heard any new news.

Following the advice from the radio broadcast, I found smaller, carry-on bags, and repacked: water, passports, money, underwear, toothbrushes. Necessities in place of niceties. I found a small suitcase for Ronit and suggested she do the same. The road forward looked more ominous now.

Ronit was concerned because she didn't have her Israeli passport with her.

I told her it probably wouldn't be a problem.

Shortly after 1500 hours that afternoon—after many telephone calls between friends, and still no official evacuation announcements on the radio—somehow a consensus emerged that it would be best, and probably safer, for foreign nationals to be together in a group. Charles offered our large house as a gathering point until we could decide what to do next.

The phone rang again. Andreas wanted Ronit to know that he made it safely to Nicosia with his family. She cried again, and told him how much she loved him.

Before we had a chance to gather, an American friend called. FBIS employees had been told to drive up the Kyrenia-Nicosia mountain pass to the UN-FINCON (Finnish Contingent) retreat: Tjikles Camp. The plan was to meet there in an hour.

"That's it!" Charles shouted. "We're leaving." He lit up our impromptu telephone tree with the news.

I took a quick shower, put on fresh clothes. Charles and Ronit did as well.

Tears in my eyes, I gave Sam one last hug and left an envelope on the table for Sabrina—a thank-you note and enough money to feed Sam for six months.

With one small bag each, a radio, binoculars, sandwiches, and water, we walked out our front door, and locked it. We climbed into the car to head for the safety of the UN camp. Whatever came next, our idyllic life in Cyprus had ended.

Sabrina and other neighbors came running over to say goodbye.

I thanked Sabrina for looking after Sam and the fish. "Help yourselves to any food or anything you need," I said, eyes tearing. We agreed to stay in touch.

Charles backed the car out of the carport, steered it down the cobblestone road, turned right, then left, onto the main road and we headed south up the mountain on the Kyrenia to Nicosia pass. As we climbed higher on the hairpin curving road, the jagged limestone slopes and rugged terrain of the Kyrenia Mountain Range came into view.

Without this modern road, I thought, getting to Nicosia must have taken days. The new road—built only a year or two before—made it easy to get from the small, northern seaside town of Kyrenia (facing Turkey, with its historic castle, ancient shipwreck, and beautiful harbor) to the bustling capital city of Nicosia, where I witnessed the Greek coup only a few days ago.

CHAPTER 15

SITTING DUCKS?

Tjikles Camp, Kyrenia, Cyprus—20 July 1974

Driving faster than normal, Charles shifted gears and sped around corners and curves. We sensed no immediate threat, but with tanks and planes in the area, who knew? We would be the last to learn if we became a target.

After the last long hairpin curve in the road, we neared the mountain top and saw the UN Finnish Tjikles camp sign on the right. Charles slowed the car and turned onto the gravel road leading up the hill to the look-out point.

Seeing the UN flag flying ahead, I sighed. "We made it."

"Safe now," Charles said, following another vehicle up the hill, into a large open parking area which appeared to be filling up fast.

A UN soldier directed drivers into tight parking spaces, so tight that we had to coordinate opening car doors with the next arrivals.

Friends rushed up, hugged and kissed.

I burst into tears when I saw Ilene and Syd with their young son, Josh, parked a few cars behind us. I ran to hug them.

"Oh, good. You're here too." Josh smiled.

"I tried to call you. No answer!" I said.

"After the first bombs fell, close by, we knew we had to get out. Went to a neighbor's house," Ilene explained. "Soldiers were shooting from our yard and Greek tanks were parked out front."

"We got out fast," Josh said.

"Thank God you made it out."

I spotted my friend Kate and her sons, and ran to welcome them. "Where's Alex?" I asked.

"He stayed home. He didn't want the boys to see him get left behind," Kate answered.

"Why would he?"

"The announcements said evacuations were for foreign nationals only."

"But he's a British citizen. Of course they'll take him."

"Our neighbor Will is trying to convince him to come," Kate said. "I saw Ronit. Where's her husband Andreas?"

I explained that he had feared for his parents' safety in Kyrenia, and promised to drive them to his brother's house in Nicosia over back mountain roads. With the Turks' invasion and Turkish checkpoints along the way, the main highway we took would be out of the question for a Greek.

She was surprised that Ronit didn't go with the family. I told her Ronit planned to return to Israel until things quieted down.

I waved to another friend, hoping to provide welcome to her and her children. I asked about her husband.

"He's at work," she said, bursting into tears. "We were forced to leave our home when the bombing started. Greek soldiers took it over."

"Where did you go?"

"A neighbor's. Two hours later, we watched our home being totally destroyed by bombs. Everything's gone. Family photos, our pets," she sobbed. "How is this possible? Our life turned to ashes!"

"I'm glad you're safe." I hugged her. To calm her. I couldn't undo the trauma, but I felt a need to console her as she mourned her loss.

Charles talked with other friends a few feet away. They were trying to quiet an elderly woman who cursed at the top of her lungs in English and another language.

"Who is she?" I heard someone ask.

"She's the mother of someone who works at FBIS. She's upset because she left her medications at home, and wants to return and get them," someone else explained.

A British woman stopped to ask if anyone knew of a nurse in the area. "My daughter started labor this morning. It's her first child. Her husband was called to fight with his unit in the Greek National Guard."

"Poor dear," I replied. "The UN will know of one."

"She's got it tough," someone remarked. "Giving birth at the best of times isn't easy."

I spotted a familiar figure walking up the gravel road. I looked around for Kate. When I found her, I pointed and yelled. "Kate! It's Alex."

Kate sprinted downhill, past the rows of parked cars, toward her husband.

I smiled, watching them hug, kiss, and walk arm in arm up the hill together toward their two sons. What a tough time they've had with Alex being taken in for interrogation, and now this frightening experience of bombs falling all around us, being forced to leave our homes. What a tough time we've all had.

Now alone, my tears flowed freely.

When the rush of traffic into the parking lot slowed, a UN soldier made an announcement about the camp's facilities. He pointed out various buildings—the UN personnel living quarters, the canteen with observation deck, the day room, showers, toilets, the cookhouse, and the radio room. "Drinking water is available in the day room or from a spigot down the hill by the entrance," he said. "Both faucets are fed by the tank sitting farther up the hill, which collects rainwater. Since the tank's exposed to sun, the water's hot. Please use water sparingly since we don't know how long the emergency will last. Please write your names, nationality, and passport number on our list." He pointed to a line forming of refugees.

"Is this an evacuation list?" someone asked the soldier.

"No. The UN keeps track of people on the premises. No word of evacuation plans. We'll keep you informed and do everything possible to keep you safe while you're here."

He pointed in the direction of a rocky hillside, dotted with olive trees and pines, and instructed us to find a protected, covered area to sleep for the night.

I looked around for Charles and Ronit. Charles stood in the long line of refugees signing the list.

I found Ronit visiting with an Israeli friend nearby. I told them we needed to find a protected place to sleep.

When Charles returned, he said he had added our names to the UN list. He assured Ronit that not having her passport with her wasn't a problem.

Charles suggested we walk around the clearing at the top of the hill to survey our surroundings and get our bearings, direction-wise, before finding a place to sleep.

"I can see why this ridge is used as an observation post," he said, looking around. "The views are spectacular from both sides of the hill."

Charles pointed north to the Kyrenia castle. "The Turks have landed and their offensive will involve air, land, and sea operations. See the corridor just below us?" he asked, pointing to the road below.

"Yes, the main road to Nicosia," I answered.

"Kyrenia to Nicosia," he said, pointing his finger south, along the road below in the direction of Nicosia. "If the Turks can gain control of this pass, they will win the war."

"The Greeks will fight back," Ronit said.

"They'll need heavy artillery and antiaircraft defense to beat the Turks. This corridor is key."

We walked back down the hill and searched for a level covered area where we hoped to sleep, as comfortably as possible.

We saw our friends Pete and Paula, putting a blanket down a few steps up the hill.

I thanked Pete for checking on me when I first returned to Kyrenia from Nicosia, after the coup.

Pete introduced us to their friends, a couple visiting from Boston.

"Hell of a time to vacation in Cyprus," I told them.

"Yes, our timing is a bit off," the wife replied.

We walked a bit farther. Charles turned back. "Let's set up there, near Pete and Paula." Charles pointed to a spot just below them. "It's easy access to the facilities. And no attack worries, now that we're in UN territory."

As dusk descended, I walked up the hill to the bathroom with Ronit and her Israeli friend. We waited in line to use the one and only toilet designated for women.

By the time we filled water bottles the sun was setting. Knowing my thin, cotton peasant dress didn't offer much protection against the prickly pine needles covering the ground, I stopped on our way back and removed the floor mats from our car to use as padding.

In dim light, we made our way cautiously along the dirt road searching for our new campsite. The terrain appeared strange under low light. Don't panic. "We're almost there," I assured Ronit.

I heard the sound of a radio and saw the outline of Charles's Afro—backlit by the fading sun—on the rise above.

We scampered up the embankment and joined our group. I arranged car mats beneath us. Charles held the radio. We listened to the latest from BBC World Service.

ON JULY 15, FOLLOWING A LARGE-SCALE NATIONAL POLICE ASSAULT ON EOKA, THE MAKARIOS GOVERNMENT WAS OVERTHROWN BY THE NATIONAL GUARD. NIKOS SAMPSON, A GREEK CYPRIOT NEWSPAPER PUBLISHER, ACCEDED TO THE PRESIDENCY AND MAKARIOS FLED THE COUNTRY. BOTH GREECE AND TURKEY MOBILIZED THEIR ARMED FORCES.

THE TURKISH PRIME MINISTER, MR. ECEVIT SAID THAT HIS FORCES HAD INTERVENED IN CYPRUS AFTER ALL DIPLOMATIC WAYS TO SOLVE THE CRISIS HAD BEEN EXPLORED.

THE UNITED NATIONS SECURITY COUNCIL PASSED A RESOLUTION DEMANDING IMMEDIATE WITHDRAWAL OF TURKISH MILITARY PERSONNEL AND URGED NEGOTIATIONS BETWEEN GREECE, TURKEY AND THE UNITED KINGDOM TO TAKE PLACE.

THE TURKISH NAVAL COMMANDER ANNOUNCED THAT CERTAIN AREAS AROUND CYPRUS ARE DANGEROUS FOR SHIPPING.

"Certain areas around Cyprus are dangerous? No shit." Charles joked. The others laughed.

I heard conversations from other groups, downhill from us. Some Brits were complaining about how their government had failed them.

"The German government got Germans out on Friday. Meanwhile the British Commissioner urged us to stay calm," one said.

"Urging British holiday makers to leave would imply that the invasion was imminent. Wouldn't it?" another asked.

"Are we sitting ducks?" someone else asked.

"Possibly," another said.

"Definitely," I muttered, under my breath.

"The Junta is to blame. They started it all," Ronit told her Israeli friend.

"Well, the Communists backed Makarios," her friend said.

"And they were pro-Arab," Ronit remarked.

"Certainly worrisome for Israel," her friend said.

"King Kissinger is determined to have NATO bases everywhere," I said. "No matter the devastation."

Charles put his finger over his lips and warned, "Shhh. Keep your voices down. Others might not agree with your opinions."

I settled down on my mat, and got as comfortable as possible on the hard ground. Ronit and her friend continued talking in whispers.

I dozed, off and on, trying to sleep. A zzt-zing sound overhead got my attention. *Probably a bug buzzing by.*

Another zzt-zing flew over, followed by a loud cracking sound.

I gasped, realizing a bullet had hit a tree nearby. I scurried to cover my head with my purse.

Moments later, a barrage of bullets assaulted nearby trees.

"Move fast to lower ground," Charles commanded.

We grabbed our belongings, scrambled north down the slope, around the hillside and crawled into a shrub covered area.

Obviously others had chosen more wisely than we.

An eerie quiet descended. I arranged our car mats to make the terrain more comfortable, and settled into what I hoped might be a bit of rest. But my mind was racing.

Reflecting on Charles's quick tactical decision at a critical time—only moments before—and his authoritative command that we move fast to lower ground; he had definitely saved our skin. Did he have "command" training or disaster management training somewhere in his background? To my knowledge he had never been in the military. The Vietnam War escalated in 1965, shortly after we married. Antiwar protests and anti-draft sentiment was building. Many young men, defining themselves as conscientious objectors, burned their draft cards and fled the country. The widespread draft resistance movement forced drastic changes to the Selective Service structure and by 1967, when we left the country, many young men were evading the draft. To avoid war. And here we sat in the middle of one.

From far away, the sound of planes flying at high altitudes interrupted my thoughts. Again, headed south toward Nicosia.

Ronit asked to use the radio to hear news in Hebrew. No new news from Kol Israel.

Later in the evening, Turkish jets flew low overhead, approaching from the north, turning east, and firing at Greek positions across the corridor.

"Super Sabre F-100s," Charles said.

"How can you tell?" I asked.

"Size, shape, power, their formation. They're impressive! Probably targeting Greek artillery fortifications across the way."

The raids were frequent and intense.

And happily not focused on us.

The Turks needed to destroy Greek machine gun nests and armed resistance in order to clear the corridor from Kyrenia to the capital of Nicosia.

After the planes left to reload, we heard sporadic shooting and artillery fire continue, back and forth across the pass—between the Turks' stronghold to the north at St. Hilarion Castle and the Greeks' emplacements occupying the opposite mountain range to the south.

A sudden loud explosion shook the ground near us.

"Sounds like twenty-five-pounders," Charles said.

"You can tell by the sound?"

"Yes, it's quick-firing and loud."

How does he know all this stuff?

I heard others talking in low voices around us. I tried to get comfortable and tried to block out the sounds by placing my purse over my head. Finally I fell asleep.

A jolting yell, from a short distance away, jarred me awake.

"I've been shot," a man groaned.

Charles immediately crawled uphill toward the injured man, who mumbled incoherently, while holding a shell casing in his outstretched hand. He kept pointing to his forehead.

"You were hit by a shell casing," Charles told him. "It probably fell from the tree you were sleeping under. Probably one fired earlier from the Sabre jet runs."

"Do I have a hole in my head?" the man asked.

"No, just a nick," Charles assured him.

"I'm still alive." The man sighed and smiled.

"You're damn lucky to be, and lucky it lodged in the tree first."

"We need to get out of here," the man said.

"Unfortunately," Charles told him, "we're stuck here. The Turks and Greeks are battling for control of the pass, and we won't be going anywhere anytime soon."

I watched Charles crawl back downhill.

Exhausted, I collapsed into a fitful sleep.

CHAPTER 16

GOOD NEWS, BAD NEWS

Tjikles Camp, Kyrenia, Cyprus—21 July 1974

The thud of metal against dirt awakened me. It was still dark, but nearing dawn. Not hearing bullets zinging past, I sat up and looked around. I heard the sound start again. Someone digging on the other side of the dirt road. I stood up to get a better look and spotted two stooped figures. Looks like Alex and Syd.

I staggered down the hill and across the road. Syd tore into the dirt with a spade and Alex with a tin can.

"Are you digging a trench?" I asked.

"Yes, for the children," Syd answered.

"I don't like dodging bullets," Alex said.

"Nor us," I said. "It was a rough night. We had to move to lower ground."

"You need to move to this lower side of the road. It's further from the Greek emplacements and safer."

I agreed and retraced my steps, across the road and up the hill where I had left Charles and friends sleeping. They were still sleeping. Lucky them!

Almost back to my starting point, I paused to sit on a flat rock nearby, and watched the trench-digging continue.

A zzt-zing whizzed past my face. Huh? What? A loud thud. Gasping, I turned and saw where the flying bullet had slammed into the trunk of a tree behind me. I hit the ground fast, crawled up the incline, and slumped to safety, facedown, between Charles and Ronit.

Several minutes of silence ticked by before a steady barrage of bullets bombarded trees all around us. I could see boots of soldiers running past. It appeared senseless, as though they were firing shots in all directions. "We've got to move," I said in a loud whisper. "As soon as it's quiet."

We lay motionless, waiting for calm. The bullets stopped. The crunch of boots and yelling subsided as soldiers ran away.

When I heard the sound of trench-digging resume, I sat up. "Let's go," I yelled, grabbing mats and belongings.

I ran, crouched low to the ground. The others followed me down the hill, across the dirt road.

Charles pointed to a low covered area, about twenty feet from the trench. "Hopefully this will be safer," Charles said.

"Anyplace is safer than the other side," Pete agreed.

As we settled into our new site, I watched dozens of weary people move their belongings from across the road in search of a safer place to wait out the fighting.

The light of day and the intense heat of the sun brought the stark realization that we sat squarely and directly in the middle of the war. We were miserable, and clearly stuck. No way out. Until the fighting stopped.

Although it was calm now, we knew there was more fighting to come. No evacuation could possibly happen until the Turks or the Greeks gained control of the pass. The Turks needed to secure it to gain access to the Kyrenia-Nicosia corridor—and the Greeks needed to hold it to stop the Turks from advancing to Nicosia.

A British man and two teenage sons, who had been vacationing in Cyprus, sat their belongings down near us. I greeted them with a weary hello.

An American family moved in near us. The father complained that people in their previous site became hysterical every time shots were fired. "Very upsetting for the wife and kids."

Planes flew over constantly. The Turkish fighters were back unloading their vengeance of rockets and bombs on the Greek National Guard positions across the pass.

Waves of planes and helicopters flew over the mountains toward Nicosia.

"Five C-47s," Charles said, watching ancient twin-prop cargo planes. Weird—as we huddle, freaked out, Charles identifies and counts aircraft?

"I'm hit," the newly arrived American man yelled, holding up a bloody hand with a hole through the middle of it.

"What happened?" I heard someone ask.

"I was pointing at a plane flying over, telling my son it was a C-47."

Pete crawled over to help the injured man and went with him to find a Finnish UN medic.

I helped his wife and children move farther down the hill to a hopefully safer spot.

A surprise zzt-zing pinned us to the ground again and a barrage of bullets kept us facedown for several minutes.

After the firing let up, the men returned. The injured man's hand was bandaged. Dark bloodstains covered his clothes.

With grim humor, the men made suggestions for decorating the hole.

"You've got a bloody hole in your hand—why not put a jewel in it?" one British man suggested.

"Or a monocle," said another, mocking the Brit. "For better vision."

Not skipping a beat, the injured man smiled. "Well, why not leave it as it is and jack off with it?"

Our entire group howled with laughter—a much needed release in our tense situation.

The familiar buzz of thousands of cicadas suddenly filled the scorching hot air. Loud noisemakers! Loudest song known in the insect world. Should the cicada chorus sing too close to a human's ear, the sound is deafening and loud enough to cause permanent hearing loss. Although they don't bite or sting, their distinctive, shrill song was an added annoyance in our miserable state.

I covered my ears until the wave of sound crescendoed, and died down.

Intense heat. Lack of sleep. The constant sound of flying insects buzzing around had us all wondering how to cope with the misery at hand.

"These damn creepy crawlies," Charles complained. "Wish someone would bomb them."

This started a discussion of who had the worst insect bite from the sleepless night before, followed by our new meme: Good News, Bad News.

"The Good News is, no deadly bites. We're alive," I said.

"The Bad News is, so are the creepy-crawlies." Charles added.

Charles went with Pete to fill water bottles. When they returned, Charles informed us that there were 153 civilians on the UN list, sixty of whom were children, and the temperature reading by the water tank showed 100-plus degrees Fahrenheit.

I thanked them for my bottled breakfast. "The Good News is, there's hot water," I said. "The Bad News is, no tea bags."

Midmorning, as I napped, I was jarred awake by the screaming sound of planes flying low overhead.

"They're not headed for Nicosia," I heard Charles say, pointing at the formation of Turkish F-100s flying in low. "Super Sabres. Get ready. Heads down."

We hunkered down and waited for the all-too-familiar sounds of rockets being fired. A loud pop, followed by a whistle. I held my breath and waited for the final all-encompassing, earth-shaking explosion, and prayed that we would survive another fierce attack.

I gasped in relief when I heard the final explosions from the rockets. I opened my eyes. "We're still alive," I said. Tears streamed down my face.

"They've gone to reload," Charles said.

"Listen," Ronit said, pointing across the pass. "They're meeting heavy resistance from the Greeks."

"I thought I heard antiaircraft shots, just before the planes dropped their load," Charles added.

"I hope no one misses their target," I said. "If anything lands on us, we're toast."

The Turkish planes returned, time and again that day, dropping their bombs on Greek positions across the pass. Every hour or so, they'd pound the hillside with heavy fire trying to knock out resistance.

"Apparently the Turks aren't going to achieve their goal as quickly as they hoped," Charles observed.

"The Greeks aren't giving up," Ronit said.

When there was a lull in the fighting, I turned the radio on to BBC World News.

JET FIGHTERS OF THE TURKISH AIR FORCE RESUMED THEIR OPERATION THIS MORNING AGAINST GREEK AND GREEK CYPRIOT OPERATIONS ALL OVER THE ISLAND.

TURKISH TROOPS, WHICH LANDED IN KYRENIA, HAVE ADVANCED OVER THE KYRENIA MOUNTAINS AND MET THE PARATROOPERS DROPPED TO THE NORTH OF NICOSIA. KYRENIA IS NOW UNDER THE CONTROL OF THE TURKISH ARMED FORCES.

THE GREEK GOVERNMENT ANNOUNCED THAT TURKEY HAS LOST 11 AIRCRAFT.

THE TURKISH GOVERNMENT ANNOUNCED THAT ALL AIRCRAFT WHICH TOOK PART IN THE OPERATIONS HAVE RETURNED TO BASE SAFELY.

SO FAR THERE HAS BEEN NO INDICATION OF THE CASUALTY FIGURE, BUT IT IS THOUGHT THE GREEKS HAVE SUFFERED MOST FROM AIR STRIKES.

THE YUGOSLAVIAN FOREIGN MINISTER ANNOUNCED THAT YUGOSLAVIA SUPPORTS TURKEY'S OPERATION IN

CYPRUS.

THE TUNISIAN GOVERNMENT SAYS THAT GREECE IS RESPONSIBLE FOR THE SITUATION IN CYPRUS.

THE AMERICAN GOVERNMENT AND AMERICAN INTELLIGENCE WERE CAUGHT BY SURPRISE BY TURKEY'S INVASION.

"Not true," I told Charles. "The Turks haven't advanced over the mountain. The pass to Nicosia is still being fought over, and the American government certainly wasn't caught by surprise. How can they report things which aren't true?"

"Hitler did it."

Seeing my startled look, Charles continued. "Planned. Propaganda. Governments do it all the time. Welcome to the world of the BBC—Big Brother Corruption."

"So as sitting ducks, we're the only people in the world who know what's happening here?" I asked.

"Yeah, that's it," Charles replied, collecting empty bottles. "I'll go do a water run with Pete while it's quiet."

I crawled around a tree to check on the trench-digging progress. Much to my surprise, it was finished and the children were sitting in it smiling.

"It's deep and wide," I said. "How did you get it done so fast?"

"Only four feet deep," Syd answered, looking exhausted from the ordeal.

Alex lay snoozing a few feet away.

"It's our fortress," Josh announced.

"Glad to know the little ones are safer," I said, receiving a show of toothy smiles from the children in the trench.

"For them it's fun and games. They don't realize the danger," Kate said, looking grim.

The kids continued to grin.

"Wish we had a deck of cards," Ilene said. "A game of bridge to distract us."

"Until the next bombing raid." I sighed.

"Have you heard any news of the Sixth Fleet?" Kate asked me. "We heard there's a list of Americans and that the Sixth Fleet is sending helicopters to pick them up."

Puzzled, I shook my head no. "Might be a list of official US employees and families. There are quite a few here. But there's no way in hell the US could rescue only Americans."

"Has anyone mentioned it to you?" Ilene asked.

"No. We're not part of the official community," I answered.

"Someone said your names were on the list," Ilene said. "It's causing quite a stir."

"News to me," I replied.

"According to the status of forces agreement, the US can't evacuate anyone," Kate said. "Only the British, Greeks, and Turks can do that."

"Sounds like someone's wish list," I replied. "I'm sure we'll all leave here together."

Sporadic shooting forced me back downhill to my mat. I lay facedown and thought about the strange conversation with Ilene and Kate. A list to evacuate Americans only? No way!

The shooting subsided, and it grew quiet again. Charles and Pete returned with filled water bottles in hand.

Charles crashed down beside me. In a whisper, I asked him about an evacuation list for Americans.

He told me Pete had compiled a list of "official" Americans on the hill, in hopes the Sixth Fleet could arrange to pick them up.

"That's ridiculous," I whispered. "What about everyone else?"

"It won't happen. But just in case, Pete put our names on the list."

"We're not official."

"I know. We'll see."

The onslaught continued, all afternoon and well into the night as the battle for the pass raged on. The corridor highway from the seaside village of Kyrenia to the capital city of Nicosia was key to winning the war.

Charles is right. Whoever controls the pass will win the war.

I turned on the radio and listened to a report from BBC. The voice on the radio reported that the Turks had wiped out the Greek opposition and were now in control of the pass.

Why are they still fighting? Why are they bombing us? I asked myself. "Bullshit," I murmured. "If only it were true, we could get the hell out of here."

CHAPTER 17

FIRE! RUN!

Tjikles Camp, Kyrenia, Cyprus—22 July 1974

In the early morning hours of the third day, the battle raged on. Turkish jets flew low passes over the UN area, launching rockets at Greek enclaves across the pass.

I cowered in fear every time I heard the initial "pop" sound overhead, followed by a whistle, and the deafening explosion. Wherever that rocket ended, horrific destruction was a certainty.

In the middle of the fierce fighting, I hoped and prayed that neither side would drop bombs short of range. A few times shells fell short of the mountain and landed in the corridor. None had hit us. Yet.

The Greeks fired from cannon emplacements and machine gun positions on their side of the pass. Following each bombardment by the Turks, surviving Greek positions fired defiant answering shots: "rat-a-tat-tat."

As the day wore on, several Greek emplacements went silent. By afternoon, only one lone position remained.

"They can't last long much longer," someone reckoned. "The Turks are pounding them."

"They're brave to stay," I said.

"Or stupid," someone else replied.

Silently, I blessed them nonetheless. *Thoughts matter.*

We listened to an announcement from BFBS.

A CONVOY FOR CIVILIANS WILL RUN FROM FAMAGUSTA TO THE BRITISH BASE. ARRANGEMENTS ARE BEING MADE FOR CIVILIANS IN THE NICOSIA AREA.

"No mention of evacuation plans for civilians in Kyrenia," I remarked.

"Do they even know we're here?" Ronit asked.

"I'm sure the UN has told them."

Ronit left to go to the bathroom. When an hour passed and she hadn't returned, I decided to look for her, and fill water bottles on the way back.

A British tourist stopped me and asked if I'd heard about the UN jeep abducted by the Greek army. Apparently Greek soldiers had kidnapped UN soldiers and taken their uniforms. Dressed as UN soldiers, they were traveling freely through Turkish areas, killing Turks. "UN soldiers can't carry loaded weapons and can't load weapons until they've been fired on," the man added.

"When will the nightmare end?" I asked him, before moving on to continue my search for Ronit.

In the blink of an eye, my world had been turned upside down. And now, turned upside down again. I continued along the dirt road, across the parking area, and climbed the hill to the toilets. No sign of Ronit anywhere. I filled bottles with water and quenched my thirst by drinking a bottle while standing near the tap. Thirst quenched, I walked back down the hill.

Almost to the parking lot, sudden gunfire interrupted my stroll. I scrambled for cover between a row of parked cars. Ahead, I noticed a man also hiding between parked cars. I watched him crawl forward in the direction of the dirt road. As he neared it, an explosion shook the ground. He waited until the dust cleared, then dashed across the road, away from the parking lot, and disappeared downhill.

I heard a loud thunk-thud sound and looked up. Less than a meter from my face, I saw a bullet lodged in the metal just above the car window.

A sudden realization made me sick to my stomach. If one car gets hit and catches fire, the entire parking lot of cars will go up in flames. They are parked so close together. *An inferno.* I shuddered at the thought. I had to get far away from the packed parking lot. Clutching water bottles, I stooped low and moved toward the road.

178

As soon as the shooting subsided, I raced north across the parking lot, over the dirt road, and scrambled downhill. I sat down under a tree, waiting for my racing heart to slow down.

I got up and ran again, hoping to reach our spot further downhill. As I neared the children's trench, someone screamed, "Get DOWN!"

I dove into the trench.

Bullets whizzed overhead. Targeting the very spot I had fled a split second before.

"Whew," I sighed, landing. *If I hadn't run when I did, I'd be dead.*

"Are you okay?" Josh asked.

"I'm fine. Sorry to spill water on you," I said, seeing my empty water bottles scattered about." I smiled at the children in the trench. I straightened my dress and wiped dirt from my face. "Sorry to crash in on you guys like this."

"Good reflexes," Josh said, handing me two empty bottles.

I waited for quiet, climbed out of the trench and walked back to my site.

"Great performance!" Charles smiled, welcoming me. "The Good News is, she made it."

"The Bad News is, she returns with empty bottles." I shrugged, collapsing on my mat.

Ronit returned about an hour later. She had been visiting with a Greek family nearby. She appeared to be in a good state of mind. She said she felt happy, knowing Andreas chose not to fight.

We listened to BFBS again.

PLANS ARE UNDER WAY TO EVACUATE FOREIGN NATIONALS FROM THE NICOSIA AREA THIS AFTERNOON. THOSE WANTING TO BE EVACUATED ARE TO FORM A CONVOY OF CARS AT THE BRITISH HIGH COMMISSION AT 1400 HOURS THIS AFTERNOON. THE CONVOY WILL THEN PROCEED PAST THE HILTON HOTEL AND TRAVEL IN THE GENERAL DIRECTION OF THE BRITISH BASE AT DHEKELIA.

DUE TO THE INTENSE BATTLE RAGING IN THE NORTH

We cheered the cease-fire report. Spirits soared.

Shortly after noon, a UN jeep stopped on the dirt road above our site. It pulled a trailer carrying an enormous covered pot.

A UN soldier announced, "Hot soup. Come and get it."

People scrambled up the incline to get their ration from the steaming pot.

I realized I was hungry. Although hot soup would just make us feel hotter, I welcomed food in any form after two days of nothing to eat.

Seeing the one and only soup ladle in use, Charles dipped a wide-spouted plastic container into the pot and filled it with soup. He filled several empty water bottles using the container as a ladle. Others requested his service, so he kept filling bottles and containers for the hungry.

After devouring the soup, someone in our group commented, "The Good News, the UN made delicious soup for us."

Someone else added, "The Bad News, it's salty fish soup and we're running out of water."

On that note, Charles and Pete left to make another water run.

When Charles returned, he told of seeing three wounded Greek soldiers who had strayed into the UN camp. "They sat huddled together under a tree, like scared animals. When shots rang out near them, they dropped their rifles and crawled away."

"How sad," I noted.

"They're doomed." Charles shook his head.

Later that afternoon, another wounded soldier wandered into the area. Young. A boy, maybe 16. Hurt and bleeding. Staring crazy-eyed, he begged me for *nero* (water in Greek). I looked around for a bottle of water to give him.

A UN soldier appeared immediately and led the soldier up the hill.

Another UN soldier explained that they would dress his wounds, give him food and water, and send him on his way. "We can't jeopardize the lives of innocent civilians by letting soldiers stay here," he explained.

"I understand," I agreed. Knowing the boy would be sent back into battle, I wept. *War? So senseless. So inhumane. So crazy.*

Turkish planes returned. Flying low overhead, they targeted the remaining Greek position across the pass.

I shuddered as I heard the sound of rockets being fired again—the pop, the whistle, and the final explosion when the rockets smashed into the side of the mountain.

We waited and listened for the familiar Greek response of "rat-a-tat-tat."

Several minutes went by without a reply.

"They got him this time," someone yelled.

But after several more minutes, we heard the reply, "rat-a-tat-tat, rat-a-tat-tat."

"That cocky son of bitch. He's fantastic," Charles bragged.

Turkish planes bombarded the Greek position several times that evening. Each time, we waited and cheered our surprise and approval when we heard the lone position reply. "Rat-a-tat-tat."

Later, we listened to news from BBC.

REPORTS FROM ANKARA SAY THAT THE TURKISH GOVERNMENT IS WILLING TO MAINTAIN DIPLOMATIC CONTACTS WITH THE US, BUT IS NOT PREPARED TO UNDERTAKE SERIOUS NEGOTIATIONS UNTIL THE OBJECTIVES OF ITS MILITARY CAMPAIGN ARE ACHIEVED.

THE TURKISH PRIME MINISTER, MR. ECEVIT, HAS SAID THAT THE PURPOSE OF THE LIMITED MILITARY OPERATION IS TO ESTABLISH A BALANCE OF FORCE IN CYPRUS.

We listened to announcements on BFBS.

> FOR THOSE OF YOU STILL STRANDED ON THE NORTHERN COAST OF THE ISLAND, WE HAVE MADE PLANS TO HAVE YOU PICKED UP BY BRITISH SHIPS, ALONG THE BEACH FROM TWO MILES EAST TO TWELVE MILES EAST OF KYRENIA AT DAWN TOMORROW MORNING—IF A CEASE-FIRE CAN BE ARRANGED.

"The big if," I muttered, settling down for the evening.

I watched luminous bullets fly back and forth across the pass. *Just like the Fourth of July.*

Charles, of course, identified them as tracer bullets and explained they have a firework charge ignited by burning gunpowder. The light from tracers helps soldiers mark their targets.

"Glad we're not their targets," I said, watching bombs bursting in air.

"I'll never again enjoy a Fourth of July celebration," I mumbled, watching the sky rain showers of colorful flames and smoke. As one explosion after another ignited, a stunning exhibition of fire killed all in its path.

No one answered. Perhaps they're lucky enough to sleep through this nightmare, I thought. *To sleep, perchance to dream.*

Long before dawn the next morning, Charles turned on the radio to hear BFBS announcements.

> FOR THE PEOPLE IN THE KYRENIA AREA, THE EARLIEST WE CAN GET SHIPS INTO THE AREA WILL BE SOMETIME THIS MORNING. STAY TUNED FOR FURTHER DETAILS.

He turned the dial to BBC.

> NIKOS SAMPSON HAS BEEN REMOVED FROM OFFICE AND REPLACED WITH GLAFKOS KLERIDES. THE COUP REGIME ENDS. A GENERAL CEASE-FIRE IS DECLARED, BUT IN MANY PARTS OF THE ISLAND, THE FIGHTING CONTINUES.

US Secretary of State Henry Kissinger took the credit for persuading both sides to agree to a ceasefire on 22 July—on condition negotiations began immediately on the island's future.

"Yeah!" refugees shouted.

Encouraged by the report, many people stirred and began taking belongings back to their cars.

I carried our mats back to the car. Charles suggested we wait there until he and the other men had a look at the action from the lookout post.

"Hopefully, we'll see those British rescue ships," Charles said as they left.

When the men returned about a half hour later, no one was smiling.

"No rescue ships in sight," Charles said shaking his head.

"Lots of ships out at sea, but all are flying the Turkish flag."

"Maybe they're making sure the cease-fire works," I said.

"Twenty-one Turkish ships," Pete announced.

"Strung out east to west approaching the island, about ten to twelve miles west of Kyrenia," Charles added. "The Turks are staging a massive invasion."

"Oh, my God!" I cringed. "Can I have a look?"

"Me too?" Ronit stood.

"Sure," Charles said, leading us up the trail to the lookout.

Taking turns using the binoculars, we uttered shock and surprise at what we saw.

Turkish ships were landing and unloading their cargo—soldiers, tanks, half-tracks, and other military hardware.

"A bit bizarre," I remarked. "Like watching documentary films of World War II."

We returned to our site on the hill before noon, and discussed the seriousness of the situation.

Helicopters flew low overhead. We watched them drop troops and supplies farther up the mountain, beyond the UN camp.

The children counted aloud as the falling parachutes unfolded in the sky. "Eighty-eight. Eighty-nine."

"The Good News, the fleet has arrived," someone said.

"The Bad News, it's the Turkish fleet," someone else muttered.

"The Good News, we're in UN territory. The Bad News, the Turks haven't heard of the UN," someone remarked.

"More C-47s," Charles said, as transport planes dropped dozens of bundles.

"Look, they're dropping more paratroopers," someone said.

I sat and watched as more parachutes dropped from the sky.

The children stopped counting.

I turned on the radio, hoping to hear what the drop of hundreds of bundles meant. But rescue of stranded citizens no longer played on the British Forces station. Instead, it played song requests from its radio audience. "Food, Glorious Food" was followed by "I Want to Go Home." Next came "Give Me a Ticket to Anywhere."

Another delay. Obviously no rescue for us today.

Sabre jets returned, flying low overhead. "Looks as though the Turks will be terminating the lone Greek position this morning," Charles commented.

In groups of three, the jets pummeled the position. Rocket after rocket smashed into the hillside emplacement.

After each air strike, we waited for a response.

The British family near us stood, to hear the response better.

I waited and held my breath until I heard a faint "rat" sound.

Minutes later, it was followed by a louder "a-tat-tat."

Emotions overwhelmed us. "Bravo!" we cheered.

"Rat-a-tat-tat. Rat-a-tat-tat."

A sudden and loud burst of gunfire nearby pinned us to the ground. Soldiers appeared from all directions, surrounding us as they fired at each other.

"Move!" I screamed. "We're under attack."

"Move! Move!" Others shouted and screamed, as round after round of machine gun fire exploded.

I scurried further downhill, away from the targeted area. I looked around for Charles and Ronit. Didn't see them. I noticed a small boy sleeping on the ground, face up and alone, a few feet from me. I crawled over to him and covered his body with mine until the firing soldiers moved on. I picked the child up and ran with others down the hill toward the ravine. It was total mayhem.

I heard Charles shout. "Quick, into the ravine," he yelled, and grabbed the boy from my arms and tossed the child to Syd, who stood at the bottom of the ravine catching children as they were thrown to him.

"Jump!" Syd shouted.

I jumped.

Charles ran back up the hill to help a young mother with two children. He jumped into the ravine and sat down across from me.

Heads down, we crouched together in the ravine as bullets flew through the air from both sides.

Heavy shooting continued. We could do nothing but sit and wait as the barrage of bullets whizzed past overhead. Powerful explosions uphill, near the lookout point, shook the ground.

Charles pointed to a house on a rise above the mouth of the ravine. It was shaken again and again by explosions. Fragments of shells, and pieces of rock and dirt rained down on us.

"Let's move farther down," Charles suggested to Syd.

"It might be even worse farther down," Syd replied.

So we stayed put, hunkering down to avoid the crossfire over our heads as Greek and Turkish soldiers exchanged rapid gun fire. As bullets whizzed past, I prayed we'd survive.

When the shooting finally ceased and debris stopped falling, Charles looked at me and smiled.

My mouth fell open and I stared wide-eyed in disbelief at the scene happening above and behind Charles's head.

Charles turned to see what I was looking at so intently.

A line of Turkish soldiers stood at the edge of the ravine with rifles aimed and ready to fire.

Dressed immaculately in wrinkle-free uniforms and polished boots, they looked picture-perfect—but perplexed by our presence.

With swift jumps they landed in the deep gully with us. They looked around in all directions, then smiled to show us they were friendly.

Frightened, we pointed at each other and yelled, "American, British, French, Israeli, Lebanese, Egyptian." Thank goodness no one yelled "Greek."

Dozens more soldiers jumped into the ravine. Their captain shouted something in Turkish. They scrambled up the other side, marched up the hill, and disappeared into the pines.

I heard a loud collective sigh. I burst into tears. Charles tried to comfort me: "It's okay. They're gone."

I smiled. "I know, I'm crying happy tears."

A few minutes later, some of the soldiers returned. Speaking Turkish, they asked for *su.* "They want water," Charles said, handing them bottles of water.

The soldiers smiled and handed sticks of chewing gum out to the children.

The children stared, wide-eyed, at the smiling soldiers. "Wow!" Josh said. "Like Action Man."

A UN soldier nearby gave the Turkish soldiers more water and led them down the ravine, away from our area.

Two more straggler soldiers joined us in the gully. Again the UN soldier gave them water and pointed them downhill.

About fifteen minutes later, three Turkish soldiers returned from downhill, wanting to set up a mortar position to protect us. UN soldiers assured them we were fine and urged them to move on down the mountain.

After they left, one UN soldier explained, "Setting up a fire position would make us a target, after all."

We thanked them for moving the Turkish soldiers downhill and away from us.

"An ambulance has arrived with plenty of water," one UN soldier explained as they passed out bottles of water and urged everyone to drink up, so we wouldn't get dehydrated.

I downed bottle after bottle of water.

"Cecil DeMille couldn't have produced a more spectacular production than this," Syd said.

"The actors playing Turkish soldiers aren't convincing," I commented. "They don't look tattered enough."

Pete stood up in the middle of the ravine, pretending to be the director. "Cut," he said. "Soldiers, back to your starting position. Wipe dirt on your uniforms. Look more ferocious. No passing out gum. Retake."

We laughed.

I looked up and down the row of people lining the gully, but didn't see Ronit. "Do you see Ronit?" I asked Charles.

Charles eyes searched the rows of people. "No, I'll walk down the ravine and look for her."

He returned after a few minutes. "Don't see her. I'll look uphill. She's probably with her friend."

As Charles's figure merged into the next curve of the winding ravine, I suddenly felt exhausted. I sighed and gave myself permission to reflect on the day's nonstop events.

An eerie quiet descended. I hoped Charles found Ronit. Alive.

The quiet was shattered by an abrupt and immense explosion downhill. North. Direction Kyrenia.

The sky darkened. Thick billows of smoke floated up the hill. I covered my mouth and nose. More explosions, more smoke.

A startled look crossed Syd's face. He was the first to connect the dots. "Fire!" he yelled, pointing downhill. "Run!"

I glanced down the ravine. *Oh, my God!* I jumped, turned, shrieked at the others, "Fire! Run! Uphill!"

I grabbed Josh's hand and the hand of another small child nearby and began running. "Fire! Run! Fire!" I yelled.

"Fire! Run!" others screamed, warning people to keep moving. Dozens of people scrambled up the ravine path in a desperate bid for survival.

Balls of fire and walls of flames overwhelmed the hill on both sides of the gully. The wildfire leaping up the hill was destroying everything in its path.

Swirls of smoke made it difficult to see. Someone stumbled and fell, and was immediately helped up—and pushed forward.

The fire exploded with intensity, spreading fast and furious due to the dry summer conditions. The heat scorched the ground around us.

I could hear the snap, crackle, and pop of tree branches devoured by the raging fire. The orange flames were getting closer. Too close for comfort!

"Move! Move!" people screamed.

Like a panicked herd of cattle, we pushed others forward, moving up, cresting the hill—hoping and praying that the ascending flames wouldn't chase us down the other side. Or at least not so damn fast.

CHAPTER 18

RED DOTS?

Frankfurt, Germany—November 1977

"Ah, hear hear. Witness the entrance of the peacock. He struts into a room as if he owns it. We all know he's renting space," Michael said archly, as we watched a distinguished-looking man pass through the lobby of the Faustkeller theater restaurant toward the art exhibit area.

The man stopped and took a glass of champagne from a roving waiter.

"Is that Tom Kool, the art critic?" I asked.

"Yes!" Michael answered.

"Cool that he came," I said.

"He's kind of hot, as a matter of fact," Julie remarked.

"And he knows it," said Michael, his eyes tracking Tom across the room.

"Hope he gives you a good review," Julie said.

"He will." Michael nodded. "I can tell he's loving it."

"How can you tell?" Julie asked.

"He's my type," Michael answered. A mischievous look played across his face.

"Your gaydar?" I asked.

"Champagne, ladies?" asked a waiter, carrying a tray laden with glasses of champagne.

"Yes please," Julie answered.

"Thanks," I said, taking a glass.

"Me too," Michael helped himself.

"Marti," I called to a woman approaching. "I'd like you to meet my friends, Michael and Julie."

"I'm Michael. That's Julie," Michael clarified with a whimsical look.

After hellos, I explained how I met Marti one evening at the Balalaika. Marti, a psychologist, educated in the States, had returned to Germany to start her private practice as a clinical psychologist. "She knows lots of the same people we all do, so don't ask names," I added with a laugh.

Marti told us of her plans to attend a psychology conference in Capri.

"Capri!" I exclaimed. "When? I've dreamed of seeing Capri."

"Next year. It's a conference to teach psychologists about art therapy," Marti said.

"Art has always been my therapy," I added.

"Perhaps you'd like to join me? We could share expenses."

"Now that's a great idea. Let's do it."

Another waiter followed with stuffed mushrooms and other goodies.

"Delicious," Michael declared, trying a Brie-and-walnut-topped bruschetta.

I spotted Diane and Steve at the entrance, approaching the exhibit space.

"Hey, Diane, Steve," I called, "I'm so glad you're here."

"Impressive show," Steve said. "You've been working hard."

"What a turnout," Diane exclaimed. "Has the television crew interviewed you yet?"

"Not yet. But two newspapers have. And Tom Kool, the art critic, is here."

"Excellent," Steve said.

"Is the Indian woman here?" Diane asked.

"Not that I know of," I answered, glancing around the room to be sure. "I tried phoning her today, but no answer."

"Is Dan here?" Diane quizzed, with a mischievous smile.

"Steely Dan?"

"You know who I mean. Dan Dan Spicy Noodles."

"He is," I answered, face flushing.

"Susan," a man tapped me on the shoulder. I turned to see my boss from my club management job.

"Hey, Wayne. I'm delighted you were able to make it."

"The whole office gang's here. I'd like you to meet my wife, Marina," Wayne said.

"Marina," I said, extending my hand. "I've heard many wonderful things about you. It's nice to meet you. I understand you're also an artist."

"I dabble in watercolor," Marina said. "Your work is brilliant. So full of life. I've never seen batik painted on canvas before. Very unique. Did you design your blouse too?"

"I did."

"It's beautiful! Wayne says you'll get rich and famous, and not need your day job anymore."

"My golf game has certainly improved since you've been my assistant," Wayne said laughing. "You do all my work."

"I'm still working on perfecting your signature. So I can give myself a big raise."

We all chuckled. I turned to see even more people arriving.

The crowd grew and mixed and mingled. Attentive waiters roamed the room with trays of champagne and hors d'oeuvres.

"Congratulations," Tom Kool said, suddenly appearing at my side with Michael. "What an exciting night. Your work is vibrant. Thanks for inviting me."

"Thanks for coming!"

"I wouldn't have missed it for anything. Your theme *My Childhood* is intriguing."

"Thanks. It's been quite fascinating, exploring the influence in my current life of things which happened so long ago."

"*Hide and Seek,*" Tom said, pointing to a large painting on a side wall, "got my attention."

"Is it confessional art?" Michael asked me.

"Definitely! Being from a large family of eight kids, I often hid in the closet to have time alone. Sometimes I hid, in clear sight, just to see if I could be invisible."

"Wow," Julie remarked. "That's different."

"Were you successful?" Tom asked.

"Sometimes," I answered.

"And to think I thought you were playing with yourself," Michael added.

"Now Michael." I smiled.

"Closets have their uses," Michael replied.

"I'm fascinated with your unique approach to batik art," Tom said. "I've been a fan of batik for years, but haven't ever seen it done on canvas. Do you use brushes?"

"Yes, all sizes, and anything else that works to apply the colors."

"How do you get the fine details?" Tom asked.

"Dental tools work great for special details."

"And you remove the wax?"

"Yes, and stretch the canvas, seal it with a coat of acrylic, and it's ready for framing."

"Interesting technique."

"Thanks! Look around. If you have any more questions, let me know."

"I need to look at that closet one again," Tom said as he turned to leave.

"I'll join you," Michael said, leading the way.

Mary Kaye and her husband approached. "Susan," Mary Kaye said. "Your art speaks volumes about life and light."

"It's a wonderful exhibit," her husband added.

"Thanks for coming."

"Congratulations!" someone said.

"Inspirational," I heard from another direction.

"Thank you!" I smiled.

"So many of your pieces take me back to my own childhood," I heard a man say. "The one I had hoped to purchase has been sold."

"Which one?" I asked.

"Mr. Monk."

"It sold?"

"Yes, there's a red dot on it and several others."

I almost felt overwhelmed at the success—but at the same time it felt expected. Especially after my wild roller-coaster ride of these past four years of ups and downs.

"I'm thrilled. I just bought *Magic Carpet Ride,*" said an office colleague.

"Oh, I like that one," said another enthusiastic admirer.

"Thanks!" I said, taking a deep breath to take it all in.

"You've come a long way," Steve said. "From the looks of all the red dots, I'd say this show is a great success."

"Red dots. Oh, my God! I think you're right," I exclaimed, looking around the room.

"I know I'm right."

"Looks like a royal flush to me," I said to Steve, an expert poker player.

Michael returned to my side. "Guess what?"

"What?" I asked.

"Mr. Kool just purchased *Hide and Seek.*"

"No shit. For real?"

"Yes, and he's invited me over for the hanging."

Hanging. Hung. A synapse or two flashed, a distraction. A red dot was placed on my *Strawberry Ice Cream* painting.

"Wow!" I said. "I wonder who purchased that one."

"What a night." Michael smiled.

The café lights dimmed, and a hush fell over the exhibit crowd.

A lone spotlight illuminated Rosetta—sitting on a barstool, lightly strumming her guitar. Elegant in a simple, silky black pantsuit and a spotted zebra head wrap, her dangling silver earrings danced as she swayed to the music.

"Tonight," she said, "we are gathered to honor the talent of an artist who dreamed big, and worked hard to make her dream come true. An artist who just got out and did it. This one's for you, my dear friend Susan."

The crowd cheered.

Silenced by the strong emotions bubbling within, I smiled and nodded. No words could possibly express my gratitude for the support of so many well-wishers.

"Don't go changing," Rosetta sang soft and slow.

I covered my heart with my hands. Eyes brimming with tears, I choked up listening to my friend sing one of my favorite songs—Billy Joel's's latest hit, "Just the Way You Are."

Michael reached out and patted my arm.

When the song ended, the crowd clapped and cheered for Rosetta. She clapped and cheered for me. The crowd joined in.

I smiled and bowed. I felt so loved. So supported by good friends, colleagues, and acquaintances. *That's love! Real love.*

Rosetta sang a mixture of jazz, blues, ballads, and classical music and wowed the crowd with her closing number "My Way."

The crowd erupted in applause when the set finished and the cafe lights came up.

Tom Kool returned to introduce me to an acquaintance. "Susan," he said, "I'd like to introduce you to Herr Schäfer, *der kulturelle Direktor für die Stadt Frankfurt.*"

"Herr Schäfer, please meet the talented artist, Susan Joyce."

"I'm honored to meet you," I said. "Thanks for coming to my exhibit."

"My pleasure," Herr Schäfer replied. "Your work is impressive. I'd like to meet with you one day about the possibility of having an exhibit with *die Stadt Frankfurt.* It would be for next year. A two-woman show with one of our accomplished local artists. Would you be interested?"

"Interested? I'd be honored." I answered.

"Excellent. Please call me for an appointment next month and we'll discuss details," Herr Schäfer said, handing me his card.

"I definitely will," I said. "I appreciate the opportunity."

"Well, now, that's a happy connection," Julie said, watching him walk away.

"Fabulous!" Michael piped in. "It's not what you know."

"It's true," I said. "You've got to grab the brass ring."

As the crowd thinned out, television and newspaper journalists crowded around and fired questions at me.

"Is this your first solo exhibit?"

"How long have you lived in Frankfurt?"

"Would you call it a retrospective collection?"

"How long did you work on this exhibit?"

"What will your next exhibit theme be?"

I answered each question thoughtfully, grateful that I could do so in my native tongue. *If I could confuse the German word for chicken with the German word for pot of tea—jeez, the mind reels.*

When asked, "What piece are you most proud of?" I stopped and thought, and answered, "I'm most proud of myself for making my dreams come true."

When the camera lights stopped flashing, I saw my agent, Erik, standing across the room giving me two thumbs up. Grinning ear to ear, he announced, "Congratulations! A sold-out show."

"Wow!" I said, "I'm stunned."

Michael took my arm in his and danced me past every red dot in the room.

CHAPTER 19

MR. PERFECT?

Capri, Italy—1978

"Wow! It's surreal," I said to Marti, pointing to the view of the island jutting out to sea. "Like a fantasy painting of seagulls swarming the rock walls."

"I knew you'd be fascinated. As an artist, Capri is a must," Marti said. "I'm so glad you came with me. Lots of famous artists have lived here over the years."

"Michael raved about it. He spent a summer in Capri, in a villa owned by a famous art dealer. Love at first bite."

"It's a gay haven," Marti said.

"No wonder he raved."

"It's a small island," I said, as the crowded ferry pulled into the Marina Grande port of Capri. "Just a speck of land. I do hope we'll all fit."

"You Americans have a strange sense of humor. That's why I like you."

I chuckled.

"Most people are day-trippers, coming to shop," Marti explained, as we pulled into port. "They'll head back to Naples this evening, after purchasing their Capri pants and leather bags."

"Ahh, good. Hopefully I can find some quiet, secluded spots to sketch."

"Hopefully I can find a rich husband, or at least an intelligent man to father a child. My clock is ticking."

"Good luck! Remember what happened to me."

"Why are you wearing your wedding band?" Marti asked, pointing to a gold ring on my finger.

"To pretend I'm a married woman," I answered. "And I am still legally married until the divorce is final."

"But why the ring?"

"I figure if men think I'm married they'll leave me alone. After all, I'm here to work. The clock is ticking for my next exhibit."

We disembarked and exited the wharf area, in the center of the lower town. We looked around for a sign telling us where to purchase tickets to ride the funicular (cable car) up the hill to the upper town.

"Over there," I said, pointing to the sign at the entrance of the ferry terminal.

We purchased tickets, wandered around the quaint alleyways and narrow streets of the lower town, and waited on the cable car to return.

The funicular whisked us upward, high above the port of Marina Grande to the town of Capri. We walked the narrow streets into the center of Piazza Umberto.

The square was filled with tourists, dressed in everything from casual shorts and fanny packs to fancy formal attire.

"This is obviously where the action is," I said.

"Let's hope our hotel is as easy to find."

"It's near the clock tower, and there's the clock tower." I pointed.

"I see the sign," Marti said. "Our hotel is the next block up, on the right."

We checked into our large suite and unpacked.

"Nice to have a balcony, and a view," Marti said, looking around.

"Great choice," I added. "Thanks for booking it."

"I always splurge for this event and stay in the conference hotel."

"It will be a nice place for me to hang out and be creative while you attend classes."

Early the next morning, after Marti left for the conference, I took a long walk up to a scenic point overlooking the marina. It was so quiet and peaceful. A pleasant surprise, after the noise of the town.

From the peak, I could see how very narrow the streets below were, and made a quick sketch of the winding streets and buildings along the way.

I walked along the hillsides, searching for the perfect spot to stop, sit, and sketch. I found several.

A lone juniper tree, standing against a whitewashed facade, caught my eye on my way back down the hill. The color of the blue berries exactly matched the deep blue of the sky overhead.

I found a comfortable stone slab across the road, and sat for a few minutes imagining the finished painting.

I sketched it out with notes on the different shades of blue.

Next, I found a secluded garden overflowing with myrtle and lemon trees. *Oh, to capture the scents of myrtle and lemons in a painting.*

I did a quick sketch and made notes to remind myself of the vibrant colors and smells.

By the time I returned to the hotel that afternoon, Marti sat sipping wine on our balcony watching the setting sun.

"How was your day?" I asked, pouring myself a glass of wine.

"Met several interesting people and one possibly perfect person."

"Here's to it," I said, toasting my friend.

Mesmerized, we watched the sun set.

"Each sunset is so unique," I said. "Depending on the colors, the clouds, the location."

"And who you're with," Marti added.

"I find a sunset romantic even when I'm alone." I shrugged.

"You would," she said, laughing.

We watched in awe as the sun dropped, then dropped more. Slower and lower, as though it were having second thoughts about ever setting. All of a sudden, it dipped down on the horizon, and disappeared into the sea.

"Wow!" I said. "Did you see the green flash?"

"Spectacular!" Marti said, taking it all in.

For dinner, we settled on a simple trattoria nearby and enjoyed a delicious seafood pasta. For dessert, we ordered *torta caprese,* then headed to a local nightclub to find another potential Mr. Perfect for Marti.

The rhythmic sound of Neapolitan music drew us inside to a filled-to-capacity nightclub, where the uninhibited were performing exotic dances.

We found two empty chairs at a table of mainly men.

Marti smiled and nodded her approval.

Before we could even order a carafe of wine, a man asked me to dance. *"No grazie,"* I politely declined.

The wine arrived and we sat sipping, watching an elderly couple caress while enjoying a slow dance.

"Love," I said. "Nice!"

Another slow song, and another man asked me to dance. *"No grazie,"* I said again.

"Wish he'd ask me. He's sexy," Marti said.

"Must be the wedding band. Italian men obviously have a thing for married women. Must make them feel safe."

"You're probably right," Marti said laughing.

"Here," I said, removing the gold band and handing it to Marti. "Enjoy! Find the most charming man in the room and ask him to dance."

"I'll need more wine to do that."

I ordered another carafe of wine.

"Music's a bit loud for me," I said, after a few minutes. "Think I'll head back to the hotel. I want to do an early morning sketch of a garden."

When Marti returned to our hotel room, later that night, she was all smiles. "Lots of dancing," she said. "Your ring is magic."

After breakfast the next morning, I hiked to the top of the island and strolled through the Gardens of Augustus, where colorful terraced gardens showcase the native flora. Unforgettable panoramas! My sketches of the gardens worked well. The panoramic views were much more difficult to capture.

Much to my surprise, I saw a monument to Lenin. He visited the island in 1908 during his exile.

The next evening, we watched another spectacular sunset over cocktails.

Marti excitedly told me about the success she was having in the art therapy workshop. "As the class progresses, I'm drawing more and more details of past traumas in my life."

"How wonderful! Art is great therapy."

"Doodling freed my memory of events. I found some buried treasures. I can't wait to try this with my patients."

The next afternoon, we hired a boat with a guide, and explored the island's many sea caves.

As we neared the opening of the famous Blue Grotto, I told Marti, "I've wanted to see this one since I was nine, when my great-aunt Gladys sent me a postcard of it. I promised myself to see it one day."

Our guide explained that the color in sea caves is determined by the lighting conditions, and in the Blue Grotto the light comes from two small holes. Daylight enters the cave through an underwater opening, located below the entrance. The water filters the red tones of the light, so only blue tones pass into the cave.

We transferred to a tiny rowboat and entered the cave through one of the small holes. The entrance was so low and narrow, we had to lie back and wait while the sailor maneuvered the boat into the cave.

It was pitch-dark as we entered the cave, but once inside we watched in awe as a flood of emerald light filled the space.

"Watch this," the guide said, placing his hand in the water.

"Wow," I said, "it's glowing."

"Eerie," Marti added.

I slipped my hand into the water, and giggled at the sight of my hand glowing with dazzling blue light.

We exited the cave and headed back to our hotel.

"What a day," Marti said.

"Nature at its finest." Remembering the razzle-dazzle display in the Blue Grotto, I smiled, and felt at peace.

With each passing day, Marti expressed disappointment in not finding the perfect man yet.

"What about the guy at the conference?" I asked one evening, while we sat drinking at a club bar.

"I haven't seen him again. He vanished."

"You obviously have never been married, or you wouldn't be looking so hard," I told her. "It doesn't happen when you're looking for it. Chances are Mr. Right is someone you already know and like. A friend maybe. Someone with similar interests. Probably not someone you'll meet on vacation in a bar.

"If you want a child, why not adopt one? Motherhood is not defined by DNA. There are lots of children who need good homes. As a doctor with a good income, you'd qualify to adopt."

"It's easy for you to say because you've been married, and been pregnant."

"And been divorced," I added.

"You're content now. But will you feel happy when you're fifty or sixty, and all alone?"

"I don't buy into someone else being responsible for my happiness. I could have a child and a man in my life, and still be unhappy. Maybe even miserable."

After another drink, Marti told me about her first love. "At age 19, I got pregnant and had an abortion. The timing wasn't right. I was in university studying hard to become a doctor, and having a child didn't fit into my life plans. All these years later, I regret my decision."

"I'm sure you made the best decision at that point in your life. If you're meant to have a child, it'll happen. Things happen for a reason. To everything there is a season."

Marti smiled. "I know you're right. You're giving me the same advice I give my patients in therapy."

A man interrupted our conversation and asked Marti if she'd like to dance.

"*No grazie*," Marti replied.

"Why didn't you dance with him?" I asked.

"I didn't want to. I'm enjoying our conversation."

"Okay."

"How many times were you pregnant?" Marti asked.

"Six, seven. I stopped counting."

"That must have been heartbreaking," Marti said.

"No, it felt good to stop counting."

She smiled, and asked, "Do you still long for a child?"

"No. I'm content with my life. If I'm meant to be a mother, it'll happen. But in the meantime, I'm living my life to its fullest."

The gold band worked magic. By night's end, Marti had danced with most of the men in the tavern.

The next evening, Marti came back from the conference all excited. "The mystery man has reappeared. We're meeting for dinner."

"Mr. Potentially Perfect?" I asked, smiling.

"Potentially." Marti smiled. "And he's quite handsome."

I spent the evening in, alone, enjoying another spectacular sunset.

> *Drifting off to sleep, I saw myself sitting in a rocking chair, holding a child and rocking her to sleep. I lulled us into dreamland by whispering loving words to comfort and quiet.*
>
> *I stroke your cheek and hold you close,*
>
> *this moment now—divine.*
>
> *And for this fleeting moment,*
>
> *I touch your head to mine.*
>
> *I whisper, I shall miss you child,*
>
> *for you I'll always long.*
>
> *The Lullaby Illusion—life's illusive song.*

The next morning, the words were stuck in my head. All day long, I tossed them about, saying them out loud, wondering why they came to me as they did in a dream.

Not wanting to forget, I wrote the words on a piece of paper taken from a note pad sitting on the desk. The irregular star shape on the pad looked like a piece of a puzzle, waiting to be put in place.

Ah-ha! I thought. *The puzzle is solved.*

Toward the end of our Capri vacation, I chose again to stay in alone one evening and watch the moon rise over the water. I marveled as it changed from yellow, to orange, to gold, to white and on to pure shimmering light. I did a sketch and made notes of the colors needed to capture the magic of moonlight over the sea.

By the end of the holiday, I had several sketches ready to become final paintings for my next exhibit.

Marti had become quite cozy with the handsome Canadian psychologist she met at the conference, and was working on getting him to visit her in Frankfurt.

En route home, from Naples to Frankfurt, I thanked her for suggesting I accompany her. "I'm inspired as an artist and I made a childhood dream come true."

"And I met my potential Mr. Perfect," Marti said, smiling. "He said he'll visit me later this year."

"Does he know you're single?" I pointed to the gold ring on her finger.

"Yes. When I told him about your ring trick, he said you're a natural."

"A natural what?"

"Psychologist," she said, handing me the ring.

"Human behavior is interesting to observe. But I suspect the wedding ring trick only works with Italian men—who want a fling, but no commitment."

CHAPTER 20

GOD?

Athens, Greece—1978

"Welcome to Greece!" Michael said, as we cleared passport control and customs, and waited on a taxi to take us to our hotel. Michael, my enigmatic but so familiar friend, much the same as a brother, but not a brother, and not a lover. Who would understand?

"Feels good to be back," I answered. "I first came to Greece in 1969 with Charles and another couple. We spent most of our time on the mainland, but we did visit the island of Ios for a week. We thought it would be a nice sea cruise from Athens. As if seas are always calm. Wrong! Turbulent weather the entire trip. Everyone got seasick. Vomit sloshed around the deck."

"Sounds delightful. Sorry I missed it."

"Eleven and a half hours later, I swore never to be on a small boat on rough seas again. We finally arrived, late at night, and went straight to a hotel and bed. The next day, we woke up in paradise.

"A beautiful island. Sandy beaches as far as you could see. So quiet! No motor vehicles allowed on the island. Just bikes and donkeys, and walkers along well-worn trails. One day we hiked to the other side of the island. Velvet sand and crystal clear water. No hotels on that side, just caves where hippies hung out. The smell of Mary Jane was potent. Laidback. Free spirits. I admired them.

"Fortunately our boat trip back was calmer. Gentle rocking all the way."

"No vomit? The way they advertise them," Michael said.

"We took the Athens subway and trains for the adventure. One day my girlfriend and I took the subway a few stops from our hotel to get our hair cut. So crowded, we were was pressed together. And someone kept pinching my butt."

Michael smiled. "Greek men have a reputation as butt pinchers."

"It hurt. I asked my friend if she could see who was doing the pinching. She said it was hard to tell because all the men were grinning.'"

Michael laughed. "Let's ride subways while we're here. Maybe I'll get lucky and get my ass pinched."

We arrived at our hotel, checked into our suite, unpacked, and went for a swim in the hotel's Olympic-size pool.

"Rather a fancy place," I observed, after a long swim around the pool. "It's a beautiful setting."

"Only the best for my confidante."

We enjoyed cocktails by the poolside.

"What if you meet a gorgeous Greek god and want to party all night in your suite?" I asked Michael. "I don't want to be in the way."

"If I meet a god, we won't need a suite. Hell, we can do it in the water. By the way, my parents are delighted you're with me on this trip."

"Next, they'll be hinting for you to marry me."

"They already have. And, I would if I could."

"But you're 'bent,' so you can't."

"Love British slang. I'm queer and you get it. That's what I love about you. Most women think I can be converted."

"I'm not into converting anyone."

"I appreciate you," Michael said.

That night, over a candlelight dinner, I told Michael about life in Greece with Charles. "We met lots of interesting people from all over the world and became good friends with some. One couple, from California, were especially fun. He sold real estate and made good money. When trying to sell a piece of land, he had a convincing closing line. He'd say. 'Remember all wars are fought over land.'"

"Selling land in Greece?" Michael asked.

"No, land in the good ole USA. He sold it from a map and a brochure. Land in the dry Nevada desert which couldn't support human life."

"Americans can be such suckers."

"I adored his wife. A wonderful, fun person. Great artist. We all loved Greek food, except for him. He wanted Kentucky Fried Chicken for every meal, every day. Lucky for him, there was a Kentucky Fried Chicken franchise on the base and one near their apartment."

"Good Lord," Michael said. "For sure you're making this up. Who in their right mind would eat Kentucky Fried Chicken when delicious Greek food is available?"

"He thought we were weirdos, eating all that strange-tasting foreign food."

"Go figure."

"Another couple we hung out with lived nearby. The man also sold electronic equipment to Americans stationed in Greece. He had worked for the telephone company as a lineman, in the States, before moving to Greece, and knew how to connect a telephone to any junction box and make free phone calls all over the world. His girlfriend loved to play cards, especially poker. So we often had poker games at their apartment, which often got interrupted whenever anyone wanted to call the States for free."

"Good guy to know."

"And there was another couple, with two adorable children. She was a Greek TV star and he was a businessman. She was definitely a peacock. Strutted her stuff like Stupefyin' Jones in Li'l Abner's comic strip. A real sex kitten. Men fell under her spell. A friend told us that 'Stupefyin' actually caused a traffic jam in downtown Athens one day, just crossing the street. In the manner of Wolf Gal, she lured men into her den and had wild sex with them."

"Was Charles one of them?"

"Probably. I of course, being the innocent Daisy Mae, didn't have a clue."

"Did her husband know?"

"I think he knew. He looked sad around her. One evening, a group of friends got together for a beach party. Couples kept wandering out into the water for a swim. Charles had disappeared and so I ventured into the water on my own. When I returned, a married couple nearby talked about the 'swinging' couples on the beach."

"Were they swingers? Were they interested in joining in?" Michael asked.

"No, they were shocked by it. I must say I felt a bit anxious about Charles's whereabouts. He was nowhere in sight. The man kept saying that his wife and I were the truly beautiful beach babes, because we wore modest bikinis. When Charles returned, I asked him about it. He said a few couples were into the scene, but most weren't."

"A mix-and-match party," Michael remarked. "Something not taught in Sunday School."

"Heavens no! Hellfire and brimstone would fall on your head if you ever had a sexual thought, much less acted on it."

"That's how I was brought up too. All about punishment."

"Fortunately, the frontal lobotomy didn't work on me. I decided that surely God wanted me to have some fun."

"Of course," Michael said.

By day, Michael visited accounts while I wandered about, sketching local village scenes for future paintings.

Given a free afternoon, I arranged for a taxi to take me to a deserted cove nearby. "Pick me up around four," I said, waving goodbye to the driver.

With the wind in my face, I walked for miles along the sandy beach—in perfect rhythm with the rise and fall of the tide. The smell of salt water soothed me. The roar of the waves welcomed me to this place and space. I felt at peace with the universe.

I stopped and deliberately dug my toes deep into the soft sand, and giggled when cool waves swirled around my feet and tickled my toes. When the sand shifted, my toes dug deeper still.

Looking in all directions, I realized I was alone on the beach. I removed my swimsuit and let the sun warm me all over. Whee! When a cool breeze brushed my bare skin, a tide of euphoria swept over me. From head to toe, I tingled with goosebumps. I'm free to be me, I thought.

As a kid, whenever I got a tingle sensation at the top of my head, I knew something important was about to happen. And it did. I remember thinking of it as my antennae—a way to receive signals from the sky.

I stooped to examine a small, silver seashell. Turning it slowly, I watched the hues change. Pressing it to my ear, I listened to its rendition of the ocean's roar. *Brilliant!*

I moved forward, deliberately placing firm footprints into the wet sand. The sea breeze slapped playfully, while I watched wave after wave make its way to the shore. "I'll paint you one day," I yelled to the sea. It roared its approval.

I sank down in the sand and watched a colony of seagulls swoop low and land nearby. Lulled by the sounds of nature, I fell sound asleep. When I awoke, I squinted at the sun. *Probably two o'clock.*

The sun squinted back, in agreement.

Seeing cliffs ahead, I ambled toward them. As I got closer, I saw what appeared to be a giant man standing in the shadow of a rock formation.

A shadow hovered overhead. Startled, I stopped and watched a large eagle glide past and land on the cliffs, above where the giant man stood.

I moved steadily forward, stopped, and stared at him. *Are you real? Or just a beautiful god walking the beach?*

Unbelievable, I thought, closing my eyes. Squeezing them tight, I counted slowly to ten, expecting him to have vanished.

But when I opened my eyes, the giant man was still there.

I moved closer. Shaped to perfection, each ripple of flesh appeared chiseled. I know, you're Michelangelo's *David.* I sketched you years ago, when you were on display in the museum in Florence.

I moved closer still, reached out and touched him.

My hands trembled as my fingers fluttered over the ripples of his muscular legs, up his thighs, and settled on his firm abdomen.

I looked up at his expressive face filled with lines of experience and knowledge, and traced each one with my fingertips. The universe unfolded before me.

"God?" I asked.

"We are the same," a voice answered.

A screeching of tires and a car horn interrupted my thoughts. I turned to look. Dust clouds gathered on the dirt road leading down to the beach.

A car approached. I quickly dressed.

The driver honked again and waved.

"*Kalispera!* Ms. Susan," he yelled over the blare of Greek music on the radio. "Have you enjoyed your day? It's lonely out here."

I collected my things.

"Did you explore the cliffs? They're mysterious, you know? One is shaped like a giant man," he said, opening the passenger door for me.

"Yes," I said, turning for one last look. "Extraordinary!"

The car bounced along the bumpy beach road toward town.

When I heard the beginning of a favorite tune, I sang along with Roy Orbison. "Only the lonely …."

The driver joined in on all the "dum-dum-dum-dumdy-doo-wah" and "ooh-yay-yay-yay-yeah" sections at the end of each verse.

That evening, over dinner, I told Michael about the mysterious giant God man communicating with me. "When I was a kid, I lived in the vivid now. I used to sit out on the Arizona desert and talk with nature often. I felt at one with everything around me. I grew older and stopped going with the natural flow. When I create art, I feel I'm in a meditative state, being fully conscious of the here and now. Today felt like being a kid again. My soul sang."

"Sounds like a beautiful awakening." Michael said.

"Spiritual and sexual," I said.

"I'd say you are clamoring for closeness. Spirituality and sexuality go hand in hand."

"I agree."

"Have you ever found another woman sexually attractive?" Michael asked. "Just curious."

I thought about it. "It's an interesting question. I can't remember ever being turned on sexually by another woman. But I think we're conditioned, by family and society, to be straitlaced. I love my girlfriends in an intense way and find them attractive, even sexy. But I can't imagine making out with any of them. "One time, when Charles and I were living in Arad, Israel, at the *ulpan*."

"*Ulpan?*" Michael asked.

"An *ulpan* is an institute of study—where students get free room and board while studying Hebrew and Jewish history. Kibbutzes and *ulpans* were originally set up to encourage young Jewish professionals to settle in Israel."

"Ah, one works on a kibbutz and one studies on an *ulpan?*"

"Right." I answered. "One afternoon, a woman who also studied at the institute knocked on our door. She introduced herself and asked if she could come in. I welcomed her. Charles had gone somewhere, probably playing poker. She told me she could feel my vibes and knew I was attracted to her, even though I was married. I assured her she had misread me, that I was just friendly. She tried to kiss me. Shocked, I asked her to please leave. She left immediately, and left the school the next day. I felt bad that she left school because of a physical rejection. I also wish I'd handled it differently. But I wasn't at all attracted to her."

"One can't fake sexual chemistry. It's either there or not."

One evening, Michael insisted we take the subway to dinner.

"I know a wonderful place in Kifisia," I said, "if it's still there. It's the end of the line going north, so you'll have plenty of opportunity to get your butt pinched."

Michael chuckled at the thought.

When we arrived in Kifisia, I was delighted to find the restaurant still open for business.

"A garden restaurant," Michael said. "Nice."

The waiter pointed us to a corner table, then invited us into the kitchen to pick our dishes from a display case of assorted meats and fish.

I chose a meat for grilling, not certain what it was.

"Delicious! Delicacy," explained the chef.

Michael ordered an assortment of fresh seafood, a plate of appetizers to start, and of course, *retsina* wine for good digestion. "Love the pine flavor," he added.

"Delicious!" I said.

"So, you're not sorry we didn't have Kentucky Fried Chicken?"

I laughed.

After dinner, I asked the waiter to show me what part of the cow my delicious meat came from.

He returned with a chart showing different cuts of meat. "Delicacy," he said. "Organ. *Criadillas.*"

"*Criadillas?* Is that the heart?' I asked, pointing to my heart.

"No, no," he said, laughing. "Testicles."

"Testicles?" I asked, feeling dumbfounded by my selection.

"Yes, testicles," he said, pointing to his.

"Balls. Bull's balls!" Michael laughed out loud.

"You like?" asked the waiter, winking at me.

"Tasty," I said, shaking my head in disbelief at what I had just devoured and enjoyed.

That night in Athens, we rode the subway home. We talked and laughed about all the strange delicacies we had tasted in our travels abroad.

To Michael's dismay, the subway wasn't crowded and he didn't get a single butt pinch that evening. "I guess I'm not as lucky as you," he said, smiling.

CHAPTER 21

IT'S TIME

Frankfurt, Germany—1978

When I returned from Greece, my mailbox was overflowing with envelopes. I collected them, unlocked the door, and carried my mail and suitcase upstairs.

A note from my landlord, taped to my door, announced that my studio apartment downstairs was ready for occupation. Yes!

I carefully put my key in, opened the door, and sighed. "Welcome home!" I said aloud. My apartment looked different. Bigger and brighter than I remembered.

I made a pot of coffee, unpacked my suitcase, then settled on the couch and opened mail. Bills, letters from friends, one from my mom, and three surprise envelopes.

The letter from mom told me that my sister was pregnant again, with twins this time. Two brothers' wives were also expecting. *God's little blessings,* mom wrote.

A note from Erik, my agent, stated that after paying all expenses on my exhibit and deducting his commission, a large sum had been deposited to my bank account from sales of my batik paintings. "Wow!" I said, looking at the bottom line figure several times. If I'm careful, I can live on this for a year. Time to find a part-time job.

And a note from Dan, said he had been trying to reach me, and would like to take me to dinner before returning to Chicago. *It's time.*

The third envelope, from my attorney, informed me of the divorce law changes. He would arrange for a court date soon to finalize the divorce, based on "irretrievable breakdown" of the marriage. Finally, I thought, I can close this chapter of my life.

I sat, sipping coffee, reflecting on the beauty of being able to travel the world, and the joy of returning home, and seeing myself and my surroundings in a different light, each time. Changed. Better because of the journey. Accepting my here and now, while the future danced alluringly, shifting ever so slightly with each new adventure.

The ringing telephone interrupted my thoughts.

"Hello," said a deep voice on the other end. "I've been trying to reach you."

"Dan, what a pleasant surprise. I just got back from a week in Greece. Just read your note. I'd love to get together."

"How about dinner tonight?"

"Great! What time? Where?"

"Let's meet at the Balalaika, at eight, and wing it from there."

"Perfect. See you there."

The doorbell rang. I dashed downstairs. My landlord stood smiling, keys in hand, ready to show me the newly remodeled studio apartment.

"Wow," I said entering the front hall. "*Vielen Danke! Es ist wunderschön!*"

After he left, I gazed around, mentally organizing the new space—my studio. Imagining where I'd place art supplies, canvases, tools, and furniture. I began moving things. I made many trips downstairs with boxes filled with supplies.

The phone rang again. I skipped upstairs to answer and smiled, hearing Diane's hello.

"Diane, good to hear from you."

"I want details of your trip to Athens."

"Great fun! Michael is a wonderful travel mate. I sketched lots of ideas for paintings. I want to do an exhibit about natural mysteries. And I ate *criadillas* in Athens."

"*Criadillas?*" Diane asked.

"Bull's balls. They're a delicacy."

"Yuk! *Mein gott!*"

"They were tasty."

"You've got to be kidding. They actually tasted good?"

"Delicious! Perfectly grilled with lemon juice and olive oil."

"Better you than me."

I told Diane about Dan's dinner invitation, about moving downstairs to my new studio, and about the upcoming court date.

"Dan? He's nice. You're going to have fun. I'll be in Stuttgart for a fashion show this week." She said she would call again soon.

I schlepped more supplies downstairs, even managed to get my desk and chair set up, and started a new painting, which I titled *God*.

Dan was having a beer at the Balalaika bar when I arrived. I ordered my usual glass of chardonnay and we chatted as if old friends, glad to see each other.

He congratulated me again on the success of my art exhibit. "Impressive! I went back for a second look, wanted to buy one. Sold out. So you're not just a pretty face."

I told him about getting the keys to my new studio. "It's exciting. Now I have a place for my art supplies. How did your photo shoot go?"

"A success. Got some great photos. What red-blooded guy wouldn't love to shoot automobiles and get paid for it?"

We chatted. I talked about my life in Cyprus and told him about my trip to Greece with Michael.

"I met him at your exhibit," Dan said. "He's quite the character!"

I told him about eating bull's balls in Greece. He smiled. "And to think I thought you'd be kissable."

I laughed. "I brush after meals."

"Good to know."

Dan asked for the bar bill from Rosetta, and asked her to call us a cab to take us across town to his favorite Thai restaurant.

We wined and dined, talked and laughed about our childhood dreams, and the importance of making them come true.

Dan had wanted to become a photographer, for as long as he could remember. His grandfather had owned one of the first Polaroid cameras. As a kid the instant image fascinated him. "Like a trick, some kind of an illusion, the way the image developed before my eyes. Pure magic! And I was determined to figure out how it worked. I did. One Christmas morning, a few years later my parents bought me a Polaroid. The next Christmas I got a 35 mm camera. I've been a photographer since."

"Did you dream of getting paid big bucks to travel the world as a professional photographer?"

"I did," he confirmed.

"Actually, my childhood dream was to travel the world as my Great-Aunt Gladys did. She sent postcards from exotic places she visited, and I slept with the postcard on my heart pretending it was a magic carpet—one which could fly me to the place pictured on the front of the card."

"Wild! Wonderful!" he said.

"So far," I said. "I've been to all the places my aunt has, except the Far East."

"As a child, did you dream of being an artist?"

"I dreamed of being an artist, a writer, a singer, a song writer. I always dreamed of creating original things. I spent most of my childhood years in the Arizona desert. I used to sit out on a big boulder in the desert with my dog Brownie, and just watch the big screen of nature. My dog Brownie had bad breath."

"Most dogs do." Dan smiled.

"Brownie had exceptionally bad liver breath. But I loved him anyway. When I was in fourth grade, I wrote a short story, with illustrations, about loving my dog in spite of his bad breath, and won first place in a writing competition. So that encouraged me to be a writer and artist. Big time!"

After another glass of chardonnay, I told Dan a bit about my marriage and my upcoming divorce date.

"I was married once, years ago," Dan said.

"Any children?"

"None that I know of. Probably just as well, since I travel so much. My ex grew tired of being alone."

I explained that Charles traveled frequently in his work, but I quite enjoyed being alone.

"Creative people need alone time," Dan said. "I like traveling alone. My camera keeps me company."

"Do you live alone now?"

"No, I live with a girlfriend. Someone I've known for years. It's a good arrangement. No strings! She takes care of my cat when I'm away."

We talked about places we'd been. Dan had traveled all over the world on photo shoots. "I've seen some spectacular places," he said. "The wilds of Africa are probably most awesome."

"The most spectacular place I've ever seen is the Göreme Valley in central Turkey. Unreal! Looks like a moonscape, with its mushroom-shaped spires sitting atop rock formations," I said.

"Fairy chimneys, Cappadocia, Turkey. I shot it a few years ago for *National Geo.*"

"Wow! I'm impressed."

"Turkey's a beautiful country," Dan said.

"A nice mix of Europe and the Middle East. I visited there often when I lived in Cyprus. The closest I got to the wilds of Africa was the Seychelles."

"Off the coast of Kenya. I visited there in '65. Another shoot for *Geo.*"

"According to natives, it's the original Garden of Eden," I said.

"They're a rich mixture of people, and have animal and plant species not found anywhere else on the planet. When were you there?" Dan asked.

"In '75."

"Just before they gained independence from England."

"Yes, I stayed at a B&B owned by a Mrs. Mancham," I said. "She was a fabulous cook and gave me a copy of her cookbook when I left. It turned out that she was the mother of the man who became the first president of the Seychelles, Sir James R. Mancham. A year later I heard on the news that he went to England, to attend the Jubilee of Queen Elizabeth II, and was deposed in a bloodless coup."

"Bloodless? I didn't know there was such a thing." Dan laughed.

"Only in paradise!" I said.

We both laughed.

"Happy people," I said. "The Seychellois sing all the time. The women sing while washing clothes, and sing while draping clothes over the tombstones in the cemetery to dry."

"I let my washing machine do the singing," said Dan.

"Did you take photos of the coco de mer seed?"

"Of course. The double coconut, grows only in the Vallee de Mai. They're the largest seeds in the plant kingdom, can weigh up to 30kg."

"I purchased one as a souvenir—the two-lobed female-shaped one. It was beautiful! Had it fumigated, polished, and even bought a certified stamp to guarantee all insects were dead.

"When I opened my suitcase at JFK to show it to the customs official, he immediately had it taken away. Bugs were crawling all over my suitcase and the customs counter. I almost cried."

"You're lucky they didn't take your suitcase away. So how did you end up in the Seychelles?"

"A long story. My soon-to-be ex and I helped crew a boat across the Indian Ocean. The boat got stuck on a coral reef near Diego Garcia, got repaired, and we sailed on to the Seychelles. Weird things were happening on the boat and we asked the Captain to release us in the Seychelles. He finally agreed to let us get off there."

"Why wouldn't he?" Dan asked.

"He wanted us to stay on and help crew through the Suez Canal and back to the Middle East. According to the laws of the sea, the boat is an island and all persons onboard are under the command of the captain. The sea captain determines who comes on and who gets off the boat."

"Wow," Dan said.

"I had a couple of wild years."

"No shit."

"Yes," I said, flashing back to earlier events. "I lost a child, but found myself. Went through a coup and a war. Lost everything I owned, but got rescued. Ship rammed a coral reef in the Indian Ocean, but I got saved from the sinking ship. My marriage died. But I survived." I sighed.

"Here's to the Unsinkable Molly Brown," Dan said, clinking my glass.

"I think that's probably true. I'll drink to that."

We clinked glasses again.

"Oh, I forgot to mention the other near-disaster that year. On our final approach from LAX to NYC, en route to Bombay for the Indian Ocean crossing, we were abruptly forced to climb and circle for hours."

"What happened?" Dan asked.

"An Eastern Airlines plane was struck by lightning on its final approach and crashed."

"Did you see it?"

"Yes. You could see the burning, twisted wreckage from the air. The pilot told us if we had arrived before the Eastern plane ours would have been the plane struck. I am lucky!" I said, smiling at the knowing.

After dinner, I invited Dan back to my apartment for a nightcap. One nightcap led to another. We shared more stories. I showed him my new studio. One move led to another and soon we were kissing passionately and making love on the new carpet of the studio floor.

Hours later, we untangled our entwined limbs and Dan noted the time. "Five! I've got a plane to catch," he said, getting up and getting dressed.

"Nice place you've got here," he said, leaving.

"Thank you! For everything." I smiled.

"I'll be in touch soon," he said, cupping my face with his hands.

CHAPTER 22

DIE? NOT I!

Tjikles Camp, Kyrenia, Cyprus—23-24 July 1974

As I reached the top of the rise, after escaping the fire that engulfed the ravine, I saw UN soldiers directing us to move.

"Get in your cars immediately," one shouted.

"Be ready to move out," yelled another.

I delivered Josh to his parents and took the other small child I had helped up the ravine to his anxious mother. *"Mana mou,"* the child comforted his hysterical mother with his terms of endearment.

"Get into your cars! Start engines! Start moving!" UN soldiers bellowed instructions to the crowd. *Total chaos!* People cried out, trying to find their family and friends, and scurried to get into cars as fast as possible.

I heard engines start, saw cars in the first row moving forward.

My eyes searched the parking lot for Charles and Ronit. "Charles! Ronit!" I yelled, running toward our car. I searched my purse for car keys. None. *I can't move the car.* "Charles! Charles!" I shouted again.

"Susan!" Charles yelled, running from across the parking lot. "Get in!"

He started the engine.

"Ronit! Ronit!" I called my friend's name again.

"I searched everywhere," Charles said, "before the fire."

"Where were you when it started?" I asked.

"Near the bathroom, looking for Ronit."

"Oh, Ronit," I cried.

The car in front of ours sat empty. No driver, no passengers. "It's blocking our exit," Charles said, realizing there was no way around the car, or out. "We're trapped."

Two UN soldiers ran over and pushed the empty car down the hill and out of the way.

Charles steered our car forward.

All of a sudden, we heard people running past yelling something about their missing car.

"The UN's pushing it," I yelled to them.

We watched the family chase their car down the road.

The convoy stopped while they got in and merged into the fleeing cars.

The British man and his sons ran along side our car. "Stop! Please! We need a lift," they yelled. Charles stopped and they climbed in.

Panicked drivers in cars behind began honking horns frantically. Even a brief pause could create panic. "Keep moving!" a UN soldier shouted.

Another stalled car brought the convoy to a temporary halt. UN soldiers came running and pushed the car forward in the line of cars, until the driver got it started. The convoy rolled on down the gravel road and away from the flaming hell the entire mountain behind us had become.

A UN soldier, standing near the exit, directed drivers to turn right onto the paved road heading south toward Nicosia.

One lone car turned left, down the hill in the direction of Kyrenia. I wondered why they went that way.

Charles followed the convoy, to the right, winding its way up the mountain corridor.

I looked back to see if all the cars had made it out. Seeing a UN jeep at the end of the convoy, I felt hopeful they had. "We got out just in time," I said. "The camp's engulfed in flames. Oh, Ronit."

"Hopefully she made it," Charles said. "I searched everywhere for her and her friend."

We moved slowly, in fits and starts. Turkish tanks rumbled past us, taking priority, heading south toward Nicosia.

"The Turks' clear-and-hold strategy worked," Charles said. "They've finally cleared the pass to Nicosia. They're now in control of Northern Cyprus."

I sat in silence, staring at the burned-out landscape, remembering the number of Turkish bombing runs it took to deafen the "rat-a-tat-tat" sound of the lone Greek position.

The convoy came to a standstill at a Turkish command post. A UN soldier spoke with the Turkish guards.

We waited in the hot sun for further instructions. Some people got out of their vehicles and walked around to check on others.

"I feel faint," I said to Charles. "I need water."

"I'll find some," Charles offered, getting out of the car.

He returned with water. "Ronit's not in any of the cars behind us," he said. "I'll check in cars ahead."

I took a few sips of water and passed it on to the British man and son, our passengers.

Pete stopped to tell us about the delay. "The Turks won't let us into the area ahead. Fighting continues in the direction of Nicosia. They say it's too dangerous. Forest fires are still burning, on both sides of the pass. The UN is trying to decide where we'll be safest for the night."

A few minutes later, Charles returned with a big smile on his face. "Ronit's safe, with her friend, in a car ahead."

"Oh, thank God!" I burst into tears. "I'm so happy."

"The UN soldiers have decided to return to Tjikles. They have no other place to go."

Car doors clunked closed and reverse gears scraped as the convoy of civilian vehicles turned around and headed back: north, down the mountain pass.

"Fires are burning out of control," I said. "A strong wind could make this corridor into an inferno."

"It could." Charles nodded.

The lead UN jeep turned left into the gravel road and stopped just beyond the camp sign and a waving UN flag.

"Oh, my God!" I exclaimed. "The camp was ravaged by the fire. All the buildings are destroyed. Only the water tank is standing."

A UN soldier instructed drivers to park cars close together in a cleared spot at the base near the highway.

Other UN soldiers passed out bottles of water and encouraged people to refill them often at the faucet by the roadside, or from the water tank above.

I must have downed five full bottles without stopping. I looked around. I wasn't the only one.

"Susan," Ronit yelled, running to embrace me.

Hugging each other tight, we laughed and cried together.

"What happened to your eye?" Ronit asked, noticing my tearing eye.

"I think something happened when I jumped into the children's trench," I said. "I'll get it checked after we're rescued."

"I want to look for my purse and camera. I left them behind when I ran from the fire," Ronit said, heading up the hill.

The most dangerous fires appeared to be across the pass, along the main highway. They were spreading rapidly.

"Our fate will depend on nature—the wind," a UN soldier explained. "We need volunteers to help dig ditches to protect us, should the fire jump across the road."

Charles volunteered with a group of others to dig ditches and pile sandbags, in hopes of keeping the fire at bay.

As I stood and watched the men work, I remembered hearing about a famous fire which jumped a big river. The Chicago River. How is that possible? I wondered. How can a fire jump a wide river? It must have been hot as lava. Perhaps the wind carried ashes and burning debris from one side to the other. The thoughts were overwhelming. We've got to make it through this night, I told myself. You will survive, a voice told me.

"Shade! How nice," I said, finding my friend Gundy under one of three olive trees which had miraculously survived the fierce fire.

Gundy told me how worried she was about her husband, Aydin. A colonel in the Turkish Cypriot Army, he was called for duty when the invasion began. Gundy poured water into her cupped hand and patiently gave water to her "children"—two small poodles sitting in a wicker basket next to her.

Kate, Alex, and sons joined us under the shade of the tree and asked about Aydin. Gundy cried. "I don't know if he's dead or alive," she answered.

Kate and Alex reached out and hugged her. "The worst is over," Alex said, trying to comfort her.

"Alex, what happened to your arm?" I asked, noticing Alex's arm in a sling.

He explained he had been in the cookhouse, trying to fix food for the children, when a bullet hit and lodged in his arm. "A UN medic removed it and dressed the wound. I'm fine," he said.

A few minutes later, a private car pulled into the area. The driver got out and hurried toward Gundy. "It's Aydin," she cried, running to meet him. They hugged and kissed.

Seeing Alex, Kate, and family, Aydin ran toward them. "I'm so happy to know you're okay," he said, embracing his neighbors.

Eyes wet with tears, I watched a Greek Cypriot and a Turkish Cypriot rejoice—both grateful to know that their family and friends had survived.

A UN ambulance pulled in and parked near the UN sign below.

"Is someone hurt?" I asked a UN soldier.

"A young woman and her husband," he answered "When the convoy left the camp earlier, they turned left instead of right, hoping to make it to Kyrenia. Their car came under fire from both sides. Her injuries are serious. We're hoping to take her to the Austrian field hospital in Nicosia soon."

"I remember seeing that car turn left," I said. "Bless her."

"Rations of food are available near the ambulance," another UN soldier announced. Refugees rushed to form a line to pick up their rations.

Ronit returned with her scorched purse and camera. She smiled. "I'm happy. I found my survivor souvenirs."

Charles and Pete returned with rations for our group—two cans of processed cheese and one-half pound of sugar. Pete brought a bottle of concentrated lemon juice from their car.

"We've got water, sugar, and lemon concentrate," Pete announced. "Cocktail time."

We passed the cans of cheese around to share. "Finger-licking good," I said.

This of course prompted more Good News, Bad News musing.

"The Good News is, the UN has provided rations of food," Ronit said.

"The Bad News is, we got cheese and sugar," Pete said.

"The Good News is, the Turks left," Charles said.

"Bad News is, they left to avoid the raging forest fire they started," I added.

We settled down to enjoy our meager meal. *At least we're eating something.*

About an hour later, a UN soldier announced, "The ambulance is heading to the Austrian Field Hospital in Nicosia. A UN jeep will follow and lead a convoy on to the Hilton hotel, which is located nearby. Anyone wanting to join the convoy should line up behind the UN jeep."

Our group discussed it, but decided to wait for a British evacuation of civilians from the northern coast, near Kyrenia. We watched as the ambulance led the convoy south.

After dinner, we listened to news—BBC's World News.

VIETNAM, WALL STREET, NIXON IMPEACHMENT HEARING …

We waited in hopes of hearing the most important news, the only news that mattered to us.

THE PLAN TO RESCUE STRANDED BRITONS FROM THE NORTH OF THE ISLAND BY SEA EARLY YESTERDAY MORNING WAS SUSPENDED AFTER NEWS OF THE CEASE-FIRE HAD BEEN RECEIVED.

MR. ECEVIT, THE TURKISH PRIME MINISTER, TOLD AN ANKARA PRESS CONFERENCE HELD AT 1700 HOURS, "THE CEASE-FIRE ON CYPRUS IS EFFECTIVE AS OF NOW."

Charles turned the dial to an announcement from BFBS and the British high commissioner.

Within a half hour, the UN ambulance returned with the critically injured couple, followed by the other cars in the convoy. I overheard a UN soldier say that heavy fighting had made the road to Nicosia impassable, and they were forced to return to the camp.

How sad they couldn't get to the hospital, I thought.

As dusk turned to darkness, we searched for a comfortable spot to rest our bone tired bodies. Charles and I decided to sleep in our car. Ronit decided to sleep with her Israeli friend nearby.

I tried to get comfortable in the back seat, but couldn't. I covered my head with my purse, to protect it from random explosions from across the pass. I tossed and turned, but kept a vigil of the UN flag, well lit by the headlights of a UN truck.

I prayed that the wind would be still, the fires would die down, and that we could get the hell out of here soon.

The flag stayed perfectly still on my fitful watch.

Sleep crept in, and tanks rumbled along the pass road. Moments later a flash of light flew over our car and landed behind us. I screamed and jumped out of the car. No sign of fire near us.

"Probably ammunition left by the Greeks, being ignited by fires," Charles said. "The car's as safe a place as any. If we die, we die."

I climbed back into the back seat of the car. "Die? Not I."

In the still of the night, I overheard Josh ask his parents if they were going to die.

His mother replied, "I don't know love, but if we do, we'll die together in comfort, as a family."

Unable to sleep, I turned the radio on low volume to the British Forces station—BFBS.

```
THE BRITISH SHIPS ARE NOW WAITING OFF THE
NORTHERN COAST OF CYPRUS TO BEGIN A RESCUE
MISSION FOR BRITONS AND OTHER FOREIGN NATIONALS
LOCATED IN THE KYRENIA AREA. MAKE YOUR WAY TO
THE NEAREST BEACH FROM KYRENIA EAST TO THE 12
MILE BEACH, WHERE THE SHIPS SHALL COMMENCE
THE RESCUE MISSION AT DAWN. PLEASE MAKE YOUR
PRESENCE KNOWN BY DISPLAYING A WHITE FLAG OR BY
WRITING IN LARGE LETTERS IN THE SAND.

HELICOPTERS WILL COMB THE BEACHES FROM TWO
MILES EAST TO TWELVE MILES EAST IN THE MORNING
HOURS. FOR THOSE OF YOU LOCATED ON THE WEST
SIDE OF KYRENIA, TRY TO MAKE YOUR WAY TO
KYRENIA OR THE NEAREST BEACH, WHERE WE WILL
ATTEMPT TO RESCUE YOU.
```

Excited by the news, I wanted to let others know. I tried shaking Charles. He grunted and turned over.

I got out of the car and walked to the spot where Ronit had planned to sleep. No Ronit.

I stopped a UN soldier walking past. "Have you heard the evacuation news?"

"Yes. British ships are waiting offshore, but we must wait on clearance from the Turks to lead a convoy through the area. It'll happen soon," he assured me.

Around 0630 hours the UN announced it would run two convoys to the Six Mile Beach, east of Kyrenia. We got into our car and lined up to go with the first convoy. Ronit joined us.

To steer cars clear of any explosives left along the road, two UN armored scout cars and two Land Rovers led the way.

More UN jeeps and armored cars followed in the rear. The convoy turned left onto the main road and began winding its way north, down the mountain pass to Kyrenia.

"Oh, my God," I said, shocked by the smoldering remains of nature in every direction. "No trees. No green. Only charred black stumps remained."

No longer a smooth surface, the main road was buckled and twisted, almost made impassable by the holes created by the recent intense artillery fight. Mangled, perforated vehicles littered the landscape.

The lead UN vehicles moved slowly back and forth, guiding cars around huge shell casings and unexploded ordnance (some more than three feet long) scattered along the road.

What would normally be a ten-minute effortless ride, took a slow and painful bumpy hour of many zigs and zags to reach the village of Kyrenia.

I gasped in horror at missing corners, walls, and roof tops of beautiful old villas. Gaping holes in the buildings revealed burned out interiors.

Scorched bodies were scattered along the road. I shook my head in disbelief. Why would anyone believe war is a solution? Senseless. I remembered the Greek boy who wandered into the UN camp, and the lost years of all young men who fought. The loss of lives, and limbs, and homes, and nature. Homes, and pets. Had Sam survived?

When we neared the corner where we would normally turn right and drive home, I saw neighbors gathered on the sidewalk waving. "Charles, look!" I said. "It's Sabrina." Seeing Sabrina convinced me that Sam had indeed survived.

Through tears, we waved and continued following the convoy through town. The vibrant town I had known and loved was gone. What I saw now was a twisted reality of death and destruction.

At the main intersection we turned right and headed east, in the direction of the Six Mile Beach. "The shops are totally destroyed," I said, looking at smashed windows. *No backgammon games, no one smoking hookahs, or enjoying a cup of tea—effortlessly passing an afternoon. Those days were gone.*

Fragments of burned-out vehicles were strewn everywhere along the streets and sidewalks.

"The fight for Kyrenia was a fierce one," Charles observed.

I stared, overwhelmed by the sight of lifeless bodies torn apart by bombs and bullets.

Driving along the beach road, we passed field after field punctuated with blackened jeeps and tanks. Life interrupted by war. Dead humans and animals lay scattered across the morbid landscape.

I sat and stared in stunned disbelief, and wept loud and long. I gasped for air as a high-pitched wail escaped my lips.

Charles and Ronit reached out and patted me.

Approaching the entrance to the beach road, the convoy stopped. The UN had received word from the Turks that the beach might be mined. A tank arrived to sweep the area for land mines.

An hour passed. We waited in the hot sun. Another hour.

"It's now safe to proceed to the beach," a UN soldier announced, motioning cars forward.

Near the beach, another soldier instructed drivers to park their cars near a closed beachside restaurant. UN soldiers offered to collect keys and drive vehicles back to the UN facility for safekeeping.

"A generous offer," I said, "but we have all that matters. The car's not important. Thank you!"

When we removed our small suitcases, I noticed a box which had recently arrived in the mail from China. I had somehow forgotten to take it inside. A jade tea set. Part of my jade collection. Not important. Just things. How quickly 'things' had gone from an enhancement to life—to just stuff. We joined others waiting in the shade of a grape arbor which covered the restaurant's patio, and helped ourselves to clusters of delicious grapes hanging overhead.

A television crew interviewed the British man who had been at Tjikles Camp near us. When they finished the interview, the crew walked toward me.

"Good morning," a journalist said. "We're from a Swedish television station and would like to ask about your experiences during the war."

"Feels good to be alive." I smiled.

"Are you European?" the interviewer asked.

"No. American," I answered.

"You look Swedish."

"My ancestors came from Europe."

He asked my whereabouts during the coup and the war and was thrilled to hear that I had experienced both. After agreeing to be interviewed on film, the camera started rolling.

"Wow!" Ronit said, when the interview finished. "You'll be on European television tonight."

"Women and children first," a UN soldier instructed us to line up in preparation for evacuation by helicopter to the awaiting British ships. The *Hermes,* the *Devonshire,* the *Andromeda,* the *Rhyl,* and a support ship sat waiting to evacuate civilians all along the northern coast of Cyprus, we later learned,

Ronit and I waited in the long line and watched helicopters land on the beach, and lift off for the fleet of ships anchored offshore.

I was fascinated by the "whomp-whomp-whomp" rhythm of the whirling blades, and the way they rotated, much the same as wings, producing the "lift" off the ground. Identical to rowing paddles on a boat, touching air instead of water they propelled the helicopter upward and forward.

As we moved to the front of the line, we stopped and thanked UN soldiers for keeping us safe. We wiped tears from our eyes. As did the soldiers.

Everything seemed emotional now. So many feelings surfaced. Shock and disbelief at the ruin and the horrific images that lingered in my mind. Sad for all the loss. A longing for all that's gone forever. Yet grateful to be a survivor.

As we drew near the helicopter landing area, a British officer checked passports. When Ronit told him she was Israeli, but didn't have her passport, he smiled and waved her on through.

She stopped to hug him, and burst into tears. "I'm so relieved," she said, "to be alive."

Members of the British Royal Navy instructed us how to board the helicopter safely. "The whirling blades are high above your heads. But it's best to duck down and keep your head down in case of wind gust, and to keep the stirred-up sand out of your eyes," one sailor said.

"Be ready to run for the landing pad as soon as the next helicopter sets down," said another, motioning me and Ronit forward.

"Please step into the life jacket," a sailor instructed. He quickly strapped the jacket around my body. "Be ready to go when I give you the signal."

I handed my bottle of water to him. He smiled. "A dream lass. You must be joking. Cool water." Bottoms up, he finished it in one big gulp.

The helicopter touched down. He signaled us to run and lowered his head to remind us to duck down.

We ran, heads down, toward the huge helicopter.

"Whomp-whomp-whomp." The whirling blades chopped overhead. Of course I'll duck down. They sound as if they can't wait to chop my head off. And I certainly won't be lifting my hand to wave goodbye.

In one swift swoop, I was lifted onto the helicopter, into a seat, and safety belts locked. Ronit was lifted into the seat next to me. The engine screamed as the chopper lifted straight up off the ground.

"Wow," I said, laughing at the "whomp-whomp-whomp" sound of the rowing blades pushing us fast through the air.

Moments later, above the blue Mediterranean Sea, I marveled at the sight of the magnificent Kyrenia Castle—once home to Richard the Lionheart. Still standing tall. After all the wars. After more than 3,500 years of invaders.

"Look!" I said pointing. "Half of the Zephyros Hotel is missing!"

"Oh, no," Ronit gasped.

Moments later, the helicopter hovered over a ship's huge flight deck. I saw women and children being lifted off a helicopter. Crew members were motioning them to move out of the way of incoming helicopters.

The helicopter carrying us dropped straight down. An empty helicopter immediately lifted up and away, to pick up more of the stranded.

Two sailors rushed forward, unfastened our seat belts, and with a swoop lowered us onto the top deck with the other refugees.

"Please move onto the platform area," a sailor instructed. "Stay within the lines. It's a lift to lower you to the decks below." The sailors corralled us and others onto the square.

"Keep arms down. We're descending," said the sailor escorting us down.

In an instant, the platform plunged downward. The helicopter and flight deck disappeared above, and walls rose around us. Moments later, we landed in the belly of the big ship.

"Please move forward to the waiting cots," a smiling sailor said.

"Welcome to the HMS *Hermes*," said another, handing each refugee a HAPPY HERMES T-shirt.

When another sailor offered English biscuits and tea, I burst into tears.

"It's quite all right. It's English tea you know," he said, smiling.

We sipped tea and nibbled on biscuits until we heard an announcement broadcast on the ship's PA speaker system.

"Anyone requiring medical attention should proceed immediately to the ship's hospital."

"Susan," Ronit said, "let's go. You need to have your eye checked."

"It's a scratched cornea," the doctor announced, after putting drops in my eye. "It will heal. A matter of time."

"Thank you! I feel so lucky to have survived the war with only a scratch."

"Others weren't so lucky," the doctor said. "One young woman on her honeymoon lost her leg. Up to the hip, from gangrene. All because they took a wrong turn."

"Was she in the car that turned left instead of right, heading to Kyrenia?"

"Yes." He shook his head. "A bad choice."

CHAPTER 22
I AM

Frankfurt, Germany—December 1978

I had just put my key in the front door of my apartment building when I heard the telephone ringing. I ran upstairs to answer it.

I smiled, hearing Diane's hello. "Just wanted to check on you. How did divorce court go yesterday? Was Charles there?"

"Yep. He sat alone on one side of the room, while I sat on the opposite side with my attorney, Herr Nussbaum. I didn't even see Charles at first. He looks different now."

"Did you speak with him?"

"No. No need. Herr Nussbaum spoke with the judge and translated details, '*jas*' and '*neins*' to legal questions. Only took a few minutes. Dreary. The only joy is knowing it's over and final."

"That fast?"

"Yep. Married for 13 years. Divorced in five minutes."

"Wow!"

"I didn't even notice Charles leave. Herr Nussbaum invited me to join him for coffee but I declined. Just wanted to be alone."

"Time to think?"

"No. time to move on. And guess who telephoned me early this morning? Woke me up."

"Charles?" Diane asked.

"No."

"Anyone I know?"

"Herr Nussbaum."

"Herr Nussbaum?" Diane asked. "Was something wrong?"

"No. He called to invite me to lunch. What an asshole."

"Maybe he wanted you to have lunch with him and his wife," Diane said.

"No, sorry. I'm not friends with his wife. He thought I was a vulnerable single woman."

"Some men haven't a clue," Diane said.

"When I heard this deep voice say, *'Guten tag!* Did you have a good sleep?'" I asked 'Who is this?' He was offended that I didn't recognize his voice. 'It's Rainer Nussbaum,' he said.

"I thought maybe something went wrong with the divorce papers and asked. He said everything was fine, that he was just calling to invite me to lunch.

"I told him a firm no. He continued talking, telling me that whenever he thought of me he smiled. So I asked him what he was doing that made him smile."

"You didn't?" Diane asked, giggling.

"I did."

"What did he say?" Diane asked.

"He said he was shaving. I told him I hoped he didn't cut himself. He laughed and said, 'Not even a nick.'

"I told him again, the answer is no! I don't need another married man in my life. He told me if I change my mind to give him a call."

"Oh how bizarre. Not exactly professional," Diane said.

"During the divorce proceedings, he appeared professional. His poor wife. Bet she doesn't have a clue."

"Probably not! How do you feel? Now that it's final."

"Relieved. Ready to send out my freedom cards and get on with my life," I answered.

"Have you told your parents?"

"Yes, I sent them a long letter months ago, explaining my situation and the upcoming divorce. Typical of my mom, she wrote back with details of people in their church and all their woes, but never mentioned my divorce news. Hear no evil. See no evil. I've always been the prodigal one. But I won't be returning to their fold.

"My parents have never been there for me. Their religion has them blinded by the light. Don't question the Good Book. They still believe what they were taught when they got baptized in the church decades ago. Can you imagine never questioning or changing old thoughts?"

"I think it's a generational thing. Especially with divorce," Diane said.

"Perhaps you're right. Whenever I visit the States, I always visit them. They act happy to see me, but if it's a church service night they go to church and leave me sitting. Even if I'm only there for a short visit, and even if I've paid a fortune to get to Podunk, Oklahoma.

"Over the years, I've supported them financially. They never had money. They believed that God would provide. And I usually did."

Diane laughed. "So they were right about that. They just didn't know who God was."

I smiled. "They're right about giving back. I am rewarded one hundred-fold each time I'm generous."

"I get back in town on Thursday," Diane said. "Let's celebrate. If you see Michael, tell him he's invited to our place for Christmas."

"It's a deal. Thanks for your support through all of this."

"That's what friends are for," Diane said.

I put music on and got to work—addressing envelopes, and stuffing 'freedom' cards into them.

The phone rang again.

"Hello," said a familiar voice.

"Michael, how are you? How was England?" I asked.

"Business as usual, but I found time for romping a bit. Are you a free woman now?"

"I am. Feels great."

"How about dinner? My car's parked on Schweizer Strasse, near Wagner's now. Shall I pick you up or do you want to meet there?"

"I'll meet you. Be there in fifteen minutes."

"Bundle up. It's snowing," Michael warned.

"I see the flurries. I will."

I grabbed a warm scarf, coat, and hat, and headed out.

By the time I reached Wagner's Weinstube I was covered with a blanket of snow, head to toe. Opening the front door, I stepped into the foyer and wiped frozen flakes from my hat and coat. I stamped loose the icicles crusting my boots. Entering the restaurant, the smell of warm, fresh German food permeated my nostrils. The large main room buzzed with the sounds of clinking glasses, chatter, and laughter. Heat sure feels good, I thought, rubbing my cold hands together. My eyes searched the room for Michael. I spotted him in the far right corner. He waved.

"Hello dahling!" Michael grinned as I neared the table. He kissed me on both cheeks, helped remove my snow-covered coat, and hung it on the wall rack to dry.

"It's not even crowded yet," I said, looking around the half-empty room.

"Give it an hour. You'll see."

"How lovely you called. I was just wondering what I'd fix for dinner. I see you've snagged the best seats in the house."

"I've ordered drinks."

"Thanks!"

A waiter arrived carrying a big clay carafe of *Apfelwein* and glasses.

Michael ordered. "*Schweinefleisch gebraten mit Kartoffelsalat.*"

"*Schweineschnitzel für mich,*" I said. "*Danke!*"

"Pork in Germany is so delicious," Michael said. "That's why I always get my usual."

"Me too."

"How did it go in court?" Michael asked.

"Dissolved in five minutes."

"Like Alka-Seltzer?"

"Yep. 'Plop, plop, fizz, fizz—oh what a relief it is.'"

Michael smiled. "I saw Charles in England last week. He said he's moving to Hong Kong with his firm and his German girlfriend, Inge. She's quite a cling-along and dingy."

"Bet he loves that," I said.

We sipped *apfelwein* and people-watched.

"Are you still being followed?" Michael asked.

"Not sure. The other night when I walked home from the Balalaika—"

"I told you not to walk home alone, late at night," Michael scolded me.

"It felt safe. Only two in the morning."

Michael shook his head in disbelief. "What happened?" he asked.

"As I passed a storefront window on Gartenstrasse, two blocks from my apartment, I noticed a policeman standing in the shadow between two buildings. He put his index finger up over his mouth to tell me not to make a sound, and motioned me to keep moving."

Our food arrived. We dove into it. After a few minutes, Michael stopped eating and asked, "And then?"

"Oh," I said, continuing the story. "The policeman nodded for me to move on. I moved a few steps forward. When I got to the next shop window, another policeman stood in the shadows there. He did the same thing, put his finger over his mouth and motioned me to keep moving forward. So, I did."

"Were you scared?"

"Yes, shaking, but I kept moving. When I reached my street corner, I crossed the street and kept walking. Faster now. All of a sudden, behind me, I heard shouts, a scuffle, and several thuds. I looked back. Two policemen had thrown a man to the ground. A police car screeched to a halt near them, and I ran all the way home."

"Did the police follow you? Did they contact you?"

"No. They were obviously waiting for the guy behind me."

"It's possible you've been under surveillance for some time."

"Or he has."

"Too bad you didn't question Charles more about Cyprus."

"I tried. Many times. He always denied any involvement in the Cyprus War. As a member of Mensa, he believes he's the most intelligent man alive, and owes no one an explanation of anything."

"Mensa I've met are intelligent, but humor-impaired," Michael replied. "Oh, by the way, *'menza'* in Spanish slang refers to a stupid, stubborn person. A real jackass."

I laughed. "He's that. How do you know that word in Spanish?"

"I've had a few Latin lovers."

"But of course."

"Another?" Michael asked, holding up two fingers and nodding to the waiter across the room, without waiting for my reply.

"European waiters are so attentive," I said.

"They take pride in their work," Michael said. "None of this 'Hi, I'm Mike and I'll be your server tonight.'"

"I used to wait on Charles much the same. He would snap his fingers and I'd come running."

"Perfect wife for a spy. Living with this German bitch will make him wish he'd never let you go."

I chuckled.

After dinner, Michael suggested a walk across the river to enjoy the snowy evening.

"On the footbridge or on water?" I asked, smiling. "I'm ready for either."

"Since walking on water requires concentration, I suggest we stroll across the Eiserner Steg bridge this evening," Michael said, extending his arm.

"A lovely idea."

Snow flurries whirled past as we walked, arm in arm, along the river bank and up the steps to the famous footbridge. We stopped halfway across to watch boats passing below, in the Main River.

"Reminds me of people," I said. "People who meet by chance and pass in the night."

"'Ships That Pass in the Night' by Paul Laurence Dunbar," Michael said, "Clouds massing, ships passing, my soul's hurt glassing. I love that poem."

"Beautiful images," I said, when he had finished. "Who's the author again?"

"Paul Laurence Dunbar. An African-American poet," Michael answered.

"Reminds me of my life, and all that is massing, passing as I reinvent myself."

"It's ongoing. We reinvent ourselves in love and in loss. We like to think of ourselves as constant, but we're always changing whether we acknowledge it or not."

Brushing snowflakes aside, we watched ships come and go, crossed the bridge, and climbed down into the old central square of the Römer. The restored fourteenth and fifteenth century buildings were shining bright under the winter's night lights and the moon.

I pointed to the building where my art would be exhibited for the city of Frankfurt. "No date yet, but that's where it will be shown," I said, smiling.

"Exquisite!"

The snow fell heavier, blanketing the town square.

"It's starting to stick," Michael said. "Let's head back before we get stuck."

We retraced our steps and made our way back toward my apartment.

At the corner of Gartenstrasse and Schweizer Strasse, I stopped in front of the Commerzbank to reenact what happened the night the police tackled the man who followed me.

"I had just crossed this crosswalk," I said. "About here, I became aware of someone following me. Aware of danger."

"On this corner?" Michael asked.

"Yes," I replied.

We continued walking down the block, and I pointed out where the first and second policemen had been hiding. I stopped abruptly, remembering something else weird that happened at the Commerzbank corner, and ended here. Why hadn't I thought of the connection before? "I just thought of something else, something weird that also happened here."

"At this spot?" Michael asked.

"Yes, it ended at the door of this empty-looking building. Let's keep moving."

We crossed the street to my block, and as we walked I told Michael the strange story.

"A friend who used to live in Frankfurt visited me from the States. She had planned on staying two weeks. But on her second day here, she got detained when she entered the local Commerzbank to change money. The teller asked her to wait while she went to get more deutsch marks.

"Within minutes, policemen in green uniforms arrived. They took her to a special police station a few doors down the street. After interrogating her for several hours, they called me asking if I could identify her. I said that she was a friend visiting me from Washington, DC. She got on the telephone and told me they wanted me to come to the station and identify her in person. She sounded freaked."

"Who wouldn't be?" Michael asked.

"I agreed to go there right away and asked the location of the station. She gave me the address and told me it was on Gartenstrasse. I questioned the location because the only police station I knew of in the neighborhood wasn't on Gartenstrasse. She told me it looked like a regular office building. No police sign on the door. I wrote the address down and headed there to pick her up. Sure enough, no sign indicated what it was. Just an address on the door."

"I've heard of unmarked police cars."

"When I got to the entrance door someone opened it immediately and ushered me upstairs. Sure enough it was a police station and it just happened to be the same building where the two policemen motioned for me to keep moving, and then tackled the man who followed me. Probably just a strange coincidence, but weird."

"Secret surveillance. Why did they detain her?"

"She resembled a member of the Baader-Meinhof gang."

"The Red Army Faction? The left-wing German terrorists group?"

"Yes. It was shocking to me to realize that the criminal police have plain-looking buildings to spy on civilians. My friend was so spooked, she left Germany the next day and spent a fortune to get her ticket changed."

"Welcome to 1984!"

"Big Brother," I said, as we turned into the entrance to my building. "Come on up. A nightcap will warm you."

I poured drinks and joined Michael on the couch.

"By the way, we're invited to Diane and Steve's home for Christmas dinner," I announced. "Will you be in town?"

"I will. Nice!"

"I love Thanksgiving, but Christmas is my favorite family holiday," I confided. "Most Christmases were spent with grandparents in Oklahoma. My family would pile into our nine-passenger station wagon, laden with a pillow and a toy each. Brightly wrapped gifts were stuffed into crevices.

"Dad did most of the driving. One time, when we stopped to get gas, he felt sleepy and Mom said she'd drive. He was asleep before we even got out of the gas station. Mom got back on the interstate in the wrong direction. As kids we didn't notice, and it was an hour before Dad woke up—and we ended up back where we'd been two hours earlier."

Michael smiled. "Did he cuss at her?"

"No, but he yelled, and took over driving. After crossing the Arizona desert, we climbed the hills into the White Mountains. Next came New Mexico, the Texas flatlands, and finally we crossed into Oklahoma. When we saw the *Welcome to Oklahoma* sign, we'd all burst into song, singing 'OOOOOK-la-homa where the wind comes sweeping down the plain.'

"Next, we would discuss what we would do first, when we finally got to Grandma and Grandpa's house. Would we have a big slice of Grandma's coconut cream pie? Or count our presents under the tree? If there was snow on the ground, of course we'd go sledding first. Snow makes the world magical. What's your favorite family holiday?"

"Probably Halloween!"

"Halloween?" I chuckled. "That's not a family holiday."

"You don't know my family. Sure seemed like it to me."

At my front door, he kissed my forehead tenderly. "You're a beautiful soul. Good night."

"Thanks for dinner and the poem. Safe drive home."

CHAPTER 24

NEVER SETTLE FOR LESS

Taunus, Germany—1979

Entering Michael's apartment, I could smell the classic beef bourguignon cooking. Michael was a great cook who loved to take the time to prepare gourmet dishes. A fan of Julia Child, he had all her books sitting on his kitchen bookshelf.

"You can skip all the sauce straining fussiness, if you want simple," he said, as I watched him strain the sauce.

"Then it's just plain ole stew. Right?"

"Traditional stew," he explained. "Still delicious, but not what we gourmets expect."

We ate by candlelight and when I finished oohing and aahing over the dark silky sauce, Michael smiled. "Not bad," he agreed.

"Perfect. A divine dinner," I said. "Thanks for inviting me."

"My pleasure," Michael said, pouring more wine. "Impossible to make a good beef bourguignonne for one."

For dessert, Michael served an elegant cherry compote with a hint of vanilla.

"This dessert is delicious," I said. "Reminds me of the exotic fruit I devoured in Sri Lanka long ago. I can still taste it."

"After how many years?" Michael asked smiling.

"1975. After the Cyprus War."

"You were in Sri Lanka?"

"Yes. We received an invitation from people we had met in Cyprus, to join them in Sri Lanka and help crew a yacht across the Indian Ocean. It belonged to a Swedish millionaire who had yachts docked in different ports around the world."

"What size?"

"Fifty-four feet."

"How many masts?" Michael asked.

"Two," I answered.

"Fore and aft? Mizzenmast and a taller mainmast?"

"Yes."

"A ketch. Two masts and multiple headsails."

"A luxurious rig. Even had a Jacuzzi, which worked great when the ship sat in dock. How do you know about boats?" I asked.

"An ex-lover. Sailor. We rocked and rolled all over Nantucket Sound. Not exactly smooth sailing, but then the relationship wasn't either. Speaking of which, the Indian Ocean is known for its turbulence. Had you sailed before?"

"Only as a passenger, off the California coast. When the opportunity presented itself, we thought 'aah'—pleasure yachting, opportunity of a lifetime."

"Or not. Tell me about Sri Lanka."

"Breathtaking," I said, "from mountains to seaside, from jungles to swamps.

"We arrived late at night and buses weren't running until the following morning. So we took a five-hour taxi ride from Colombo, in the southwest, to the port of Trincomalee on the northeastern side of the island."

"A long ride through jungle," Michael said.

"Our driver stopped at a house along the way to pick up a toolbox. 'Just in case,' he told us. He stopped again, about an hour later, to allow a herd of elephants to cross the road."

"As if he had a choice. Did you see four-legged tigers?" Michael asked.

"We saw several wandering in a field. But we didn't see any Tamil Tigers. I think they're active again now, but back then it appeared peaceful."

"Since '76 all hell is breaking loose there. The Tamils are demanding a separate, sovereign state. Good you got out when you did. So you sailed from Sri Lanka across the Indian Ocean and up through the Suez Canal?"

"That was the original plan. We spent weeks in port, preparing supplies for the trip and waiting on charts to the Seychelles. We ended up sailing without charts because the ship's agent couldn't get them and the captain was anxious to get going. He assured us he could navigate by the stars. He said he'd done it before."

"Without charts? From Sri Lanka to the Seychelles?" Michael asked.

"He looked identical to Sinbad the Sailor, so I assumed he could."

"The Indian Ocean is vast."

"I found out," I said.

"You crossed the equator."

"In monsoon season."

"Monsoon season? Why would anyone in their right mind cross the Indian Ocean without charts in monsoon season?" Michael asked.

"Oh, they wouldn't. But we didn't discover that we weren't dealing with right minds until much later."

"A bit late for discovery."

"Sinbad was a brazen Brit. His eyes lit up in rough seas, and we were hit by storm after storm. We lost the main mast when it split in two during a fierce storm. One day we watched a massive waterspout pass us to the right.

"Once sitting out a storm and howling winds, we spotted a ship port-side heading straight toward us. The captain quickly steered us aside, and got on the radio to alert the ship of our close proximity. No answer. We hoped they had spotted us on their radar. It looked to be two ships. We soon discovered it was a minesweeper."

"No wonder they wouldn't answer."

"Next, our generator quit. We actually drifted for days with a broken rudder. We lost the mizzenmast to the wind."

Michael's face showed amazement. "And then?"

"After the generator quit, the food in the refrigerator spoiled and Sinbad's girlfriend thew it overboard."

"One way to attract sharks."

"Oh, it did. They circled the boat scarfing up spoiled food."

"And then?"

I smiled, remembering what happened next.

"It was amazing. The sea was calm. The boat rocked gently side to side. I lay on my stomach, sunning on deck and listened to the water lap the side of the sailboat. I raised my head and watched the sea, smooth as glass, behind the boat. So peaceful!

"A sudden movement in the water caught my eye. A dorsal fin surfaced. I saw another. I sat up and watched fin after fin rise out of the blue ocean. 'Dolphins!' I shouted to the others, and ran downstairs to get my camera.

"When I returned, a pod of dolphins surrounded the boat. No sharks in sight. The dolphins began entertaining us. They dove, surfaced, and bounced about in play.

"I kept taking photos and they posed for me. It was as if they understood our thoughts. So, I suggested we toss a ball to them. Someone tossed a ball. Before it could even hit the water, a dolphin tossed it back with its nose. They played ball for some time, tossing it back and forth to each other, or to us on deck. As if bored with the game, one dolphin tossed it back on board and the pod swam away. Absolutely magical!"

"Wow!" exclaimed Michael. "I thought they only did that at Sea World."

"Me too. I still have photos of the dolphins in action that day."

I stopped, sipped more wine, and continued. "One of the few good days at sea. Most were miserable. We drifted for days, in storm after storm. Seas so rough we chained ourselves to the railing, when we were working on deck, so we wouldn't be thrown overboard. As we neared the equator, it got worse. The waters churned for days on end."

"Long rough time at sea," Michael said.

"Too long," I replied. "Each day I asked, 'When are we going to cross the bloody equator?' We finally did and the currents moved us forward."

"And then?"

"Our engine sputtered and died, and we drifted toward a land mass called Diego Garcia. We broadcast 'mayday' forever. They ignored our distress calls for days. Once there, we got stuck on a coral reef and had to be dragged off the reef by the American and British navies.

"Diego Garcia," Michael said, smiling as if he knew the place. "I know about Diego Garcia. My sailor friend was stationed there. I did research on the place. It's a secret NATO military base, near the Maldives. Has one of five monitoring stations for satellite navigation."

"That's the one," I said, amazed he knew about such an obscure place.

"It has quite a history," Michael said. "NATO forcibly removed the entire population to other islands in the area, so the British and Americans could have a military base there."

"A huge base, used for refueling bombers and an important listening site for NATO."

"I didn't know they allowed civilians there," Michael said.

"They don't. In fact, they refused to acknowledge our existence until the end. We were so close to land, we could hear their radio station blaring and see vehicles and people moving about. They came to our rescue when we neared land. A small motorboat came by and offered to help guide us in. They asked if we had any drugs on board. We all shook our heads no. They advised us to throw drugs overboard in plastic bags, if we had any."

Michael laughed. "Well, did you?"

I smiled, remembering the crazy ordeal. "Yes," I answered. "The two men in the small boat later collected the plastic bags filled with hashish."

"Bet they loved that."

"The yacht got snagged on the coral and started taking in water starboard."

"You know why it's called starboard?" Michael asked.

"No," I answered.

"It's the side on which the boat is steered, because most sailors were right-handed, and the word star was originally 'steer' in old English."

"Interesting," I said, thinking about it. "How strange that the Brits drive on the left side of the road. You're a walking, talking encyclopedia."

"Did you and Charles fly back to the States from there?" Michael asked.

"Not allowed! They arranged for parts to repair the boat, and then sent us on our way. No women were allowed on the island. Only men."

"No wonder my old lover loved that assignment."

"Of course, there's always an exception to the rules," I said.

"You were allowed on land?" Michael asked.

"Yep. The British governor of the island invited us to dinner one evening. We were told to bring a change of clothes and offered a shower at his place. We women were taken to his house first. We enjoyed a nice long shower, got dressed in clean clothes, and waited on the men to arrive. After a few glasses of wine, the governor informed us the men wouldn't be coming. We asked why. He said he didn't know. So we had dinner and returned to the boat."

"Sounds like a dirty old man to me."

"He definitely was. While taking showers, we both felt eyes watching us. When we returned to the boat, the guys were furious. They were told that the governor wouldn't allow them on land."

Michael shook his head. "A selfish bastard!"

I stopped for a moment, and thought about that unlikely event in my life. "I swear," I said, "sometimes I think parts of my life are just my wild imagination. Maybe they didn't really happen. But the governor gave me a souvenir, which I still have. An 'Official First Day Cover, 1975 Seashore Plants' envelope. I take it out and look at it, from time to time, to remind myself that this amazing adventure happened to me."

"A reality check?"

"Yes." I smiled.

"How about coffee and a brandy?" Michael asked.

"I have a long drive home," I answered.

"Stay here. You know you're welcome. The guest room has fresh linens, and my mother will be thrilled to know you spent the night. She's forever hopeful I will straighten out."

"Hope springs eternal! OK, I'll stay the night," I said, clearing dishes from the table while Michael made coffee.

Later, while sipping cognac and coffee, I remembered another part of the story. "By the way," I said, "the captain's girlfriend looked like a young Liz Taylor, but wasn't very intelligent. She wore skimpy clothing, even when we went shopping in the local souk—market. One day, an angry crowd of people gathered and threw stones at her."

"They actually stoned her?" Michael asked.

"Chased her out of the village and back to the boat. She thought it was funny and laughed about it. The captain cussed her out for her lack of respect for the locals. They fought about something which happened before we arrived. They screamed and yelled at each other for hours."

"What did you do?"

"We holed up in our berths and let them go at it. From what I gathered, she had sex with the captain of a boat docked nearby, a few days before we arrived."

"So, this is why your captain wants to get out to sea fast."

"Yep. The other crew member was her brother. After setting sail, we learned even more. Their father, a famous Israeli physicist, had sent the brother along to protect his daughter from Sinbad. He had committed a crime in England and could never return there."

"Persona non grata," Michael said.

"Exactly. One day, out of the blue the bimbo asked me if I knew who Charles was."

"Same question you got in England, at the refugee party."

"Same question. When I told her that Charles worked for a Swiss firm selling electronic equipment, she howled laughing. When the captain heard her, he told her to stop teasing me.

When I told Charles about the strange conversation, he informed me that she had spent time in mental hospitals. 'Try not to upset her,' Charles told me."

"And you're in the middle of the Indian Ocean and there's no getting off."

"Exactly! No escape. On tenterhooks, I just tried to get along with everyone. Knowing she did the cooking, I made sure she tasted things before I'd eat anything. She got so weird she stopped speaking to everyone onboard, and communicated by writing letters and delivering them in person."

"Wow! A real weirdo! Good you took the *über*-cautious approach. You're damn lucky to be alive. Weird things happen at sea. Most people have no idea."

We moved into the living room and Michael played his new Peter Allen album. "I told you about seeing him live in London," Michael said. "I'm absolutely in love with this man."

"Isn't he married to Liza Minnelli?"

"Not anymore."

"He's your type?" I asked.

"He has to be, if he was married to Liza."

I laughed, sat back, and slowly sipped my brandy.

Michael adjusted the volume, and we listened to Peter Allen sing his hit, "I Could Have Been A Sailor."

"Sailed the seven seas—" Michael sang along. "—but settled for safer harbors—."

"Wow!" I said when the song had finished. "An amazing song! The lyrics are brilliant. So introspective. Many people think much the same. 'I would have, could have, should have, if only I had, done this' in life. They always have an excuse for why they can't do something."

"But not Susan," Michael said, nodding. "You take chances and live life to its fullest."

"The way I see it, in our lives we're given a blank slate. It's up to us to make it happen, or not."

"Here's to you, kiddo!" Michael raised his glass. "Never settle for less."

"Not my style," I said, clinking glasses.

Much, much later, we said our good-nights and headed to bed. Separate beds. But I could see Michael's mom smiling a hopeful smile.

CHAPTER 25

SHOP AROUND

Frankfurt, Germany—1979

"Imagine getting paid to learn and travel," I said to my friend Rosetta one evening, while sitting at the bar of her club.

"How did you find this job?" Rosetta asked.

"This woman, in charge of training for an international computer company, introduced herself at my last exhibit and asked if I'd be interested in working for her company. She said she wanted someone creative to teach professionals computer programs. I explained that I knew nothing about computers but would like to learn, and would only be interested in a part-time job. She assured me they would train me and were in fact looking for a part-time consultant. She gave me her card. I called, interviewed, and she hired me on the spot."

"Good money?" Rosetta asked.

"Great money!"

"Can I go with you on your next trip to France?"

"Why not?" I answered. "I'll work by day, and by night we'll wine and dine in a fine French restaurant."

"Sounds good. What do you hear from Dan?" Rosetta asked.

"He calls from time to time," I answered.

"He's smitten with you."

I laughed. "He told me I could have been a Playboy bunny. Good line!"

"He's photographed a few."

"He's nice, but too far away. Interesting men are everywhere. I met two bankers on the U-Bahn yesterday. After introducing themselves, one invited me to dinner next week."

"Go girlfriend! Oh, by the way, your slick-looking English guitarist friend stopped by earlier this evening looking for you. Said he's tried calling several times."

"Trenton?" I asked.

"That's him. Said he's in town for a gig, and he'll stop in later."

"Great! Thanks!"

A serious-looking businessman entered the club and sat on a barstool near me.

Rosetta nodded in his direction and immediately made him comfortable. "What would you like to drink, hon? Your usual?"

He nodded.

Rosetta walked away, then turned back and smiled. "Robert? Right?"

"You've got a good memory," he said.

"A pint of Bavarian *Weizen* coming up," Rosetta said.

"Impressive," I said. "How can you possibly remember what your customers drink?"

"I always remember what handsome men drink," Rosetta said, smiling at him. Robert smiled at me. A cool, calculated smile.

Rosetta returned with his pint and introduced Robert to me. "Susan's an artist. Her last exhibit was a great success," Rosetta bragged.

"I collect fine art," Robert said. "Perhaps you can show me your work sometime."

"All sold!" Rosetta said laughing. "You'll have to wait 'til the next one."

"When and where?" Robert asked.

"May. Frankfurter Künstler Jahresausstellung. Stadt Museum."

"The annual exhibit at the city museum? That's impressive!" Robert said.

Robert chatted with Rosetta, finished his drink, paid his bill, and left. He returned a moment later and handed me his business card. "Put me on your list. Give me a call."

After he left, Rosetta said, "Aloof men drink only craft beers. A certain kind of snobbery. He's a big tipper, though."

"No wonder you remember his name and brand," I said.

"Good for business."

"Certainly is."

An airline crew arrived and sat together at one of the bigger tables. I found myself staring at one particular man.

"He's a good looker," Rosetta said.

"I think I know him. He looks identical to someone I knew in Cyprus."

"What's his name?"

"Miles, a pilot with Cyprus Air. He and his wife were our neighbors before the war."

"I'll find out," Rosetta said, going to take their drink orders.

When she returned, she snickered. "That's him. He's blown away by my psychic ability."

I turned to see Miles staring at me. Recognizing me, he smiled, got up from the table and walked toward me. "Susan?" he asked.

"It is I," I replied, smiling. "How are you?"

"Fine. Fancy meeting you here. What a surprise!" He gave me a hug. "Where's Charles?"

"We're divorced. He lives in Hong Kong now."

"Oh my! Do you live in Frankfurt?"

"Yes, in Sachsenhausen. How's Tina?"

"We divorced," he said with a sigh, "not long after returning to England from Cyprus. The war proved tough on our marriage. We adopted two children, but even that didn't help."

"How's she doing?"

"Busy. Parenting is hard work. I see the children when I can. I'm often flying."

"Who do you fly with now?"

"British Air. Perfect for me. Good company. Why don't you join me and the crew at the table? I know the captain and others want to meet you."

Miles introduced me to the flight crew. One young woman, a stewardess, looked like a younger version of Miles's ex-wife, Tina. I could tell they were romantically involved.

The crew asked lots of questions about the Cyprus War, life in Frankfurt.

I told them about my life as an artist, and invited them to attend my next exhibit.

"We're in town often," the captain said.

"Congrats!" Miles said, leading a toast to my success.

"I'm following my dream," I said. "At last."

The crew clinked glasses and cheered.

The captain moved from his seat at the other end of the table and settled into a seat next to mine. He chatted about numerous holidays he had taken in Cyprus over the years, and rambled on about feeling the loss.

"It was paradise," I said.

"*Paradise Lost,*" he added. "Do you know the poem by John Milton?"

"Not by heart. It's a long one."

"Only ten books and ten thousand lines of verse," he said smiling.

I chuckled. "I've conquered several chapters of Psalms, but never tried to recite ten thousand lines."

"Psalms? Why Psalms?" he asked.

"When I was a kid, I got paid to learn Bible scriptures."

"So you had incentive?"

"I did," I answered, smiling. "Money is a great motivator."

Miles glanced at his watch, and signaled to the crew that it was time to leave for the airport.

"Lovely to see you, Susan," he said. "Glad to know you're doing well."

"You too," I said, giving him a hug.

Before leaving, the captain handed me his card and invited me to dinner on his next trip to Frankfurt. I accepted.

"The hits keep coming," Rosetta said after bidding the crew a good night. "That captain is the cat's meow!"

"Oui! Oui!" I added.

"Mercy me!" Rosetta said, laughing.

I decided to call it a night and head home when Trenton waltzed into the club, his bass guitar in tow.

"Hoped I'd find you here," he said, giving me a kiss on the cheek. "Tried calling, but you're never home."

"I've been busy," I said smiling. "Good to see you."

"I promised I'd be back for more fun and games," Trenton said, winking at Rosetta.

"Have you met Trenton?" I asked Rosetta.

"Oh, yes," Rosetta said. "Trenton stops by when he's in town."

He ordered drinks and told Rosetta about first meeting me, at a bar across the river. "I got paid to entertain on stage, while this one held everyone's rapt attention. Holding court, she was. So, from the stage, I asked her 'What's a nice girl like you doing in a hole like this?' Without skipping a beat, she said. 'Checking out moles.' 'Touché,' someone said, and the crowd howled laughing."

"A lively group," I confirmed.

"Bloody hell, they were all snockered. Cheeky comedian, this one," Trenton said, patting my cheek and smiling at Rosetta.

"You can dress her up, but can't take her out," Rosetta said with a laugh. "How long are you in town this time?"

"The weekend, then back to the UK. I'll return for the music festival, and Susan of course."

We said good night to Rosetta and strolled back to my apartment. I showed him my studio first.

"It's perfect," he said, looking at some of my work. "You've done some nice pieces here."

We climbed the stairs to my apartment, sat on the couch and talked about life for hours.

He told me about his musical gigs, and his full-time job with a musical instrument company.

I told him about my exhibits, my recent divorce, my new part-time job and the travel that went with it.

"You have been busy," he said. "Sounds like the best of all worlds."

"I do love getting paid to travel."

"Getting paid to travel and perform is a sweet deal for me. But," he hesitated, "it makes family life more difficult." He went on to explain that he and his wife led separate lives, but decided to stay married for the sake of their four-year-old daughter. "We were childhood sweethearts. Her father is the local vicar."

The local vicar, I thought. "A priest?" I asked.

"Yes, for our local church."

"Are you religious?"

"Heavens no," he said laughing. "But the wife is."

"Oh." I hesitated, then asked, "Are you happy?"

"I love my daughter. My wife's a good mother."

"Do you love your wife?"

"For being a good mother. Look, she got pregnant and joined the Pudding Club. Have you ever heard of it?"

I shook my head no.

"It's an old British expression for being pregnant."

"Oh," I said laughing.

"I belted up. We did the honorable thing and got married. The parents are happy. What else matters?"

"Your happiness? It's your life. Your choice. We're in very different situations. My ex tried to divorce me on grounds I didn't produce a child. Today, I'm grateful I didn't have one with him. An unhealthy marriage. For me, the honorable thing was divorce."

"Not to worry," he said, stroking my cheek. "I won't get you preggers. I always wear a French letter. An eraser."

"An eraser?"

"A Trojan. A rubber Johnny. To protect," he assured me.

Trenton ended up staying the night, and the weekend. His Cockney accent had me laughing hysterically. Some jokes I got, others not.

"Fun-buns!" he said once, kissing my breasts.

I laughed so hard, I had to get up and go to the bathroom.

Between bouts of laughing, petting, and extended kissing, Trenton would leap out of bed, put on his tight white briefs, grab his guitar, and sing to me. Some songs were romantic. Most were outright silly.

"You have a great voice," I said.

He nodded. "Thanks ever so," he said bowing.

"Why the tighty whites?" I asked.

"Protects the instrument," he explained.

"Who's the comedian?" I asked, laughing. "You Brits have a reputation for brilliant repartee, but sometimes it's hard to grasp with the accent."

The next morning, we enjoyed breakfast in bed.

"Do you like bangers and mash?" he asked, looking serious.

"What?" I sat up.

"Bangers and mash."

"I don't know," I replied. "Maybe we can do that next time."

Trenton howled, explaining that bangers and mash is a traditional English dish made from sausages and mashed potatoes.

I laughed, and laughed some more.

He got up, got showered, and packed his bag.

Before leaving, he sat on the arm of the sofa and beckoned me to join him on the couch.

"I want to sing a special song for you. You're in a great place in your life. So listen up."

He began strumming the chords of an oldie, and slowly added the melody notes.

"'Shop Around,'" I said, "Smokey Robinson and the Miracles."

He smiled, nodded yes, looked me in the eyes, and sang the song to me.

"When I became of age, my mother called me to her side …."

I swayed to the music, listened to the words, and joined in on the chorus. Words of wisdom, I thought, advising young people not to be stuck on the first one who comes along. But who ever listens to mother?

After he finished crooning the last line of the song, he stopped, and whispered.

"Keep your freedom." He leaned forward and kissed my forehead.

"My plan exactly." I nodded, and waved him goodbye.

After Trenton left, I put on Billy Joel's *52nd Street* album and cranked up the sound. When the song, "My Life" came on, I cranked it even louder and danced away. "You can speak your mind, but not on my time." I sang along. "It's my life."

I especially liked the line, "You wake up with yourself."

I thought about the lyrics long after the music stopped and allowed the thoughts to drift to my life, and my situation as a single woman.

Discovering lust: I was clueless about sex when I got married. Feels good to explore sex and not feel pressure to get pregnant.

Shopping around: I like that idea. Figuring out what makes me tick. It's not the biological clock. I smiled.

Time for coffee. Time to paint wax on canvas.

CHAPTER 26

SURPRISE!

Frankfurt, Germany—April 1979

My telephone rang early on April 1, 1979, my thirty-fourth birthday.

The first call came from McAlester, Oklahoma. "Happy birthday, birthday girl! How's my favorite April Fool?" Aunt Wilmoth asked.

"Aunt Wilmoth. What a lovely surprise!"

"I can't forget your birthday. I helped change your diapers. You were the cutest little bundle of joy."

Aunt Wilmoth, my aunt by marriage to my Uncle Duvel, always remembered my birthday no matter where I lived in the world. She loved to travel and often rendezvoused with me in exotic places. I felt especially close to her and often referred to her as my second mother. Aunt Wilmoth also loved to chat.

"Are you following doctor's orders, after your back surgery?" I asked.

"I'm taking it easy. Haven't jitterbugged yet."

"It's hard to keep a good jitterbugger still."

She wanted to know all about my love life and asked if I had special plans for my birthday.

"I think my friends are up to something," I explained. "In Germany if you want to celebrate your birthday, you have to organize it. So I planned to cook a Mediterranean feast for my friends. They all love Greek cuisine. But when I telephoned to invite them, each one said they had other plans."

"Everyone?" Aunt Wilmoth asked.

263

"Yes, everyone. So I think they're planning a surprise."

"An April Fool's joke? As a kid, you were the one playing jokes on others."

"They're all acting secretive."

"You're probably right. What will you wear? Something special?"

"Maybe I'll surprise them and wear my birthday suit."

"Your birthday suit? Dear me!"

"Is Uncle Duvel home?" I asked, changing the subject. But an idea was born.

"No, dear. He's working in the Gulf this week, overseeing a drilling project. But he said to wish you a happy birthday. He'll be home next weekend."

"Tell him thanks and give him a hug for me."

"The church choir is scheduled to sing in Germany end of May. I'll plan on spending a few days with you."

"Wonderful. I'll show you around Frankfurt."

"That would be nice," Aunt Wilmoth said. "Remember when you escorted us to Luxembourg?"

"Of course. A fun trip."

She fondly began recalling the time I drove my aunt and uncle, and another couple to visit the place where my uncle and the other man had fought with allied forces to liberate Luxembourg from the Germans in 1945.

"An important trip for Uncle Duvel. Perhaps," I chuckled at the thought, "I could wear a colorful, silk scarf to accent my birthday suit."

"Dear me! I do hope you're joking. Did I tell you about the time—" Chatting away, Aunt Wilmoth told me about a time she forgot to pack a designer silk scarf that perfectly matched a silk suit, for a cruise she went on. Fortunately, she had packed plenty of other outfits to wear.

I listened, inserted an occasional, "Oh no," and listened some more. She talked some more about how excited she was to be touring Europe with the church choir.

I told her I looked forward to seeing her smiling face, and thanked her for always remembering my birthday.

"How could anyone forget you? You're very special," she replied.

We said our goodbyes and I gently placed the telephone back on the hook.

I sipped one cup of coffee after another as I answered the ringing phone.

Birthday greetings came from near and far, again and again, as family and friends wished me a special day. Being an April Fool is fun! Friends remember my birthday.

Looking good for thirty-four, I thought as I looked at myself in the hall mirror. *Surprise! Won't they be surprised? I can't wait to see their faces.*

The thought of surprising my friends had me smiling and giggling all day.

My friend Gray called to say his previous plans got canceled and he'd like to take me to dinner.

"Are you sure?" I asked, suspicious of his last-minute change of plans.

"Absolutely!"

"But I thought you had important family matters you had to deal with."

"I changed my mind," he said. "I'll pick you up at seven."

Nice! I smiled, reflecting on first meeting Gray, not long after my first exhibit. A mutual friend had introduced us, suggesting that Gray, a German American journalist, interview me for a television show about the arts.

He telephoned one evening out of the blue and suggested we get together at a local café. We chatted away, as if old friends, getting to know each other.

He interviewed me several weeks later, attended my second exhibit, and became a fan of my work.

I finished a sculpture of a tall female figure titled *I Am*. Her outstretched left hand reached skyward. Her right hand touched her head, as if she stood thinking on her feet. A space between her full lips made her appear to be speaking. Words of wisdom? Perhaps.

After cleaning up the studio, I went upstairs, poured myself a glass of juice and sat on the sofa thinking about the past year and all the twists and turns of life. Staring at the budding tree outside my window, I reflected on personal change and growth, and jotted down my thoughts.

> *A day to remember, to stop and reflect*
> *challenges, changes, closely inspect.*
> *Life's twists and turns. The ins and the outs,*

the smooth, the rough, the roundabouts.
Growing. Becoming the best I can be.
Sharing with others the unharnessed me.
Time is the essence, the substance of life.
Life's the illusion, we continue to splice.
A beginning, a middle, a climax. THE END?
Hey, hold it a minute. Did that frame just bend?

I laughed when I finished writing the last line.

The buzzer announced Gray's arrival. I ran downstairs to let him in.

"You're not ready," he said, seeing me in jeans and a sweatshirt.

"It won't take me long to change clothes. Come on in."

"But we'll be late," he said.

"No hurry. It's my birthday! How about a glass of bubbly?"

I returned with a bottle of champagne and filled our glasses.

"Happy birthday!" Gray said, raising his glass to mine.

"Thanks for celebrating it with me." I clinked his glass.

"Where would you like to go for dinner?" he asked.

I grinned. "Look, I know what's going on," I said. "I know about the party."

"Party?" he asked, trying to look dumbfounded.

"The surprise birthday party for me."

Gray shrugged his shoulders, shook his head, and smiled.

"So, I've planned a surprise for everyone," I announced. "Time to rock and roll."

Gray drove up and down several streets, looking at street signs and addresses. He acted as though he was lost.

"Funny, we're blocks from any restaurant," I said, as Gray parked the car in a residential neighborhood near my apartment.

"I need to stop at a friend's place and pick up a book I left behind. We can walk from there."

Right, I thought, smiling.

As we entered the walkway to the building, I recognized Serena's house. I stopped Gray and asked, "You left your book at Serena's place? Why, that's convenient."

He rang the doorbell. The downstairs door was ajar. He pushed it open, and motioned me inside. We climbed the stairs to Serena's first-floor apartment. It was dark.

All was quiet. I listened. "Whispers," I said, smiling and nodding.

The front door clicked open a crack. He motioned me forward, into the dark apartment. I could hear people breathing.

"Surprise! Surprise!" My friends shouted. "Surprise!"

The lights went on. "Happy birthday!" they chimed in unison, beaming.

I smiled, looking at the beautiful faces of my friends all around the room.

One button at a time, I opened my cream-yellow London Fog raincoat. Unbuttoning the last button, I threw the coat wide open and showed my naked body.

"Surprise! Surprise!" I whooped, flashing at them. I grinned, prancing past. A loud gasp filled the room. A hush fell over the place.

Someone broke the silence, "Oh, my God!"

Diane giggled and waved. "Go girl!"

"Touché!" someone else shouted.

Michael howled laughing. "You can dress her up, but you can't take her out."

My friends looked shocked, definitely surprised. They shook their heads, laughed loudly, applauded, and gave me a thumbs-up.

Diane's husband, Steve, asked, "Can you run that past me again?"

"Sure," I said, opening my raincoat and flashing them again.

"Stunning!" Michael said.

"Where's my camera crew when I need them?" Gray asked.

"Lordy, lordy! You go girl!" Rosetta said, laughing herself silly.

I took a bow, then headed down the hall to the bathroom and changed into a party dress.

When I returned, the room erupted in laughter and applause again.

The dining table was laden with a buffet of my favorite foods. Michael handed me a glass of champagne.

Rosetta led the group in singing "Happy Birthday to You."

"Hey, Sue girl, what ever gave you that idea?" Diane asked later.

"I've always wanted to do that," said Serena. "But never had the nerve."

"My aunt gave me the idea this morning when she telephoned."

"Your aunt?" Julie asked.

"Yes, I told her I thought my friends were planning a surprise party for me. She asked if I would wear something special, and I remembered I owned a special suit."

"Your birthday suit?" Marti laughed.

"Easy decision. It didn't require pressing," I said.

The roomful of friends cheered again, and we moved and grooved to the music of the Bee Gees, the album featuring "Stayin' Alive."

"Ah, ha, ha, ha," we sang along.

CHAPTER 27

MAINHATTAN

Frankfurt, Germany—1979

"Carlo says Frankfurt's nickname is 'Mainhattan,'" Michael announced, as we sat waiting on Apfelwein and steak tartare.

"Because of the skyscrapers? I thought it was nicknamed Bankfurt," I said.

"It's the financial center of Europe with banks and the stock market. And like Manhattan, it's an international, multicultural metropolis."

"Is Carlo the cute banker who works for Commerzbank?"

"No, he's the gorgeous banker who works for Commerzbank." Michael placed his hand over his heart.

"You've got it bad."

"And he's baaad." Michael baaed like a sheep.

"I'm glad it's a city that invests in culture. Otherwise, I might not be having another exhibit with the Stadt."

"Your batik sculpting will be exquisite on display in the Römer museum."

"It's exciting to explore a new medium. How did you and Carlo meet?"

"The Grüneburgpark. A good pickup place."

"One moonlit night?"

"Broad daylight."

"I thought Grüneburgpark was for joggers."

"We were jogging."

"In your pin-striped suits?" I asked.

"Only briefly! Carlo always says, 'Life is to be livid.'"

"My Israeli friend Ronit says 'livid' instead of lived. And she says 'closes' instead of clothes. I smile and never correct her. I love hearing foreigners speak English."

"Carlo's accent makes English sound downright sexy."

"It's amusing the way information is translated."

Michael smiled."I remember a sign I saw once in a bar in Japan. It read, *Special Cocktails for Ladies with Nuts.*"

I laughed. "I remember a newspaper ad from *The Ceylon Daily News*. It read, *Chickens for sale! 140 Hens, 2½ years at Mental Hospital.*"

"I've seen some real doozies in my travels," Michael said.

The waiter appeared with our order.

"*Wunderbar,*" Michael said.

"My favorites," I replied.

Michael ordered another *Apfelwein.*

"Is there anything you don't like about Carlo?" I asked, after the waiter left.

"He's a bit uptight sometimes," Michael said, "so I have to help him relax."

"You're good at that."

"Tell me about the tourist film you're starring in."

"I'm only an extra. I'll be lucky if I get to speak a few lines. My first shoot is tomorrow morning. It's an interesting idea for a film though. It's based on illusion. Potemkin Villages."

"Sounds very interesting," Michael said.

"A busload of international tourists think they're seeing authentic rural villages when in fact they're seeing painted facades that collapse after the tour bus moves on.

"Clever ruse! Government props up images to hide unpleasant realities."

The Frankfurt Stadt gave the film director a list of English-speaking artists living in the area. The director wants us to make up our own lines as arrogant, sightseeing tourists."

The waiter arrived with our drinks and food.

"Diane and I went to Amerika Haus last night to hear Erica Jong speak," I said. "She's promoting her new book, *Fanny.*"

"Erica of 'zipless' fame?" Michael asked.

"That's the one. I think she hit the nail on the head with *Fear of Flying.* My sexual experiences continue to teach me about myself. It was an interesting evening, hearing her speak and answer questions. I became a bit turned off when she described her joy at having a daughter instead of a son. I thought, she's doing exactly what men do when they brag about having a son to continue the family name. I expected her to pass out cigars."

"Or cigarillos. So you weren't impressed?"

"I'm impressed with her accomplishments. She's quite egotistical though. So tell me, were you impressed with Gray?"

"Gray?" Michael asked, hesitating.

"Yes. Gray. You met him at my birthday party and chatted with him."

"He's intelligent. Charming! A bit too curious though."

"He's a journalist. Of course he's curious."

"Asked me lots of questions about you and Charles."

"Charles? Why would he ask about Charles?"

"He knows him. He knows about Cyprus."

"You're kidding! He's never mentioned knowing Charles to me. He knows we're divorced. He knows what I've told him about Cyprus, but he doesn't know that I think Charles was involved."

"He's umbrageous." Michael loved fancy words.

"As in shady?" I asked.

"Yes. Full of shadows. Not Mr. Right for you!"

"You think he's married?"

"Yes. But he might tell you otherwise. He wants to get to know you better."

"Why?"

"Charles. Cyprus. I think someone thinks you're writing about Cyprus."

"Maybe one day. For now, I'm working on my art."

"Did you and Charles ever talk about putting the Cyprus story out there?"

"Friends encouraged us to tell our story, right after the war. I did research and we talked about it. When someone in the film industry offered to meet and discuss it as a possible film, Charles said a flat-out 'no!' When I asked him why he didn't want to tell the story, he refused to talk about it."

"Another reason to believe he was involved?"

"Yes. It was obvious that he couldn't talk about it. Shortly after that, we left for Sri Lanka for 'pleasure yachting.'"

"I can see the chemistry working between you and Gray," Michael said.

"He invited me to go skiing with him next weekend."

"No harm in that. Just keep your eyes and ears open."

"I will. By the way, after listening to Erica Jong's talk last night, I had a wild-horse dream. Same dream I used to have as a child. In the dream, I'm a wild pinto running free across the Arizona desert—gracefully galloping across the plains, jumping over sagebrush, and racing up the side of rocky terrain."

"Horse dreams indicate you're allowing your emotions and sexuality free rein. Did the horse in your dream speak?"

"Neighed a lot!"

"That's the voice of your unconscious. Excited cry of a wild one. Dreaming and taking time to reflect on your dreams is important. Wish I remembered more of mine. They're not as interesting as yours."

"How can you know if you don't remember them?"

Michael raised his eyebrow, and two fingers, signaling the waiter for more drinks.

A distinguished-looking businessman approached our table. As he neared, I recognized him. He smiled.

"Jurgen," I said. "What a pleasant surprise! I thought you were in Madrid this week."

"Change of plans," he said, bending down and kissing my cheek. "Darling, how are you?"

"I'm fine. Nice to see you. Would you like to join us?" I motioned toward Michael. "I'd like you to meet my good friend Michael. He's the friend I've told you about."

Jurgen stopped and stared wide-eyed at Michael, obviously shocked.

Michael looked up and smiled. "Hello, Jurgen. Please join us."

"No, no," Jurgen protested. "I've got a meeting." He quickly turned and walked away, and out the door.

"Wow!" I said. "That's weird. He's in a real hurry. I was hoping you'd get to know him."

"Obviously uncomfortable," Michael said reaching for my hand. "Susan, I know Jurgen."

"You do? How? I just met him a few weeks ago."

"I know. When you told me about Jurgen, I hoped and prayed it was a different one. After all, there must be at least two million Jurgens in Germany."

"What are you telling me, Michael?"

Michael hesitated, but said, "I also know Jurgen intimately. I'm sleeping with him as well."

"Oh, my God. What a shock!"

"For me as well, sweetheart," Michael said, still holding my hand. "Jurgen is a typical, married European male. AC/DC."

"He's married?" I asked.

"That's what he told me."

"He told me he's divorced."

"Well, at least he gave us the same name to use."

Stunned by the news, I shook my head in disbelief. "Mind boggling," I said.

"Are you all right?' Michael asked.

"Yes, I'm fine. How about you?"

"No problem for me. Just a trick."

"A treat for me. He's a very sexy man."

"I'll walk you home," Michael said as he signaled for the bill.

"A good idea!" I said, offering to pay my share.

"Heavens no. We talked business, didn't we?"

"Of course. Banking business," I agreed.

A cold wind hit us as we exited the Weinstube.

"How about stopping by the Balalika?" Michael asked. "I want to show you something there."

"Sure, we'll surprise Rosetta."

"The world is full of pusillanimous people," Michael said, taking my arm. "People lacking the courage to be honest with themselves and others. As a result others get hurt. You've taught me about courage. So much so, I've decided to quit my job and start writing."

"Quit your job?" I stopped walking. "Wow!"

"I'm in the planning stages, building a nest egg."

"That's wonderful!" I said, reaching up and kissing his cheek. "From what I've read of your work, you're a talented writer."

"So far my life is just a rough sketch of what it could be. An inchoate idea, not yet developed. The more I listen to Peter Allan sing 'I Could Have Been.' I find myself wanting to be all I can possibly be in this life."

"Michael baby, how're you doing?" Rosetta greeted Michael as we entered the club. "A nice surprise. It's been a while."

Michael gave her a big hug. "Good to see you. I've been traveling."

"How're you doing girlfriend?" she patted my arm.

Michael told her about his recent business trip to England and about his plans to quit his job and write.

"How exciting! Will you stay in Germany?" Rosetta asked.

"Not sure. Time will tell."

"I hope so. If it's where you need to be."

Rosetta brought us drinks.

"I hope you haven't repainted the men's room," Michael said.

"Heavens no! Why would I do that?" Rosetta asked.

"Glad to hear it," he said. Excusing himself, he headed for the men's room.

"Why on earth would I paint the men's room?" Rosetta asked me, puzzled.

"No idea," I said.

When Michael returned, he motioned for me to follow him.

"Best graffiti in the world," he announced, "You'll have to sit down to see it."

"Sit on the men's toilet?" I asked.

"Yes. It's written on the bottom part of the door."

"What if someone needs in?"

"I'll stand guard."

I turned on the light switch, put the lid down, and took a seat. When I found the graffiti Michael referred to, I laughed out loud. Scrawled in deep-purple bold letters, it read:

'FUCK ME! BEAT ME! MAKE ME WRITE BAD CHECKS!'

When I came out of the men's toilet, Rosetta stood waiting her turn to get a good laugh. She said, "Lord have mercy" between bouts of loud laughter.

"That reminds me of our friend Theo. What do you hear from him?" Rosetta asked me.

"He loves living in Vienna," I answered

"Who wouldn't?" Rosetta questioned. "Is he still acting?"

"He is. I'm planning to visit him soon and hoping Michael can join me."

"Gotta see Vienna before leaving Europe," Rosetta told Michael.

"To Vienna!" Michael said, raising his glass.

CHAPTER 28

FOG

Frankfurt, Germany—1979

Gray telephoned often. He always had a good excuse for stopping by or getting together. What started as a friendship quickly turned into something more intense.

As the relationship evolved, my candid conversations with Gray about creative projects propelled my work forward. He became my number one fan and always appeared eager to discuss my latest ideas.

Unlike Charles, who never once asked about my art. And unlike Charles, Gray said he cared about my well-being—physically, mentally, spiritually—and appeared in tune with my needs.

My dreaming increased, and I kept a dream journal on my bedside nightstand. Some dreams inspired me with fresh ideas for art, while others warned me of impending dangers. Through these I recognized uncomfortable realities.

Since I knew I had nothing to do with the unraveling of Cyprus, I felt free to talk to Gray openly about it—in my ongoing search for the truth. He often brought the subject up, but only when we were away from my apartment.

One afternoon as we sat together on the couch in my living room, I mentioned I thought the US and Israel were involved in the Cyprus affair. "What do you think?" I asked him.

He sat silent, looked surprised by my question. Instead of answering, he placed his fingertips over my lips, suggesting I don't say more.

"It's a nice evening. Let's go for a walk," he suggested.

Seeing his serious look, I nodded. "Good idea!"

We grabbed our jackets and began walking. We strolled in silence for several blocks.

When we stopped in a park near my apartment, he answered my question. "I think you're probably right about Cyprus. But your apartment may be bugged. Let's only talk about Charles and Cyprus when we're alone and outside."

Startled at the thought, I looked long and hard at him. "Why would anyone bug my apartment?"

"Probably has something to do with Charles and Cyprus."

"But we're divorced."

"You weren't when you lived in Cyprus with Charles."

I let his answer sink in, and studied his facial features for a few minutes. "It's strange," I said.

"What?" he asked, looking at me.

"You and Charles have that same foreign look. You could be any nationality. Italian, Lebanese, Israeli. Well, not Chinese."

He placed his index finger tips on the outside corners of his eyes and stretched them out resembling slits.

"Me no look-a Chinese?" he asked.

"No. No Chinese," I laughed.

"So you've done research on Cyprus," he said.

"I did, after the war. Spent hours collecting bits and pieces of the puzzle."

"Are you planning to write about it?" Gray asked.

"Just searching for the truth."

"Do you still have the research material?"

"No, I gave it to a friend for safekeeping."

"I'm surprised Charles didn't want it."

"Oh, he did. But I refused. It's my research."

"What do you hear from Charles?"

"He lives in Hong Kong with his new German wife."

"Who does he work for now?" Gray asked.

"An ad agency. They're expecting a baby soon. Did I tell you about the baby dream I had?"

"Don't think so."

"In my dream, I sat across from Charles's wife and baby on a train. The baby looked just like me. The wife glared at me and said that Charles had a hissy fit when he saw the baby looked like a miniature me."

"That's a strange but funny dream."

"I woke myself up laughing."

Gray chuckled.

"Speaking of strange dreams," I said, "I had one about you the other night. You were crawling around on hands and knees in a freshly painted child's room, picking up wooden block pieces and arranging them in a certain order."

"A wooden puzzle?"

"Yes. You were concentrating, inspecting and turning each piece carefully. Only after a through inspection did you put a piece firmly into place."

"Did I have on diapers?" he asked, laughing.

"No, you wore a dress suit and tie."

He nodded. "I have puzzle dreams often."

"Since I had the dream, perhaps I'm the one stuck in a puzzling life situation? I had an interesting dream one night while visiting Capri. In the dream I sat reciting a poem while rocking a baby to sleep. The next morning, the poem was stuck in my head and I grabbed a note pad sitting near the telephone in the hotel room, and wrote it down. When I removed the note from the note pad, I noticed a star shape. It reminded me of a puzzle piece."

"A piece of a puzzle?" Gray asked.

"Yes—the missing piece to complete the puzzle."

He suggested we head back to my apartment. While walking back, I asked Gray how a double agent works.

"Double agents spy for two different governments."

"Right. Like Mossad and the CIA?"

"Yes, and often transmit disinformation used in counter-espionage operations."

"They pass along useless information? Lies?" I asked.

He nodded yes. "Sometimes."

"How do they get recruited?"

Gray stopped in his tracks, surprised by my blunt questions.

"I need to know," I said. "You know all about the business."

"I'm just a journalist." He smiled.

"So how do agents get recruited?"

"Some approach foreign intelligence agencies and offer information."

"They just walk in and tell what they know?" I asked.

"Yes."

"And others?"

"Others get 'spotted' when the agency identifies people who appear to have access to information on a regular basis."

"Someone who visits military bases on a regular basis?"

"Yes. And someone who knows technology, and speaks foreign languages."

"Oh," I said, nodding my head.

Several days later, Gray stopped by for a drink. I prepared a tray with cheese and crackers, and poured two large glasses of wine. We sat and sipped together.

"Are you married?" I asked, and watched him squirm and almost choke on a piece of cheese.

He hesitated. "My family life is difficult to explain," he said. "My wife and I share a long and complicated 'East-West history' together. Divorce is out of the question."

"Are you Catholics?"

"No. It's more complex than that."

"Not explainable?"

"No."

"Does she know about us?"

He hesitated again. "I'm sure she does at some level. She knows every-thing about me."

I sipped more wine and thought about his evasive answers to personal questions.

"Shortly after Charles and I divorced," I said, "I received a letter from him telling me he had to divorce me because I asked too many questions."

Gray smiled. "You certainly do that."

I often felt Gray's presence before he arrived at my front door, even though we hadn't made previous plans to get together.

"Sometimes," I told him, "I feel we are mirrors for each other. Showing the good, the bad, the ugly. Although the mirror never lies, it doesn't always tell the truth. Because sometimes we hide the truth from the mirror."

He nodded in agreement.

"Perhaps we knew each other in a previous life. If you believe in woo-woo."

"As the matter of fact, I do," he replied.

One night, several weeks later, I awoke from a dream in a sweat, feeling chilled. I felt Gray's presence beside me, stroking my cheek. His London Fog raincoat dripped water on me. I turned on my bedside light and the vivid image faded. I wrapped a robe around me and wrote about the chilled, wet feeling.

> *Your thunder shakes me wide awake.*
> *Your raincoat drips, I shiver and shake.*
> *You stroke my cheek, as you sit near.*
> *Please understand, your message is clear.*
> *I agree, and wipe the storm from your face.*

Erase the fears, my fingertips trace.

When I saw Gray several weeks later, he apologized for being out of touch and said he tried telephoning me one rainy night from London.

"London?" I questioned him. "You were in London?"

"Yes, on business."

"I'm stunned," I said. I got up and retrieved my dream journal from the bedside table. I showed him the poem.

He read it, over and over. He shook his head, and said, "Spooky!"

As we sat on a bench in a park another evening, I shared the bizarre dream I had years ago, about Charles being in Sofia, Bulgaria, with a strange woman.

"You saw the event as it happened?" he asked.

"Yes. Charles later admitted he had an affair with a stewardess from Sofia. This while I was lying in bed eight months' pregnant in Cyprus."

This led to a long discussion about "sexpionage."

"I remember reading about the Profumo scandal in the early sixties in Great Britain. It brought the Macmillan government down," I said.

"Because it involved the Secretary of State for War," Gray said.

"Christine Keeler. The cabaret showgirl. Sleeping with Profumo and at the same time sleeping with the naval attaché at the Soviet Embassy."

"And passing British defense secrets to the Soviets."

"It caused quite the stir in London town. Another married man bit the dust."

"If Charles is an agent," Gray said, "he was probably spotted when you lived in Israel."

"If he was, I wasn't aware of anything unusual happening."

"He's Jewish, intelligent, a linguist, an electronics engineer. Perfect."

"He denies his involvement in Cyprus and even wrote an article about not being a spy."

"Did it get published?"

"No idea. He sent me a copy of his original writing."

I continued working on my art and teaching computer classes on American bases and in international company offices around Europe.

I took my friend Rosetta with me on a trip to a Canadian base in southern Germany. That evening we drove across the border to France for dinner in a three-star French restaurant.

We talked about fine dining in France versus good dining in Germany. "The French have a way to make everything taste divine," Rosetta said.

"Even frog legs and slugs," I added.

"Snails," she corrected me, smiling.

"Of course. Even slugs would taste good in a French butter sauce or in flaky French pastry."

"True." Rosetta laughed. "How's your banker friend?"

"Which one?"

"The sexy one with the big eyes and large sensuous lips."

"He's fine. We still get together sometimes."

"If I were you, I'd be getting together with him all the time."

"He's a playboy. Plans to get married soon and still screws around. Not my idea of good mate material."

"Have you heard from Dan lately?" Rosetta asked.

"He telephoned me last week. He's getting married."

"Go on girl, not Dan?"

"Yes, Dan. He's marrying the gal he's been living with forever. He's a good guy. I wish them luck."

"Are you still involved with Gray?"

"Yes, but his complicated personal life is taking its toll. Need to let go. Even my dreams tell me so."

"Girlfriend, whatever you do, don't give up this part-time job. I love coming to France with you."

The next morning, over breakfast in our hotel, I noticed a large black poodle sleeping quietly under a nearby table while his owners enjoyed their coffee and croissants.

"Europeans are so civilized when it comes to allowing pets in restaurants," I commented.

"Dogs are certainly quieter than babies."

"He looks like your dog Jet. He's well trained."

"Or dead." Rosetta laughed.

"Someone once told me about a woman who visits London often and takes her little dog with her."

"England? They have strict quarantine laws."

"I know. So she gives him a sleeping pill and then wraps him around her neck like a fox stole and they wave her on through."

"Lord have mercy." Rosetta laughed. "A wrap dog."

"Must be a German spitz. They're small."

"My Jet's way too heavy for that. Lordy, I could break my arms and neck trying to get him wrapped."

We shared a big belly laugh, finished our breakfast, and drove home to Frankfurt.

We discussed people, places, and things which help move us forward in life and those that hinder or delay our progress.

When I dropped Rosetta at her place, she thanked me for taking her along. "Let go of whatever doesn't work in your life. Except for trips to France."

I assured her I wasn't ready to give up French cuisine anytime soon. "Especially escargot."

That night I had a disturbing dream about being lost in the woods with Gray.

*We wandered around for hours on an overgrown path, getting
ourselves deeper into a thicket and dark forest. The farther we went,
the more lost we became. Finally we came to a fork in the path. I felt
certain the left fork would lead us out. Gray said he felt exhausted
and would wait for someone to find us. I told him we could die waiting to be rescued. I said I would take the left path and find the way.
After walking a short distance, I saw a clearing. When I stepped into
the clearing, I recognized the surroundings. I knew exactly where I
was and where I needed to go. Excited, I returned to lead Gray out
of the woods, but he had disappeared into the fog of night.*

The next morning I replayed the disturbing dream in my mind. I immediately telephoned Michael and invited him to lunch to discuss the dream.

Over lunch, I shared the dream details.

"How did you feel when you were in the middle of it?" Michael asked.

"Lost. Worried. But I knew I'd find a way out if I listened to my gut
instincts. And the minute I saw the left path I knew I needed to follow it,
even if it meant leaving Gray behind."

"How did you feel when you made it out of the woods?"

"Happy!"

"Describe the different paths."

"The path Gray and I were on together was not clearly defined. It was
overgrown and rocky—difficult to navigate. Similar to a maze. The left
path I chose to get out of the woods, was smooth, easy to move on."

"How do you feel now?"

"Relieved. Fortunate to believe in dreams and to listen to mine. They've
been warning me to move on alone, for some time.

"Last week I had a dream about living with Gray in New York City, in a
lovely high-rise apartment. I decided to go for a swim in the building
pool. When I entered the elevator, I became aware of a putrid smell and
saw smears of brown on the walls and stains on the carpet.

"The elevator man said a friendly 'Good morning' and smiled.

"I held my nose to ward off the smell, and asked him if he smelled the shit.

"'It's always smelly,' he said, surprised that I hadn't noticed the stench before.

"When the elevator doors opened to the pool. I disrobed and dove in. When I surfaced at the other end and opened my eyes, I saw dozens of turds floating in the water. I screamed and thrashed, and quickly climbed out of the pool

"A barman offered me a cool drink. I shook my head no and pointed to the filthy pool. He shrugged. 'No more than usual.'

"I ran down the emergency stairs to our apartment and quickly unlocked the door. I took a long shower to cleanse myself of the crap."

I stopped talking and sat still for a long time. "It's not a healthy, honest relationship," I finally said.

"Perhaps it's run its course," Michael suggested.

"It has."

"Someone is trying to find out how much you know about Cyprus. Is it possible Gray's a plant?"

"It's possible. But Charles never told me anything. I only know what I feel."

"Perhaps Charles kept you in the dark to protect you."

"I think Gray is doing the same."

"Probably is. Have you contacted Theo about us visiting him in Vienna?"

"Yes. *Arsenic and Old Lace* opens on the first of next month. Theo's playing the role of Mortimer's insane brother. A perfect role for him," I said.

"Fun! Let's attend the premiere," Michael said.

"Great! I'll make the arrangements."

CHAPTER 29

GET CHECKED

Vienna, Austria—1979

Clickety-clack, clickety-clack. I listened to the rhythmic sound of the train wheels moving along the track as we glided toward Vienna. Michael sat sleeping in the window seat opposite mine.

The train picked up speed, and I watched the Austrian countryside fly by.

Michael stirred and turned his face to catch the sun.

Reflecting on my love for Michael, I smiled. *A dear friend! Handsome! Intelligent! Witty! A good travel companion, too.*

Michael smiled a sleepy smile, eyes half-shut, as if he heard my thoughts.

"The Austrian countryside is beautiful," I said, seeing Michael's eyes open. "Castles, vineyards, cattle grazing, and quaint sleepy towns."

"Certainly put me to sleep," Michael said, sitting up straight. "If only I'd been born straight. I could fill you with dancing sperm and we could make a child together. That would make my folks happy."

"Only if we got married in the church and raised cute little Sunday School kiddos," I reminded him. "Theo is looking forward to meeting you. I'm sure you two will hit it off."

"He didn't want to meet me in Frankfurt," Michael said.

"He felt humiliated by his performance."

"It happens to the best of us. I've made some real faux pas on stage. And in daily life. Gaining one's balance, after the false step, is the important part. How long has he been in Vienna?"

"Only a few months. He left Frankfurt after splitting with his mate. He ended up doing some theater work in Amsterdam, until he landed a full-time job with the English theater in Vienna. Glad we're here for his opening night."

"Opening night can be the worst or the best. But it's always exciting."

"Hopefully he won't be too nervous," I said.

"He'll do fine in English. He's a good actor."

"Ah yes! I remember it well. I invited you to Café theater to meet him."

"He played King Lear."

"The show had just started."

"Act I, Scene I," Michael said, "I do know my Shakespeare."

"He said his opening lines in German," I said, remembering.

"Yes," Michael said. "He was doing fine until, 'Inzwischen werden wir bekunden unsere dunkleren Zwecke—' He forgot his lines."

"No wonder."

"The crowd waited patiently," Michael said.

"Wanting him to remember."

"He slipped and said 'Oh, Scheiße.'" I laughed.

"The crowd cheered because he was speaking German."

"And he got back on track by speaking his lines in English until he remembered them in German."

"Even the reserved Germans laughed and clapped for him."

"Unfortunately after that he only accepted roles in English."

"Can't say as I blame him."

The train slowed to a stop in one small village, but soon was up to speed again. Sleepy towns. Vineyards. Zipping past.

"Have you seen the Lipizzaners perform?" I asked Michael.

"Only in films," Michael answered.

"Their stables are smack-dab in the middle of the city."

"Well then, we must see them."

The train slowed again as we passed through a small, dreary village.

"Austrians from small towns sure look sad and serious," Michael said. "Let's hope the Viennese are more lively."

"Oh, they are. Vienna is a vibrant city."

The train slowed to a stop on the track.

"We're getting closer," I said. "Vienna is fab! You're going to love the old stone buildings with tile roofs and chimney pots, the old churches and steeples, the narrow cobblestone streets, the rows of cafés with divine sweet shops."

"Sounds European." Michael smiled. "Too much of a good thing could kill us. Let's OD on chocolate."

"We're almost there." I pointed out the window.

When we arrived, we took a taxi from the train station to our luxurious old hotel located in the heart of Vienna. I oohed and ahhed, pointing out sights to Michael along the way.

"Impressive," Michael said.

"Wow!" I said. "Our hotel's next to the Albertina gallery."

"Only the finest for my confidante."

Unpacking my toiletries, I saw a familiar design on Michael's hand soap.

"I remember this soap from our trip to Greece. Do you carry it with you everywhere?" I asked, pointing to a soap bar wrapped in red and black paper with a picture of a flamenco dancer on it.

"It's Maja soap, named for the beautiful señorita, or maja, fanning herself. I love it. Always buy tons of it when I visit Spain. Smell it," he handed the soap to me.

"The smell is a combination of the best fragrances from everywhere. Carnations, nutmeg, roses."

"It's a turn-on for lovers."

"Perhaps I should use it."

That evening we rented a horse-drawn carriage, with a driver wearing a traditional bowler hat, to take us on a tour. The carriage carried us along the Ringstrasse, the grand boulevard encircling the city center, and delivered us to the door of Vienna's English Theatre.

Entering the theater lobby, I told Michael, "Theo wants us to stick around after the show and attend the cast party. He wants us to meet the stars."

We were handed a program and found our seats.

I looked at the program cover with the title of the play, *Arsenic and Old Lace,* and admired the artwork on the cover. "Fun!" I said, pointing to the graphic of an empty bottle with a lace skull beside it.

"Did you see the film version with Cary Grant?" Michael asked.

"Yes. Hysterically funny."

"Exciting writing. Love the dry, satirical humor. Vintage!"

From curtain up, Theo's supporting role as the insane brother had us laughing throughout the production.

"Amazing how he resembles Boris Karloff," Michael whispered.

"And the star, David Cameron, looks a double of Cary Grant. Handsome guy," I said. "According to Theo, he's the ex-husband of Hildegard Knef, the famous German singer and actress."

"Oh, my! I adore her. She's a good writer too."

Beginning to end, the production was brilliant! During several curtain calls, the audience gave standing ovations. We clapped and cheered extra loudly for Theo's performance.

After the show, the cast mingled with invited guests and the laughter continued. We enjoyed meeting the actors and the production team.

Theo went out of his way to rave about me to David and to let David know that Michael and I were just good friends. I enjoyed David's British wit. But no sparks flew between us.

"A fun evening," Michael said as we caught a cab back to the hotel.

As we passed under an arch of the former Hapsburg palace in the center of the old city, Michael said, "I agree, Vienna is fab!"

"And tomorrow you'll see the Lipizzaners perform live."

"Great!"

"Theo will join us for a late lunch at a small restaurant he recommends near the school."

"Founded in the 16th century, the Spanish Riding School is the oldest riding school in the world," the guide continued. "Originally built for the imperial family, the riders decided to stay on and do public performances when the monarchy ended. It takes many years of training to become a rider."

"Interesting," Michael said. "I didn't know the Lipizzaner breed was originally a war horse."

"And General Patton saved them at the end of World War II."

After the tour of the Spanish Riding School, we watched the famous baroque horses and riders perform their elegant horse ballet. From trots in place to hops on back legs, to fancy pirouettes, their moves were majestically choreographed.

"Awesome communication between horse and rider," I whispered.

"Lipizzaners are natural acrobats," Michael whispered back. "Extraordinary balance and fine motor skills."

"How do they ever learn all that fancy footwork?'

"Many years of patient training."

We sat on the edge of our seats when eight stallions performed together. The Dancing White Stallions looked as if they were floating in the air as they pranced and danced together.

"What graceful creatures," I said, watching their long silver manes and tails swing and sway with their moves.

"What a ceremony," Michael commented as the show ended.

"Beautiful living art!"

Theo sat waiting for us at the restaurant. We congratulated him on his outstanding performance. Obviously pleased with the success of the show, he said, "Not bad. Not bad at all."

"You were fabulous," I raved on.

Theo's first question was, "So what did you think about David?"

"He's handsome, just as you promised. And he's great fun. I thought you were going to invite him to join us for lunch."

"I did, but he had another commitment."

Grinning, I told Michael how Theo always tries to fix me up with handsome men. "When I went to see Theo perform on stage in Amsterdam he tried to fix me up with a tour guide who invited us to see—"

"—Amsterdam by night," Theo finished my sentence. "Well, you're a beautiful woman and he was absolutely gorgeous. Unfortunately not my type. And Amsterdam by night sounded so romantic."

"Until he introduced himself as Heinz 57," I said laughing. "Whatever that's supposed to mean."

"He's spicy," Theo said, "and he said he could get down with the night crowd. So I encouraged Susan to stay on the boat and enjoy Amsterdam by night. I could tell he was a gentleman and I had plans to attend a party at the Mister Leather convention."

"Did that line throw Heinz 57 for a loop?" Michael asked.

"Heavens no," Theo said. "Confirming my gayness encouraged him."

"I stayed for the night tour and enjoyed a bike ride home with Heinz," I said.

"How romantic! Did you have tantric sex?" Michael asked.

"No, nothing sacred," I said. "An interesting man. A writer and quite the scholar. His tour guide gig pays his rent."

Theo walked back to the hotel with us. In parting, he announced, "Volker, my ex, has AIDS. His diagnosis is bad. He's going downhill fast."

"Oh, Theo," I said, "I'm sad to hear that."

"Have you been tested?" Michael asked Theo.

"No, I'm afraid to. I don't have any symptoms yet."

"Pandemic," Michael said. "A very destructive disease."

"If I die, I die. In the meantime—"

"Get checked," Michael suggested, as we said our goodbyes.

We toured the Albertina museum and walked the narrow cobblestone streets of Vienna. Michael took dozens of photos of old stone buildings with their tile roofs and chimney pots, and old churches and their steeples.

I took an amusing photo of a vacuum cleaner accidentally left out in the ballroom of the Schönbrunn Palace.

We strolled past rows of coffeehouses and sweet shops. We stopped at several and definitely overdosed on chocolate.

"In all the world, so far," I announced, "Vienna is my favorite city."

"It's fabulous!" Michael agreed.

On the train ride home to Frankfurt, Michael announced that he would return to the States to write and perhaps do some acting. "This weekend has convinced me it's a must."

"When? Where?" I asked.

"Los Angeles to start. I have a friend there. Paulo, a fellow screenwriter. We met in Spain a few years ago."

"When you were buying a suitcase load of Maja soap?" I asked.

"That's when I first became aware of its magical powers."

"Oh, Michael! I'm happy for you. Sad for me. I'll miss you. How soon will you move?"

"I've given notice and plan to leave within three months. I'll get your box back to you before I leave."

"My box?"

"You know, your 'Cyprus box.'"

"I haven't thought about it in months. I stopped being followed shortly after giving it to you."

"Did you mention it to Charles or Gray?" Michael asked.

"They've both asked several times. Gray wanted to know if I was planning to write about Cyprus."

"What did you tell him?'

"No plans, but who knows. I'm still trying to figure it all out."

Before Michael left Europe to return to the United States, I hosted a surprise dinner party for him. When he entered my dark studio friends yelled, "Surprise!" Michael began stripping.

We encouraged him to "Take it off! Take it all off." He stopped midway and put his shirt back on. "I can't compete with this April Fool," he said, hugging me.

We enjoyed a Mediterranean feast with bottle after bottle of retsina, and danced the night away to Billy Joel's greatest hits. Rosetta and I surprised Michael with an original love song we had written together about the joy of knowing Michael.

Obviously touched, he said, "Thanks for being my family."

"We'll miss you, Michael," Diane said, hugging him goodbye.

"Write when you get work." Serena laughed, kissing him.

"Or when you get published," Julie said.

After other friends departed, Michael stayed on and spent the wee morning hours talking with me about his hopeful next chapter in life.

"Sounds exciting," I said, wiping tears from my eyes. "My life will be boring without you."

"Your life will never be boring," Michael said, stroking my cheek.

"Are you nervous? About the unknown?"

"It's like jumping off a cliff and hoping wings will carry me to a fresh start."

"Your wings will carry you far. Life's too short not to go for the cliff-jumping adventure."

"Promise me you'll visit me in LA."

"I promise," I said, wiping a tear from Michael's eye.

CHAPTER 30

GOIN' STRONG

Frankfurt, Germany—1980

Walking through the noon-hour rush of pedestrians on Niddastrasse past carts and racks loaded with fur coats, I stopped and took a deep breath of the permeating pungency of the garment district of Frankfurt—the area where designers, small retailers, and manufacturers show their fashion wares.

A coat display in a shop window showed a slim style for the new red leather look.

"Entschuldigung!" I apologized, bumping into a furrier pushing a rack.

"Kein Problem," he replied, rolling the newest collection of coats forward.

The smells and sights and a cacophony of sounds bore witness to noon in the hustle-bustle of a major European city.

Beads of perspiration trickled down my forehead. Hot for September. *Have I lost my mind? Lunch with Charles is a waste of time. Especially with my busy exhibit schedule. Hard to believe I've had three successful shows so far this year, and another is scheduled for October at the International Theatre Workshop in Bad Homburg.*

As I pushed forward toward Kaiserstrasse, the massive Frankfurt am Main Hauptbahnhof came into view.

I stopped and admired its sensible architecture—and the effective way German trains always run on time. God knows I'd missed a few, when I'd only been a minute late arriving.

Nearing the restaurant, I replayed yesterday's telephone conversation with Charles.

He said he needed help putting the pieces of the puzzle together. (I wondered how he spelled need. Perhaps k-n-e-a-d?) He mentioned wanting to be friends, and then said he had something important to tell me about Cyprus.

I explained I had no spare time. Besides, no one can solve someone else's puzzle.

He said he would be returning to Hong Kong and insisted we meet for lunch at my favorite Chinese restaurant to discuss the latest on Cyprus.

After a long pause, I agreed. I heard a click and realized he had hung up before I could change my mind.

As the Tse-Yang sign loomed ahead I slowed to a stop. *You can handle it. Take deep breaths.* I pushed the heavy glass door open and stood for a moment in the dark foyer, letting my eyes adjust to the dimly lit restaurant.

Stepping forward, I looked around the crowded dining area for Charles. No sign of him.

A silver-haired man sat alone at a table in the far back corner reading a newspaper. *That can't be him.* The man lowered his newspaper and looked at me, and returned to his reading.

I glanced around the room again. No Charles. *Great! I'll use the bathroom and leave.*

Walking past the corner table, the distinct smell of a Camel cigarette.

The silver-haired man looked up. "Susan?" he questioned, standing to face me. "You look so different. I didn't recognize you." He leaned forward to kiss me.

I stepped back.

"Please," he said, pulling a chair out for me. "It's the short hair. I like long hair on you."

"Thanks!"

"What would you like to drink?" he asked as the waiter approached.

"Chai, green tea."

"May I recommend a perfect wine to go with Chinese food?"

"Just chai."

"A bottle of Dynasty, two glasses please, and a pot of chai," Charles gave the waiter our order. "After moving to Hong Kong, my taste buds changed," he explained. "Dynasty wine pleases the refined Chinese palate."

I nodded.

"So, how are you?" he leaned forward.

"I'm fine," I answered.

"I'm pleased you agreed to have lunch with me."

"A quick one." I glanced at my watch. "Do you like living in Hong Kong?"

"We actually live on an island near Hong Kong on the waterfront."

"Do you still work for the firm?"

"I'm writing a book about dealing with China."

"Trading with China?"

"Yes. It's an exciting time to be there. Countdown time now that Britain and China talks have begun on the future of Hong Kong."

The waiter returned with our drinks. Charles inspected the label, and performed his usual wine-tasting ritual. Nodding his approval, the waiter filled two small glasses with wine.

"I'll order now," Charles said, ordering numerous dishes from the menu.

"I'm not that hungry."

Charles ignored my comment with a wave of his hand and ordered more.

"*Prost*," he said, raising his wine glass.

"Cheers." I raised my cup of tea.

"How are your parents?" Charles asked.

"Still religious! And yours?"

"Still not. My father has cancer and isn't handling it well."

"Sorry to hear that. I always liked your parents."

Charles nodded and reached for a cigarette.

An awkward silence ensued as he lit it and took his first puff.

I stifled a cough.

"I saw your last two exhibits," Charles said.

"You did?"

"Yes."

"Where?"

"In a gallery in London and here at the Amerika Haus. Better than I expected."

"Practice does make one better," I replied. *What a jerk.*

"How many have you had?"

"Five so far. Another one is scheduled for this fall at the city museum."

Charles nodded.

The waiter arrived with steaming bowls of hot and sour soup.

"*Guten Appetit,*" he said, bowing, before walking away.

Charles tasted the soup and announced, "Delicious as ever."

"A bit hot." I stirred my bowl.

"That's why it's called hot and sour," Charles piped in.

I glanced at my watch again, waiting for the soup to cool.

"Are you keeping track of time?" asked Charles.

"A gift from my aunt," I said, admiring my watch.

Charles finished his cigarette and stubbed it out in the ashtray on the table.

"Isn't it interesting that Chinese restaurants always play American music?" I observed.

Charles stopped to listen to Louis Armstrong's famous version of "Hello Dolly."

"You're lookin' swell, Dolly," Louis sang.

"It's nice to have you back where you belong," Charles said, reaching his hand out to touch mine.

"Oh, please." I pulled my hand away. "Have you had a fight with the wife?"

The waiter returned with a tray laden with steaming dishes of shrimp, vegetables, noodles, a Szechuan-style spicy pork, wonton, and a chicken in soy sprouts with oyster mushrooms.

Charles quickly filled his plate from the assortment. "I highly recommend the wonton. It's as fine as any I've tasted in Hong Kong or Peking," Charles said.

"You should know."

"And I still work for the ad agency, if that's what you mean by the firm. They transferred me to Hong Kong to manage the Far East office."

"Have you mastered Chinese?" I asked.

"Almost."

"You've always been good with languages."

"I only speak four well."

"That's modest, but handy in your line of work."

Ignoring my comment, Charles collected noodles with a twirl of his chopsticks. "Delicious!" he announced, pouring more tea and wine. "Do you still have the research material on Cyprus?"

"No, I got rid of it long ago."

"Really? A smart move."

"Look, I know that International Links is a shell company."

Charles dropped his chopsticks on his plate. "What are you talking about?"

"It took me a while to figure it out. Do you know Gray?"

Charles glanced around the room cautiously, picked up his chopsticks, and continued eating.

"Do you know Gray?" I asked again.

Again, he ignored the question.

The waiter returned to clear empty dishes.

"*Hat's geschmeckt?*—Did you enjoy it?" he asked.

"*Geschmeckt sehr gut,*" Charles said.

"I have good news about Cyprus. You've come into money. The Cyprus government's finally going to settle our claim."

"Whose name is on the claim?" I asked.

"Mine, of course. But half of it is yours. We were still married then."

"We were still married when we had the Swiss bank account, but I never received a franc from it. And we were still married when you withdrew all the money from our US account. I never saw a cent of that either. And I've never received a pfennig from our German account. So why should I expect money this time?"

"I'll make certain you get your share."

"Does this mean you're finally going to pay your half of the divorce bill, as well?"

"I didn't pay the attorney fee because I changed my mind about getting divorced."

"No! You didn't pay the attorney because you wanted life to be tough for me. After you tried to snuff me in Brussels and I walked out—with less than five dollars in my pocket—you thought if you left me penniless I would come crawling back to you. You thought I would miss the moneyed lifestyle. Well, you're wrong."

Charles placed his chopsticks carefully on his plate and reached for another cigarette.

"And," I continued, "I certainly don't miss the smell of cigarettes at meals."

Charles lit his cigarette, took a puff, and looked at his watch.

"Being alone," I said, "has given me lots of time to think. I've discovered that more is sometimes less."

Charles continued puffing on his cigarette.

I stared at the red velvet wall behind him.

Charles asked the waiter for the check and took his wallet out to pay. He opened it to a photo of a child sitting in a stroller. "This is my daughter," he said, showing me the photo.

My eyes focused on a smiling little girl in a frilly pink dress with matching bonnet. "She's—"

Charles interrupted, "I can finally forgive you for not giving me a child."

"What?" I asked, stunned by his remark.

"Yes," he answered.

I took several deep breaths. "The photo of your daughter," I said quietly, "reminds me of a dream I had years ago, when we lived in Brussels. A dream about me pushing a child in a stroller past a snake pit in a garbage dump."

Charles looked puzzled. "You and your crazy dreams."

"You were the child in the stroller. When I awoke, I knew our marriage was over. Broken beyond repair. You were never honest with me and used 'not having a child' as an excuse to end the marriage. If having a child makes you happy, I'm glad for you. I hope you spend time with her."

"I'm gone much of the time with my work."

"Good you have a photo."

"Surely you want children?" Charles asked. "Someone to look after you later in life?"

"Being creative makes my life work. I don't feel anything is missing. I feel fulfilled. If I'm meant to have children, it will happen."

I sat for a moment more, picked up my handbag, pushed my chair back, and stood to leave.

Charles put his cigarette out.

"Thanks for lunch, Charles," I said. "I wish you a good life."

Charles stood, awkwardly silent.

I turned and walked away.

Emerging into bright sunlight, I took another deep breath, sighed, and burst into song. "It's great knowing that I'm growing, glowing, goin' strong," I belted it out, loud and clear, replacing the original lyrics with my own words.

As I sang and danced my way along the smooth sidewalk, I smiled and waved at curious onlookers.

CHAPTER 31

WHY NOT?

Frankfurt, Germany—1981

Michael's departure left me feeling in a state of flux—about my life and its direction. I missed his wonderful sense of humor, his adventurous spirit, and his physical presence in my life. I missed traveling in style as his confidante. Although we communicated often by telephone, through correspondence, and sometimes in dreams, being at Wagner's without Michael was downright boring—like life without electricity. Unplugged. Powerless.

My last art exhibit, a show for McCann-Erickson Advertising Agency, was well received and I felt good about my breakthroughs in batik sculpting. But my creative flow had slowed and I wondered if I'd ever get it back up to speed.

I continued teaching computer classes part-time, and began writing short travel articles about places I visited. Something new and exciting. Putting my adventures into words on paper, telling a story.

Friends invited me to travel with them to Malta. A travel magazine asked me to do an article on the Republic of Malta to showcase its charm.

After reflecting on my father's many sermons from the Book of Acts, delivered from his Pentecostal church pulpit, about Saint Paul's shipwreck and subsequent landing on Malta, and reading about the Megalithic Temples—the oldest freestanding structures in the world—my planned trip sounded exciting. Ah, back to the clear blue Mediterranean Sea.

We arrived in Malta on a beautiful clear day, rented a car, and set off immediately to check out the beach cove near our rental house.

The following day we explored Valletta. Making notes of my first view of Valletta Grand Harbour, encircled by walled fortifications, and the colorful, bobbing fishing boats, I took dozens of photos—historical monuments, churches, domes, medieval walls, ornate coats of arms, colorful gates, wildflowers, stunning statues, and quaint village streets.

The Megalithic Temples spread over large areas of the hills of Malta and according to the guidebooks are older than Stonehenge and the pyramids. I didn't feel anything sacred, but snapped lots of photos of old rocks.

We visited the old city of Mdina. I walked alone down a narrow cobblestone street into the open square showcasing the late 1600s Saint Paul's Cathedral. "Impressive!" I exclaimed, seeing its striking facade and magnificent, painted dome.

Leaving the lavish interior of the cathedral, I stepped out into the plaza and looked at other building facades in the square.

The afternoon light danced on one old, hand-carved wooden entrance door to a shuttered building. I snapped a quick photo of the door and hoped I'd captured its essence.

When I returned to Frankfurt, I wrote my impressions about Malta, and submitted it along with several of my photos to the magazine editor. She liked my article, and to my surprise chose one of my photos to accompany it.

After publication, I saw she had placed the photo of the old, carved wooden door at the top and center of the page. She gave me credit as the writer and photographer. *Not bad, I thought—artist, writer, and now photographer.* It was a beautiful door.

I met Diane and Rosetta at the Balalaika one evening. We chatted about life in general and I shared news from Michael's latest letter. "He's still in LA, still working on a screenplay, taking art classes, creating original woodcuts and making prints from them. He says to say hello."

"Exciting," Diane said.

"I miss Michael. Is he acting?" Rosetta asked.

"No mention of acting. He's involved in an intensive personal development program, called Silva."

"I've heard of that," Diane said. "It's a meditation program to help you visualize and tap into your greatest potential."

"Sounds like a religious experience," Rosetta said.

"Certainly spiritual. He's in training now to teach the method and wants me to come visit him in LA and attend a workshop."

"Are you going?" Rosetta asked.

"I could use a fresh jolt of energy. Why not?"

"Have you heard from Theo since you got back from Vienna?" Diane asked.

"Yes, sad news," I said. "He has full-blown AIDS and is going downhill fast. He's returning to the States to spend his final days with his family."

"Oh, no," Diane said. "I'm so sad to hear that."

"Me too," said Rosetta. "Theo was a talent."

"A wonderful friend, too," I said, shaking my head.

"What about your Israeli friend Ronit? Isn't she coming to see you soon?" Diane asked.

"This week. She arrives on Thursday. I want you to meet her."

"Oh, I'd love to," Diane said.

"Me too," said Rosetta.

"I'll arrange it, lunch or something while she's here."

"So when will you go to LA?"

"End of the month. After Ronit's visit."

"Do you keep in touch with the Cyprus folks?" Rosetta asked.

"A few. They're scattered all over the globe. All reminisce about paradise lost. One American friend from Nicosia stayed in touch for several years. I last heard from her after her boxes of belongings arrived in Philadelphia. Only her nightgowns were missing. She commented that she hoped they improved some Turkish soldier's love life."

"What happened to Ronit's Greek husband?" Diane asked.

"Ronit initially stayed on in Cyprus following the war, searching for him. She eventually found Andreas. His father was held captive by the Turks. His sister was injured and in the hospital. His brother and wife were homeless. The Israeli Embassy found a place for Ronit and the family to stay. Life was tough. Some months later, Ronit decided to return to her parents' home in Israel and wait for Andreas there.

"After several months, she lost all contact with him. She sent many letters, in care of the embassy, but never heard back. Eventually, they divorced and she married an Israeli. They have twin boys. She's happy, loves being a mother, and sends photos of the twins often. Ronit's a real clotheshorse, so I expect her to arrive with lots of suitcases."

"Zsa Zsa." Rosetta laughed.

I met Ronit at the airport. We hugged and kissed, and both laughed out loud when Ronit's five suitcases arrived at the baggage carousel.

"How long can you stay, Zsa Zsa?" I asked.

"Only five days," Ronit said. "My mother-in-law's looking after the twins."

"A suitcase a day? Wait 'til you see my teeny-tiny apartment."

"I don't pay for excess baggage, so I brought plenty. Just in case," Ronit said.

"Did you bring me jars of Greek olives?" I asked, laughing. "Wonderful to see you again. You're as beautiful as ever with your shining dark eyes and hair. Love your fashionable leather pantsuit. You're still a clotheshorse, I see."

After lugging suitcases upstairs to my apartment, I showed Ronit my art studio and my latest works. "For my next exhibit," I explained.

"How many have you had?"

"Six. Working on number seven."

"Wow! You made your dream come true. How did you get your first exhibit?"

"My friend Diane invited me to a restaurant for dinner one evening and introduced me to the restaurant owner. He dabbled in art, and knew many actors and artists who frequented his restaurant, located downstairs from the Frankfurt theater.

"There were a few paintings hanging on the walls, but he expressed interest in getting more to brighten the space.

"Diane suggested using the restaurant walls as exhibit space for artists to show their work. She suggested an opening night to bring new customers into the restaurant. He thought it was a brilliant idea, and asked me if I'd like to show my work there. Needless to say, I was thrilled and quickly said yes."

"That's luck," Ronit said.

"Serendipitous for certain."

I made fresh coffee and we talked for hours about Cyprus, the coup, the war, and the aftermath.

"Although it happened years ago, it feels like yesterday," I said.

Ronit described her long and tortuous search for Andreas, after the invasion, and enduring the second phase when the Turks invaded again in August 1974. "His family blamed me and all foreigners for the war. It was miserable being with them, feeling I had to stay until I found Andreas."

"I'm sure they blamed the American government. I think Charles was somehow involved."

"Unfortunately Cyprus sits in a strategic location—at the crossroads of Europe, Asia, and Africa."

"Cypriots have long suffered and been sacrificed in the struggle of the 'Big Powers' to control influence in the Middle East."

"I still have my scorched purse and charred camera. They're prize souvenirs to remind me how lucky I am to be alive," Ronit said.

"We are lucky. I still have my HMS *Hermes* T-shirt."

"I lost mine in Cyprus."

"Remember our helicopter ride over Kyrenia?" I asked.

"A wild ride."

"Sad to see the destruction."

"But the Kyrenia Castle survived."

"Once again, after thousands of years of foreign invasions."

I told Ronit about seeing Charles at the Chinese restaurant and knowing I would never see him again. "It felt good to close that chapter of my life."

"Do you think you'll ever go back?" Ronit asked.

"To Cyprus?"

Ronit nodded.

"One can't ever go back. And I don't feel a need to."

"Didn't Charles go back?"

"Yes, through Turkey. I'm not sure why. He said he went back for our belongings, but I think he went back to find something he'd left behind."

"What?"

"Something personal. Something important to him. I probably won't ever know. He didn't even tell me he had plans to go. He called from England, after he made it out of Cyprus safely."

"Were you in England?"

"No. In Virginia awaiting his next assignment."

I cleared cups from the table, and suggested we have some wine to celebrate our reunion.

"*L'chaim!*—To life!" we cheered, clinking our glasses together.

"I remember you felt certain the Turks would invade," Ronit reminded.

"I knew they would. My gut said so." I described the dream I had, in the early morning hours before the invasion, where I drove our car down a steep hill and the two right tires flew off. "When I managed to steer it to safety, I knew I'd survive."

"It's a miracle we did. I remember the dream you had in Cyprus about seeing Charles with another woman in a strange city?"

"Yes. Sofia, Bulgaria."

"Was it true? Was he there? Did you ask him about it?"

"Yes. It was true. He later admitted he had an affair with an airline hostess from Sofia, during the time I spent long months in bed—trying to have a baby."

"Charles wasn't honest."

"No, he wasn't."

"And you had another strange dream, just before the baby died."

"Before I was wheeled into surgery. I stood in a dark, cold tunnel. A voice with a small light led me out. It was the same voice which saved my life the night the gas went out on the heater."

"I remember. You insisted on having an autopsy done on the baby to determine the approximate time of death."

"I knew when his spirit departed. I looked at the clock and noted the time. And the autopsy later showed the baby died at that exact time."

"Your dreams are amazing!"

"Cyprus was a difficult time for all of us. And a time of awakening for me."

"It was especially difficult for me financially," Ronit said. "I remember you insisted on giving me money to live on when we said goodbye."

"Lucky I had money on me. I went to the bank and withdrew most of our Cyprus pounds just two days before the war started."

How fortunate you are that the Cyprus government wouldn't allow you to buy the old hacienda."

"A blessing in disguise. Life is often like that."

"Even your marriage to Charles?"

"Yes, my marriage to Charles got me from LA to here. And I like where I am now."

We smiled, knowing we were blessed.

Ronit shared a photo album of her family and pointed to each member as she told stories about them. Her husband, Zvi, the joy of her life, worked as an airplane mechanic for El Al. They met at the Tel Aviv airport shortly after she returned to Israel. "He's everything Andreas wasn't," she said smiling. "We never fight over anything."

"He's smart to let you have your way. Handsome too. Looks European with his reddish hair and green eyes."

"He's an Ashkenazi Jew. His family came from Eastern Europe."

"Your boys are a mixture of you and Zvi. They're adorable."

"Do you have anyone special in your life?" Ronit asked.

"Lots of great friends. You'll meet Diane and Rosetta on Friday. No special man, if that's what you mean. I'm sure it'll happen one day, if it's meant to be."

Ronit unpacked gifts she had brought from Israel.

"It's gorgeous!" I exclaimed, admiring a silver mezuzah necklace designed by an Israeli artist.

"To bless you wherever you go," Ronit said.

Next came two animal drawings from Ronit's twin boys.

"Delightful! I'll frame them and hang them in my studio for inspiration."

Ronit handed me a gift-wrapped package. Tearing it open, I saw a traditional solid brass menorah. "From my mother, to say *toda*—thanks for everything. I know you're not Jewish, but a home needs a candelabrum."

Ronit presented a colorful tablecloth and napkin set. "From me and Zvi."

"Perfect for dinner parties."

"And another one from me." Ronit handed me a large basket filled with goodies.

"Dead Sea Cosmetics?" I said, laughing as I unpacked a mud facial care gift package.

"To keep you looking young and beautiful forever," Ronit said, giving me a hug.

"Ronit, do you remember when Andreas's mother read my coffee grounds?"

She nodded. "I remember it well."

"She said there was a bird in the bottom of the cup, but never told me what it meant."

Ronit hesitated. "I know. She didn't want to worry you."

"So she knew the baby would die?"

"Yes. She told me when a bird pattern appears in the bottom of a cup, it means death."

"She was certainly right about that."

"She read my grounds often, and sometimes refused to tell me what she saw. According to Andreas, she was a master at reading meaning into coffee grounds. Strangers came from faraway villages to have her read for them."

Early the next morning, after breakfast, we crossed the Eiserner Steg bridge, and viewed the Rententurm, a guard tower and the oldest standing building in Frankfurt.

Ronit stopped a stranger passing by. "Can you please take our photo? We're friends reunited after the Cyprus War."

The man smiled, probably not understanding a word except 'photo' and took several shots of us smiling and hugging each other.

We thanked him, and continued strolling through the historic Römerberg. We stopped in the square with its restored houses. I showed Ronit the window where my art had been on display for the Town of Frankfurt. She took several photos of me in front of the window.

We walked along the Zeil pedestrian shopping street and settled on a nice restaurant for lunch.

Again we talked about Cyprus and the war, and how lucky we were to have survived it without a serious life injury.

"I certainly learned about how nature works in time of crisis," I said. "I had just started my period the day before the war started. As soon as the bombs started falling, it stopped. It was as if my body knew it wasn't the ideal time to be menstruating."

"Remember how we all had the shits between bombing runs?"

"Good thing we had multiple toilets in that house."

"Remember the British woman who had gone into labor that morning?" Ronit asked.

"Yes, with her first child. I learned later that her labor pains stopped until we were safe aboard the HMS Hermes."

"I saw her mother on the ship." Ronit said. "She was so happy, knowing her daughter delivered a healthy baby boy within hours of our rescue, and named him Hermes, after the ship."

Leaving the restaurant, Ronit spotted a Hertie department store. "I promised the boys I'd bring toys and clothes from Germany. You know how expensive things are in Israel."

Hours later, we caught a cab back to my apartment. Ronit's new purchases filled several large shopping bags.

"You'll need to purchase another suitcase if you buy anything else," I said.

"No problem. Baggage is free for me."

The next day, we took a train to Heidelberg and visited the old castle. "A breathtaking view," Ronit said, looking down from the old ruin. She asked another tourist to take photos of us together.

We caught a train back to Frankfurt and enjoyed a late lunch and afternoon with Diane and Rosetta at Romanella's Italian Restaurant.

"Your friends are special," Ronit said, on our trolley car ride home.

"My family." I smiled.

As we walked the two blocks home. I remembered something I wanted to show Ronit.

"I have a surprise for you," I said, as we arrived at my apartment.

"A surprise? I love surprises."

I removed a large envelope from my bookshelf, filled with typed pages of writing.

"What's this?' she asked, looking at the stuffed envelope.

"I'm writing a children's book. Slowly but surely it's coming along. The idea came to me a few years ago in a dream."

"A dream? A children's book?" she asked. "What's it about?"

"An elephant and his extraordinary adventures. After Charles and I split, I became quite ill with pneumonia. I was sick for some time, spent weeks in bed. Lots of time to dream and think about life."

"Like Cyprus."

"Yes. And, just as friends there—like you—took care of me then, my friends here looked after me and nursed me back to health. One night, an elephant appeared in a dream. He was standing at the foot of my bed singing a song to me."

Ronit giggled.

"The next morning, I felt better and stronger, and found myself singing the song all day long. I didn't want to forget the words, so I wrote them down in my dream journal."

Ronit nodded and smiled.

"The following night, the elephant appeared again. He had lots of important things to say. I wrote the words down, and was surprised to reread it and see it was all in rhyme."

"Fun!"

"It didn't make sense at the time, but I kept my dream journal handy and anxiously awaited another visit from the singing elephant."

"Did he show up again?"

"Many times. Over the years. And each time, I made notes of our conversation."

"Still in rhyme?"

"Always in rhyme. Would you like me to sing the song for you?" I asked.

She nodded.

I began singing.

> *"An elephant won't forget you when you're happy.*
>
> *An elephant won't forget you when you're sad.*
>
> *'Cause an elephant knows the secret is remembering it all—*
>
> *Learning from the good times, and the bad."*

Ronit clapped her hands together. "Great," she said. "I didn't know you wrote songs."

"As a kid, I used to make up songs all the time. After the divorce, I decided to be open to learning and doing all sorts of things. I've become a Jill of all trades."

"When will your book be finished?"

"Soon, I hope. I did a few batik illustrations, but they're not exactly right for the book."

"What's your elephant's name?"

I smiled, pulling out the title page. *"Peel, the Extraordinary Elephant—by Susan Joyce,"* I said proudly.

"You named him Peel."

"Yes, of course—elephant in Hebrew."

"Oh, my God, now I remember our conversation in Cyprus when you told me about seeing the elephant sign at the Haifa Zoo. You said then—"

"—if I ever write a story about an elephant, I'll name him Peel."

"And now, all these years later, you're doing it," Ronit said.

We shopped every day during Ronit's stay. There would be many gifts from Germany.

By the end of her five-day visit, Ronit had six stuffed-to-overflow suitcases packed for her return flight home. I insisted on taking a photo of her loading them into the taxicab. Of course they all didn't fit into the taxi trunk, so some got loaded into the backseat.

With hugs, kisses, and tears, we promised to stay in touch forever and I waved Ronit goodbye.

CHAPTER 32

DREAMS

Neu-Isenburg, Germany—1984

Katie, a bubbly Brit with red hair and a lively personality, invited friends and family to her home to celebrate a "special" birthday. I explained to Katie that my aunt and cousin were visiting.

"The more the merrier," she said, insisting I bring them along.

Since Katie was my boss at the computer company, we had traveled together on several business trips, becoming good friends in the process. We shared similar views on the spiritual realm of life and often discussed topics such as multisensory perception, death, past lives, astral projection, spirit guides, enlightenment, and visions.

Once I traveled to England with Katie's family to bring a Great Dane puppy back to Germany. Great fun!

Another time, I drove to southern Spain with Katie to spend three weeks in her mother's villa there. One night while there, Katie and I had the same identical vision. We dreamed of seeing her father die in another bedroom in her mother's villa. Years later, he died of a heart attack in that bedroom in the home.

"Ursula! Di!" I exclaimed, hugging Katie's mom and sister. "How lovely you were able to surprise Katie with your visit."

"We arrived from London this morning. I'm sure she expected us to show up. We usually do," Ursula said.

"Couldn't miss her 'big' one," Di added.

"The apartment is beautifully decorated. Did you two have a hand in it?" I asked, pointing at flowers and colorful balloons.

"Several hands," Ursula said.

"My cousin Duvel and my Aunt Wilmoth," I said, introducing my family. "Duvel's touring Europe with his high school choir. They just won first place in the International Choir Competition."

"Impressive!" Di said.

"Congratulations!" said Ursula.

"I'm the chaperone, so I made sure they got plenty of sleep every night," Aunt Wilmoth added.

Duvel smiled and said, "She looked in on my sleeping pillow. We partied every night. Still won first place."

Everyone smiled, including Aunt Wilmoth.

After a catered sit-down dinner, the guests mingled.

I sat at one end of the large dining room table, chatting with a friend. When laughter erupted around the table, I noticed a charming man with boyish good looks, holding court at the opposite end of the table.

The guests seemed captivated with his stories about German civil servants—*beamters*. He told of visiting the German immigration office, on numerous occasions, to get his work permit. Using his wineglass as a prop for the official stamp of the *beamter,* he demonstrated how they used it to officially stamp paperwork several times—to show how many stamps were actually required to make a paper properly official.

With his final stamp and his *"Nur so,"* the stem of the expensive wineglass broke.

Not skipping a beat, he deftly placed the empty bowl of the glass back on the stem, where it remained after he removed his hand. In awe and silence, others sat enraptured by his performance.

I smiled and decided he shouldn't get away with it so easily, so I tapped my end of the table with the palm of my hand. The cup toppled from the stem.

He caught it and placed it back on the stem again.

Again, I nudged the table and the cup toppled.

"Oh, no!" the seated guests groaned.

I smiled. He smiled back.

The party continued and the charming man apologized to Katie for breaking her expensive wineglass.

"Have you met Doug?" Katie asked me, motioning me closer.

"My aunt introduced us," I said.

Doug told Katie how I disrupted his brilliant *beamter* performance.

"I couldn't let you get away with that one," I said.

We laughed.

Katie told Doug about traveling to Gibraltar with me. "The rock apes went ape over Susan."

"The famous Barbary apes?" he asked.

"Yes. They roam free and entertain the tourists. Susan sat down on a stone wall to have me take her photo with the harbor view behind. I counted one, two, three. She smiled, looking very relaxed, when out of nowhere, two male apes sauntered up and sat down beside her."

"One on one side and one on the other," I said, chuckling. "I felt nervous with them sitting so close. They're big apes."

"Did you get the photo?" Doug asked Katie.

"Yes, but more apes kept coming, sitting down near her on the wall, and they all played with their privates," Katie said, laughing.

"Perhaps they wanted their picture taken too," Doug added.

"The guidebook warned tourists not to make any sudden moves, because the apes can become dangerous if teased. So I kept sitting there, trying my best to be calm," I said.

"A crowd of onlookers gathered and started taking photos. The apes continued sitting on the wall playing with themselves. Big as life!" Katie said.

"Probably bigger!" Doug said.

"One ape, sitting next to Susan, played with her long hair with one hand, while he jacked off with the other. A tourist yelled, 'Hey, you got a new boyfriend.' I got a great shot of that one. So great, the local photo place asked if they could make prints of it."

"Finally one ape got up and disappeared over the rock wall. The others followed. The crowd applauded and followed the apes over the wall," I said.

"So, you're a pinup?" Doug asked, smiling.

"With rock apes."

Doug and I chatted and laughed for the remainder of the party. I learned he managed a team of photographers and traveled all over Europe. He learned that I taught computer classes and also traveled.

"Let's plan a rendezvous," he suggested, handing me his business card.

I found my purse and gave him my card.

In parting, we agreed to get together soon.

On the way home from the party, Aunt Wilmoth told me she was quite impressed with Doug. "He's a fine young man," she said. "I hope you get to know him better."

"I plan to," I said.

The following day, I drove my aunt and cousin to the Wiesbaden Cathedral, to attend the final concert of Duvel's high school choir tour.

Early the next morning, I drove them to the airport to catch their return flight to Houston.

"I'll telephone when we get home," Aunt Wilmoth promised.

"And she wants details of your rendezvous with Doug," Duvel said, laughing.

"Only the juicy bits," Aunt Wilmoth said, hugging me goodbye.

"Great being with you two. Love you." I waved them goodbye.

One evening, about a week later, Doug telephoned to invite me to dinner. We met at a local Italian restaurant in Sachsenhausen.

Over dinner, we got to know each other with lots of questions and answers.

"What do you do besides teach computer classes?" he asked. "That's boring."

"I'm an artist and a writer," I said. "I'm working on an exhibit, and I have a fun idea for a children's book."

"Oh," Doug said. "What's it about?"

"A young elephant who wanders away from his herd. Through his travel adventures—some good, some bad—he learns and grows. The idea came to me in a dream. Story of my life. Dreams have always played an important part in my life. So when a singing elephant showed up one night, I decided I'd better pay attention. I began recording our conversations and the elephant kept showing up. So, I kept writing."

"Wow!" Doug said. "I also keep a dream journal, have for years. I find the more I write the more I remember. Are you also illustrating the book?"

"I've done several batik illustrations for it, but with writing and doing the art, it's taking forever."

"Maybe I could do the illustrations. I draw great elephants."

"You're an artist? You do? Show me."

Without skipping a beat, Doug pulled out a pen, tore off a corner of the paper tablecloth, and quickly drew a sketch of an expressive elephant.

"Wow! He looks identical to the elephant in my dream. All his senses are accentuated. Are you serious about illustrating the book?"

"Why not? I love doodling and drawing."

"Great! I'd love you to do them."

"Do you have a publisher?" Doug asked.

"Yes, my friend Alberto wants to publish it."

"I met Alberto at Katie's party," Doug said. "Isn't it strange?"

"What?"

"Of all the dozens of people I met at the party, I only exchanged business cards with you and Alberto."

I smiled. "Alberto made too much money last year and his accountant suggested he invest it. So he suggested investing it in my book project."

"Does he know publishing?" Doug asked.

"No," I replied. "But he is a good businessman."

So we agreed and began a mostly agreeable, but sometimes frustrating, book project together. The more we worked together, the more I liked him. He fit in the vision I had imagined for my life.

I introduced Doug to my friends. He introduced me to the team of photographers he managed.

We often met for lunch or dinner to discuss the book, and to get to know each other better.

Doug had a girlfriend, but no commitment, since she was also seeing an older man. I had several male friends, but all had complicated private lives. Not mate material.

And so, we saw each other more and more frequently.

One Sunday afternoon Doug rang my doorbell. Delighted to see him, I welcomed him in.

"What's that delicious smell?" he asked.

"I'm making duck ala orange."

"Duck à l'orange," he corrected my French pronunciation with a smile. "Are you expecting a guest?"

"No. I make special meals just for me. I like to cook. You're welcome to stay for dinner."

"Are you sure you're not expecting someone special?"

"You!"

"Lucky me."

Over dinner, I told Doug about my friend Michael and my visit with him in LA, and attending Silva workshops.

"I've taken the Silva courses too." He went on to tell me how he went just to prove there was nothing to it.

"A doubting Thomas?"

"Yes, I was skeptical, until I went and realized I could clearly see the individual cases being worked on and knew the exact problem and solution for each."

"It's amazing how focused and aware one can become when we tune out the static."

I cleared the table and brought out dessert.

"You baked this special too?"

"No, I purchased it at the local *Bäckerei*."

We talked more.

"Do you remember last year's air show crash at Rhein-Main?" I asked Doug.

"I heard about it on the news. A Canadian Starfighter crashed. The pilot ejected safely, but the fighter hit a car."

"Yes. I had a meeting scheduled at Rhein-Main that day. If I hadn't listened to my gut feeling, I would have been in or near the plane crash."

"Your intuitive instincts warned you?" Doug asked.

"Yes. I was ready to get in my car and leave, but each time I got to the car a voice told me to go back to the apartment and wait. I thought maybe I had left notes or something important behind. So I kept going back inside and waiting. Finally the voice told me it was okay to go. So I got in my car and drove in the direction of the base. When I got to the roundabout, the road to the airport was closed off by the police. Ambulances were carrying bodies from a wrecked car. A family of five died."

"If you hadn't listened to your voice, you'd be dead."

"Probably."

We talked about places we'd lived. I told him about my Cyprus years, the facts in a nutshell, and showed him photos and souvenirs from my Cyprus box. "I think my ex was somehow involved in the ordeal."

"How?"

"Probably an agent."

"For whom?"

"That's the mystery. Probably for both Israel and the US."

"Aren't they the same?"

"Good point. I was followed for a while. Someone wanted to know how much I knew. Fortunately for me, Charles never shared his other, secret life. I told you about my good friend Michael. He kept this box in his place for safekeeping because Charles kept asking about it and wanted me to give it to him. I refused."

"Are you afraid of Charles?"

"I am. He tried to snuff me once in Brussels, by placing his thumb on my windpipe. After that I never trusted him, because I knew he knew how to kill."

"Good reason not to trust. Whoa! You've had quite a life."

Doug mentioned he had taught art at international schools in England and in Malta.

"Malta? I wrote an article about Malta for a travel magazine," I said.

"You did? When were you there?"

"1981."

"I lived there then."

"Where?"

"In Mdina."

"Mdina is charming."

"Can I read the article?"

"Sure."

I got my writing files out and handed the article to him.

He kept looking at the photo and looking at me. "You took this photo in 1981?"

"Yes. I took dozens of photos while there. It surprised me when the editor chose that one."

"That was the front door of my apartment," Doug said, looking up at me. "I lived behind that door when you took that photo."

"You lived in the square? Near Saint Paul's Cathedral?

"Yes. In 1980-81 I taught art at the International School there."

"Wow!" I sat down and quietly let it soak in. *Unbelievable that I snapped a photo of his front door at the exact time he was living there.* I felt calm, happy all over.

"Good article," he said. "Is Michael still in LA? Still teaching Silva?"

"No, he left LA. He lives in San Francisco now, teaches attitudinal healing at a center there."

"I've read about it. How to let go of fear and embrace love."

"He's coming for a visit with his new 'soul mate,' Marc. They met after Michael moved to San Francisco. At an AA meeting. They'll stay in my studio for a few days, then travel to France. Michael and I used to drive to France often for Sunday lunch. I'm looking forward to meeting Marc and seeing Michael again. I'd love for you to meet them."

"I'd love to. Let's plan on it."

CHAPTER 33

ROSE GARDEN

Frankfurt, Germany—1984

To honor Michael's return to Germany and to welcome Marc into the family of friends, I invited friends to my place for a dinner party one evening.

Serena arrived early in the afternoon to take Michael and Marc with her to a local AA meeting. She assured me they'd return in time for the party. And they did.

Michael and Marc had been sober for a few years, but Serena had been sober for less than a year now.

I had watched her struggle for years, with her repeated efforts to stop drinking. Her problems with alcohol affected her life in a negative way.

As her friend, I talked with her about it numerous times and on several occasions took her car keys away to keep her and others safe.

She always assured me that her car knew the way home.

One evening she stopped by my apartment to chat. She had just come from an AA meeting and wanted to talk about the Serenity Prayer, the Twelve Step Program, and the 'Higher Power' concept.

"Sounds like a wonderful, powerful program," I said.

"Will you be my sponsor?" she asked.

"I can't be your sponsor. I don't belong to the program and I drink."

"I know. They want me to choose someone in the program. But I want you to be my sponsor. I want a positive spirit, like you. That's Step One in the program."

"I do know the Serenity Prayer. I've recited it often in my life."

"So will you be my sponsor?"

"I will. But I'm not going to stop keeping a good bottle of Chardonnay in my refrigerator."

"Oh, thank you," Serena said, giving me a hug.

Serena stopped by my place often, after her daily AA meetings. One evening, seeing my glass of wine on the coffee table, she smiled coyly and asked if she could have a glass of wine too.

"Sure," I answered, "but you'll need to pour it for yourself."

She went into the kitchen and returned a few minutes later with a wineglass filled with water. She sat down, sipped her water while I sipped wine.

"Thank you," she said, smiling.

"I knew you could do it," I clinked glasses with her.

Knowing Michael as a food and wine connoisseur, friends brought Michael's favorite food dishes, wines, and French brandies to the party. The serving table was laden with numerous colorful and diverse dishes.

Serena brought her famous Jamaican beans and rice dish.

One German friend brought *Handkäse mit Musik.*

Another brought a *Spätzle* noodle dish.

Diane brought a white asparagus soup.

"Spargel!" Michael said, "My favorite!"

I had prepared a traditional pork roast with a creamy sauce.

"Soaked in milk?" Michael asked.

"But of course." I said. "It's your original recipe."

"I brought the cake of my ancestors." Rosetta declared, presenting her Black Forest cake.

We laughed, sipped water and wine, dined, and talked long past midnight.

"Marc's a wonderful man," I told Michael, after the party wound down. "You're blessed."

"We're both blessed." Michael smiled. "Feels good to be content. In the past my *raison d'être* was running around, cruising parks and bars, looking for 'Mr. Goodbar' and sexual satisfaction. Marc and I helped each other find and unlock inner happiness."

"It shows in your eyes, your smiles. I'm happy for you." I hugged him.

"I knew Marc was the one for me when we talked dishes and cutlery and showed our prized family collection of china dinnerware sets. We were both missing pieces in our Autumn Roses set."

"Did he have your missing pieces?"

"He had the missing sugar bowl of the set. I had the creamer. I was missing two dinner plates. He had two extras."

"So, you're dish queens." I laughed.

"Two happy dish queens. Happy is a whole different world."

"More balanced."

We smiled.

"Nice to see you looking so content with Doug. He's a keeper."

"He is. We're letting the universe show us where we need to go."

The following weekend, Doug and I met Michael and Marc in the Alsace area of France, at a restaurant near the hotel where they were staying.

Marc raved about the hospitality of the French.

"The French?" Doug questioned. "That's not my experience, but I guess I've only been in Paris."

"The Hotel des Berges staff are very attentive," Michael said.

"We have a view of the Ill River," Marc added. "Illhaeusern is charming."

As we neared the old Alsatian farmhouse building housing the restaurant, Michael read the restaurant sign hanging overhead. *"L'Auberge de L'Ill.* Famous for its food and three Michelin stars."

The maître d' showed us to our reserved table near a window.

"This is the old part," Michael explained. "I always ask for the same table. Lots of memories here."

Since Michael had dined here before, on several occasions, he recommended his favorites—the famed mousse of frogs' legs and the supreme of squab with cabbage and goose liver.

"Squab?" I asked.

"Virgin pigeon," Michael answered, laughing.

"Ah, I get it. Biblical, for young," I said smiling.

Michael nodded yes.

"How's the *Poulet de Bresse?*" Marc asked Michael.

"Best in the world." Michael answered.

We started with apéritifs. Now that Michael and Marc no longer imbibed in alcohol, they took a sip of their drinks, and passed them on to me and Doug.

"As a recovering wine connoisseur," Michael explained to Doug. "I can now get high just sniffing corks."

"We're cheap drunks," Marc said, laughing.

By the time the entrees arrived, 'Bon appétit' had been uttered at least a dozen times.

"*Les Fromages,*" the waiter announced, bringing a tray full of cheeses.

By now, both Doug and I were feeling quite tipsy from all the extra alcohol Michael and Marc passed on.

"For dessert," Michael said. "may I recommend my favorite *La pastilla tiède au chocolat fondant.* And of course coffee comes with petits fours and chocolate."

Impressed with Michael's selection of Chateau Toutigeac 1981 Bordeaux, and equally impressed with the label design, I requested the empty bottle as a souvenir of our time together.

Before we left to drive back to Germany, I asked the maitre d' to take a photo of us under the *L'Auberge de L'Ill* hanging sign.

We hugged and kissed, and said our goodbyes.

"Come visit us in San Francisco," Marc said.

I looked at Doug. Doug smiled.

"We will," I said.

On a cold winter morning, many months later, Michael telephoned to let me know he had tested positive for HIV. "I have AIDS," he said.

"Oh, Michael," I gasped for air. "Is it possible the tests results are wrong?"

"No. I've known for some time, but kept ignoring it. Marc insisted I see a doctor. A cluster of cases have been discovered in California. I won't be here forever. None of us will, not in this body."

I wept. "Oh, Michael."

"I'm okay with it. I've accepted the verdict and figure with the meds I've got at least another year. Maybe two. I'm focusing on all the good things in my life. You. Marc. Friends. I'm determined to make the most of my time this go-round. No more 'I could have been' for me. Plenty of time to finish the screenplay."

"How's Marc doing?"

"Great! So supportive. Glad we chose each other. Getting tested and knowing the results have given us both peace of mind. I was sick for so long with flu-like symptoms I just couldn't shake."

"How long have you been ill?"

"About six months now. I probably contracted it while living in LA. But you know damn well I romped about gardens in Europe for years and never protected myself. We gays called it sexual freedom. Zealots call it our curse. I've had a good life. No regrets.

"I have a wonderful doctor. The medications make me feel sick sometimes, and tired, but they help my T-cell count. Marc and I have joined a gay church called MCC."

"MCC?" I asked.

"Metropolitan Community Church. A home for 'queer' spirituality. Several of our members have died of AIDS. It's a place of support where members help one another during the painful times. People helping people brings joy."

"It sounds like a wonderful church."

"It is. How are you and Doug doing?"

"Fine. The children's book is almost finished, and we're planning a trip together to California. To San Francisco. We'll meet in LA and drive 101 north. To visit you and Marc."

"I'm excited. Plan on staying with us."

"Are you sure it won't be too much?"

"Heavens no! We insist."

Michael asked about Diane, Steve, Rosetta, Serena, and others in Frankfurt.

I filled him in on news of our mutual friends.

"It's okay to tell them," he said. "I need positive thoughts and good energy."

"I love you," I said.

"Susan, listen. It's important. This isn't all there is. No matter what happens, we're connected forever. You're part of my heart. We'll always be in touch. We'll always communicate. Just on a different level. You can count on it. Remember when you received the 'lullaby' poem in a dream?"

"Yes, in Capri."

"You received it because you're open and receptive. Most people limit their existence by clinging to old beliefs. By letting go of the old, you've made room for the universe to give you unlimited gifts of knowledge."

"Oh, Michael!"

"I do have a special request. Will you sing the poem at my memorial service?"

"It's only a poem."

"A heavenly poem. You're the only white woman I know who sings like Mahalia Jackson and has a tight 'black ass.' I'm serious. Will you sing it?"

"I'll sing it," I said, softly starting to cry.

"Just know I'll always be available to answer any question that ever crosses your mind."

"If anyone has answers, it's you, 'Mister Walking Encyclopedia.'"

"Marc and I look forward to seeing you two soon."

"I'll call when we have details of our arrival time."

I slowly put the telephone back in place and sat down on the couch. Not Michael! Why Michael? Maybe tests were wrong. Maybe the blood work got mixed up. He's too young to die. Maybe a cure will be found.

I picked up the telephone and called Diane. No answer.

I thought about this new, strange disease that was in the air—everywhere. It had swept many creative souls into their dusty graves. People I had known for years. Friends and family members became infected. Medical research continued searching for information, but no cure had been found. No treatment killed the monster germs that attacked their weakened immune system. No hope in sight.

I telephoned Doug. No answer.

Thinking of Michael, I could smell his Maja soap. *Fresh. Pure love.* I smiled. Lucky me to have known and loved Michael.

I prepared a bubble bath and got in to soak. I cried and laughed, then cried some more.

I wondered whether we're preordained to meet certain people and visit certain places? Is it random? Fate? Random fate? Are these meetings a result of past decisions and random coincidence? Past lives? Or normal cycles of change in human life?

Some life experiences were like threshold moments. Moments when life propelled me forward and things changed forever, deep within.

Meeting Charles and voluntarily crossing into a new and exciting chapter—taking me far away from my birth family, my culture, and opening my eyes to a bigger world view.

Leaving Charles meant crossing into a dark world of unknown uncertainties where moments snapped from frightening to enlightening, and then back again. A chaos that brought lasting change.

Meeting new friends like Ronit, Serena, Julie, Diane, and Rosetta, and feeling their love and support during my crucial changes made for lasting friendships. My new family.

Knowing and trusting Michael pushed me forward on so many levels, that my perception of life totally changed.

Getting acquainted with lovers. Dan, Trenton, Gray and others exposed my inner desire to explore sex and learn the difference between lust and love—before committing to another long term relationship.

When the water grew cool, I added more hot water and more bubbles, and soaked until my skin had wrinkled.

As a young woman, I had set out to explore, to travel the world. The more I explored, the more I discovered myself. So much of my life followed a serendipitous path of spiritual discovery.

Meeting and getting to know Doug as if the universe designed a unique plan for a more creative, more vivid life.

Or more "livid." I smiled, reflecting on Ronit's favorite expression: "Life is to be livid."

I lifted the bathtub plug and watched the bubbles burst as the water drained away.

I had just finished dressing when my doorbell rang. Doug had stopped by to invite me to dinner.

"Are you okay?" he asked, wide-eyed, hugging me.

"It's Michael. He has AIDS."

Doug held me closer and let me cry into his broad chest. "How is he handling it?"

"He said he's fine, that's he's accepted the verdict and is focusing on the good things in life."

"An amazing man. A great teacher."

After dinner, Doug stayed the night. I lay awake for a long time, my mind racing around thoughts, searching for answers. Images of memories zooming past fast as I tossed and turned.

Doug held me until my breath became steady. We fell asleep taking deep breaths together.

I was visiting a nursing home. Some of the patients sat outside chatting with Michael in a lovely rose garden. As dusk fell, Michael walked with me along a footpath lit by rose-shaped lanterns hung on lampposts.

"I'm the lamplighter," Michael proclaimed, "responsible for replacing burned-out light bulbs." He removed a dead bulb and replaced it with a bright, new one.

The dream flashed me back in time, when I visited Reims, France, with Michael one weekend—shortly before he left Germany to move to LA. We visited the cathedral and were surprised by the lack of people there on a weekend. Michael and I wandered off in different directions.

I stood for some time under a stained glass rose window and found myself mesmerized by the way the raised source of light, from the window, brightened the entire cathedral interior. A force nudged me toward a side altar where candles sat awaiting a light. I lit one prayer candle and felt in awe of the amount of bright light it produced. Since the cathedral was empty of other people, I heard myself softly singing "This Little Light of Mine," a song from my childhood and Sunday School. I vowed to let my light shine brightly to end darkness in the world.

The dream flashed forward to the garden again where Michael continued to light lamps, and continued to instruct me on the importance of being a lamplighter. One light faded and died as we neared it. Michael instructed me to change the bulb. I did."

The next morning, I told Doug about the dream.

Doug touched my cheek and smiled. "Sounds peaceful," he said.

"Peaceful. I felt a warm glow inside and out."

CHAPTER 34

ALL THERE IS?

Los Angeles, California—1985

The *Fasten Your Seat Belt* sign flashed on. Returning to my assigned window seat, I adjusted my seat belt and settled in. I accidentally bumped the arm of the man seated next to me and excused myself.

He nodded and continued writing notes on a pad of paper. Probably heading to an important meeting.

I had hoped to finish another chapter from *Love in the Time of Cholera* by Gabriel García Márquez, but a passage from the book kept echoing loudly in my mind and I found myself reading the passage again and again.

"… that human beings are not born once and for all on the day their mothers give birth to them, but that life obliges them over and over again to give birth to themselves."

I turned the thought over and fell asleep thinking about it.

> *Rush hour had just begun on the Ventura Freeway. Only three o'clock, but commuters were already creeping onto the ON ramps. With luck, I'll be home before four. Elevate my feet, rest, and prepare dinner. Stepping on the gas made cars rush toward me, rather than move my car forward. I felt a sharp pain and a tear, thin fabric ripped inside me. Warm liquid began leaking between my thighs. Oh God, I pleaded. Please, not again. Feeling faint, I slowed the car and brought it to a halt on the road's shoulder.*

"Her temperature is 106," said a female voice.

"I can't get a blood pressure reading," said another.

"Is her doctor on his way?"

I felt a terrible stabbing pain in my stomach.

And like magic, I slipped out of my body. No fear, only calm. The pain disappeared. A golden light warmed me as I floated upside down on the ceiling, watching scenes from my life float by. A piano played a song from my childhood. "Let it shine," I sang along.

Bobbing heads attached to bodies, dressed alike in green gowns, were moving around inside a large white room with shimmering, stainless steel lights. I heard human voices from far below.

Floating down, I saw they were gathered around a body, covered in white on a bed. They moved legs and arms—pushing and pulling the limbs of a body.

"There's no pulse," said one voice.

"Is Dr. Sullivan on his way?" asked another.

"Is her next of kin here?" someone asked.

"Dr. Sullivan's on his way."

"Her husband's in the waiting room."

"Has he been told?"

"We're waiting on the doctor."

They continued to mechanically force the arms and legs to move.

"I'm afraid she's gone," said a voice, sounding exhausted.

The bobbing heads moved away from the body.

Floating down closer, I recognized the body. They're working on me. I need to let them know I'm still here. Still alive!

"What's her religion?"

"Doesn't say."

I re-entered my body. The pain returned. I was lying on a hard bed, in a room filled with spotlights. "Ow!" I said, opening my eyes.

A sea of eyes stared back at me. "Oh, my God!" they murmured in unison.

"I'd like to speak with my doctor," I said, sitting up straight, before slumping back on the bed and falling sound asleep.

"We'll be landing in Los Angeles shortly," a flight attendant's voice awakened me.

"Aaa-ah," I said, adjusting my seat forward to its upright position. I took a deep breath and slowly exhaled.

"No need to feel nervous," said the man seated next to me. "Odds are good we'll have a safe landing."

I laughed. "I'm not normally a nervous flier. It's something about returning to LA."

"Is LA your home?"

"No. Used to be. I was born here."

"A real California native? That's unusual these days."

"We're a rare species. Are you here on business?"

"I live in Burbank."

"Beautiful downtown Burbank?"

"Close. Up the hill. Do you know the area?"

"I do. I used to work in Hollywood, lived in Sunland."

"Just up the hill. Where do you live now?"

"Frankfurt."

"Germany. How interesting. I was stationed at Rhein-Main a few years ago. I loved it. Especially the *Apfelwein Stubes*."

"Frankfurt's a great city. So conveniently located. One can drive to France for lunch."

"And, if one doesn't drink too much good French wine—"

"—one can drive home again," I completed his sentence, with a smile.

"How long have you lived there?"

"Many years."

"Lucky you!"

"It's home."

"Are you here on business?" the man asked.

"I'm meeting my mate. We're driving to San Francisco to visit friends."

"Will you take the Coast Highway?"

"Highway 101 all the way."

"A beautiful drive."

The plane turned a sharp right turn. I looked out the window, searching for clues as the plane circled a blue-gray sky.

"It's normal, flying into LAX," he said. "Guess the pilot had to make a quick move. A go-around. Probably to avoid other aircraft."

"Oh, dear," I said, taking another deep breath.

"A smart move," he said, smiling.

Watching white clouds roll past, I reflected on my near-death experience, and dying. *What happens when we die? The final curtain? Does the mind, and all of our memories, die with us? Does death extinguish our "little light"?*

> *The doctors and nurses had declared me a goner. Clinically dead. My heart had stopped beating. No blood getting to the brain, yet I was still aware of my physical surroundings. An illusion? I remember it vividly. As if it happened yesterday, not years ago. I saw everything happening in the operating room and scenes from my life. Just floating around like a cloud. Out of my body. No heartbeat! No pulse! No oxygen to the lungs. No reflexes. No vital signs!*
>
> *I smiled, remembering the shocked look of the medical team when I reentered my body, opened my eyes wide, and demanded to see my doctor.*

The plane accelerated and ascended. My fingers tightened on the armrest.

"It's okay," the man said. "Planes often circle LAX before landing."

"It's a good thing there's a good cloud show today."

"We'll climb higher and circle back, possibly land on another runway."

"You must fly often to know the landing routine."

"I'm a pilot. It's normal procedure. Flying into LAX is always a challenge. It's the fifth-busiest airport in the world."

"No wonder I try to avoid it."

"Might be a bumpy landing. There's a strong crosswind, whipping the tail around."

"Thanks for the warning! Fortunately, I have a guardian angel," I said.

"A good thing to have. When did you leave LA?"

"1968. After the Watts Riots and the aftermath, I saw life in America in a different light. I worked for Pacific Telephone at the time of the riots, and one morning on my way to downtown LA for a meeting the police stopped my car. Two other telephone company employees were riding with me. A white woman and a young black woman. The police yanked the black passenger from my car, pinned her against it, handcuffed her, and repeatedly banged her head against the rooftop. I screamed at them to stop. They told me to shut up or they'd do the same to me. She had done nothing wrong. None of us had. We were just riding to work. It was so horrible, and so unnecessary. I realized then that justice didn't exist if you were a person of color in LA."

"An idealist? Not always a practical way to view life. Injustices happen everyday, somewhere in the world."

"I know," I said, "but I grew up believing America was different. That we were a 'just society.' After the Watts Riots, the tension in LA became electrifying. Things that had been swept under the rug before were exposed. It became a war zone. Six days of riots, burning buildings, snipers, police brutality. For me, the illusion of a 'just society' was shattered. A song out about that time said it all. 'Is That All There Is?'"

"Peggy Lee. I remember that song."

"She made it a hit. It made me wonder how people in other countries lived. Side by side? In ghettos? Definitely a turning point in my life."

"'Break out the booze and have a ball. If that's all—'"

"Exactly! So my ex and I quit jobs, sold everything we owned, and set off to see the world."

"How did your family and friends react?"

"A mix of admiration and befuddlement. No one understood. They still don't. I knew there had to be more to life, for me anyway."

The flight attendant made the "landing soon" announcement, and I adjusted my seat back to its upright position and looked again out the window.

Miles of freeways. Wrapping over and under each other—like ribbons twisting and turning as one intercepts another. Spotting the intersection of the Golden State Freeway and the Pasadena Freeway, I pressed my head against the window.

"Do you recognize any landmarks?" he asked.

"I think we just flew over Eagle Rock," I said.

"You're right. We did. How long will you be in LA?"

"Just long enough to meet my mate, rent a car and head north to spend time with a very special friend. He's bedridden, but still has his wicked sense of humor. He's in the final stages of AIDS. I look forward to laughing with him again."

"A horrible disease. I know. My mate's also HIV-positive."

"I'm so sorry," I said. "Bless you both."

"Ladies and gentlemen, welcome to Los Angeles, City of Angels," the flight attendant announced.

We gathered our belongings and said goodbyes.

"I wish you and your mate well," I said, as we reached the passenger terminal.

"Have a good visit with your friend," he said.

I stopped in the ladies' restroom to freshen up. While washing my hands, I felt eyes staring at me in the mirror.

A gorgeous black woman, dressed seductively to show off her curvaceous body, smiled at me.

Wow! Must be a movie star. I smiled back.

The other woman winked at me.

I lifted my eyes and observed her strong facial features. *Is it a she? A he? A transvestite?* I continued scrutinizing.

She nodded, applied eyeliner and lipstick, swiveled her hips, adjusted her jeweled belt, and smiled again.

I combed my hair, collected my carry-on, and turned to leave.

Remembering the old Virginia Slims advertising slogan, I stopped and gave her a thumbs-up.

She gave a thumbs-up back.

You've come a long way, baby!

EPILOGUE

After the Cyprus War, I kept in close contact with several friends from my Cyprus days.

Ilene and Syd returned to England and lived in the English countryside, until Syd died of a heart attack while walking down a busy street in London. After Syd's death, Ilene moved to southern France. Their son, Josh, is now a master carpenter in Wales.

Kate and Alex lived in London for a couple of years until Kate became ill with cancer. After Kate's death, Alex returned to the Greek side of Cyprus. He managed a restaurant there. We stayed in touch for years after Kate's death, but eventually lost contact when he remarried. Ilene sent me an e-mail telling me of Alex's death in Cyprus on July 28, 2012. Thirty-eight years after the Cyprus War.

My Cyprus neighbors Beth and Patrick returned to England after the war, but when they retired a few years ago they purchased a summer home on the Greek side of the island.

Their landlord, Sabri Tahir, one of the best-known figures in Northern Cyprus—renowned for his friendship with the novelist Lawrence Durrell, who describes him as a "rogue" in *Bitter Lemons*—went on to become the mayor of Girne (previously called Kyrenia) after the Turkish invasion in 1974. Charles visited Sabri and stayed with him when he returned to Northern Cyprus in 1975. Sabri survived a car-bomb attack in 1990 and a gunshot wound to his leg in 1996 that left him partially paralyzed. On May 10, 2000, at age 76, Sabri was murdered by a former bodyguard while working in his hotel office.

My cleaning gal, Sabrina, stayed on in Kyrenia. I corresponded with her and sent money to feed our cat, Sam. She stayed in touch until Sam died in the early '80s. She assured me he died of old age, not starvation.

Gundy, our German friend, and her husband, Aydin, a Turkish officer, stayed on in the Kyrenia area following the war.

Pete and Paula returned to the States following the war. I kept in touch with them for several years, but after my divorce lost contact with them.

Most of my friends from Cyprus returned to live in their homelands.

To my knowledge, Ronit is still living in Israel. I lost contact with her in the early '90s, but continue to search for her on various social network sites, hoping one day to be in touch again.

The fate of Andreas is unknown. Ronit lost contact with him after their divorce.

From time to time, Ilene shares news of others who survived the Cyprus ordeal.

Cyprus is still divided by a Green Line. Nicosia is currently the only divided capital city in the world. I read recently that Cyprus is the first country in the world to run out of land water. Unfortunately, the ongoing conflict between the Turkish and Greek communities has their political leaders ignoring this drastic situation. The land is dying.

After moving to Europe I made many new friends, and our friendships have survived to this day.

My friend Gertrude, the doctor, died in Frankfurt Germany in 2011. I will always be grateful to her for being my friend and saving my life.

Serena, who introduced me to Gertrude, still lives in Frankfurt and continues to thrive as a musician, mother, grandmother, and AA member. She's now 29 years sober.

Diane and Steve still live in Germany. Diane teaches art and English. Steve, a world champion poker player, often travels to the Turkish side of Cyprus for poker tournaments. On his last trip to Kyrenia (now Girne) he took photos of my old neighborhood.

Mary Kaye, my psychologist friend, retired and moved to the Southwest of the US.

Julie divorced her lousy husband and moved to Washington, DC, where she met and married a photojournalist. She's the proud mother of two independent daughters.

Marti, my psychologist friend whom I accompanied to Capri, met a musician while on vacation in the Far East. They married, had a daughter together, and later divorced. She's happy being a single parent.

Rosetta still performs at her jazz club—the Balalaika—in Sachsenhausen.

Trenton is probably still entertaining in his tighty-whites. I still laugh at my ignorance about strange British expressions and cuisine.

Gray retired and moved on.

Michael left this physical plane on October 20, 1986, but lives on forever in my heart. He often whispers answers to my many questions, and whenever I smell Maja soap I smile, remembering Mr. Walking Encyclopedia—the greatest spiritual guide anyone could ever wish for.

Doug and I moved to Oregon in 1986. We visited Michael several times before his death. Being with him each time was a great gift.

Doug and I married in 1988 and moved to North Carolina, where we adopted our son, Jesse. We now live in a small beach town in Uruguay.

Wagner's continues to serve the best *Apfelwein* in Germany. I know because I tasted it in October of 2008 when we attended the Frankfurt Buchmesse, and traveled around Europe visiting old friends, including Katie and her mother in the South of France.

Katie passed in 2009. The brightness of her spirit shines in my heart forever.

Acknowledgements

Thanks to my many friends who helped refresh my memory of the shared experiences during the Cyprus years and my years in Europe, and encouraged me to share my journey with others. Though most chose to remain anonymous, this book could not have been written without their words.

During the writing of this book, I've received support from family members and friends—writers and readers. Special gratitude goes to all who read and reread the manuscript at various stages, commented on draft after draft, and asked questions which alerted me to what was missing in the book.

My heartfelt thanks to all for your insights and suggestions. You've contributed greatly to the success of this book.

If you've enjoyed this book, I hope you will review it. You can chat with me at http://susanjoycejourneys.com/

If you love memoirs, join the We Love Memoirs Group: https://www. facebook.com/groups/welovememoirs/ You'll get a warm welcome!

ALSO BY SUSAN JOYCE

Good Morning Diego Garcia — A Journey of Discovery

Peel, the Extraordinary Elephant

Naro, the Ancient Spider

Post Card Passages

Alphabet Riddles

ABC Animal Riddles

ABC Nature Riddles

ABC School Riddles (editor)

Made in the USA
Monee, IL
07 July 2026

56551789R00208